W9-BTI-039

"*My French Family Table* is focused around our
favorite subjects—cooking and enjoying food with your
family—and it is just as gorgeous, colorful, and warm as
her first book. We also love how Béa makes gluten-free
baking so natural, easy, and effortless. Truly inspiring!"

**—David Frenkiel and Luise Vindahl,
authors of *The Green Kitchen* and *Green Kitchen Travels***

"In *My French Family Table*, Béatrice Peltre has once
again brought together a collection that balances tradition and
contemporary tastes, the realities of the everyday kitchen
and a subtle sense of luxury. With warmth and her distinctive,
deft touch, the recipes feel wholesome, special,
and thoroughly personal."

—Tara O'Brady, author of *Seven Spoons*

"In *My French Family Table*, Béa reminds us of the
importance of the table. To gather together for the meal, which
need not be fussy or complicated, is really what is central in
feeding a family. But the food is what brings us to the table, and
Béa never disappoints there. The recipes are simple
yet inspirational, and tucked in between her poetic words
and stunning photographs are countless tips and tricks
for making each recipe a success."

**—Ashley Rodriguez, creator of the blog *Not without Salt*
and author of *Date Night In***

my french
family table

BÉATRICE PELTRE

my french family table

RECIPES FOR A LIFE FILLED WITH
FOOD, LOVE & *JOIE DE VIVRE*

Roost Books
Boulder
2016

Roost Books
An imprint of Shambhala Publications, Inc.
4720 Walnut Street
Boulder, Colorado 80301
roostbooks.com

© 2016 by Béatrice Peltre
All rights reserved. No part of this book may be reproduced in any form
or by any means, electronic or mechanical, including photocopying,
recording, or by any information storage and retrieval system, without
permission in writing from the publisher.

9 8 7 6 5 4 3 2 1

First Edition
Printed in the United States of America

⊗ This edition is printed on acid-free paper that meets the American
National Standards Institute Z39.48 Standard.
♻ Shambhala Publications makes every effort to print on recycled paper.
For more information please visit www.shambhala.com.

Distributed in the United States by Penguin Random House LLC and
in Canada by Random House of Canada Ltd

Designed by Toni Tajima

Library of Congress Cataloging-in-Publication Data

Peltre, Béatrice, author.
My French family table: recipes for a life filled with food, love, and joie
de vivre/Béatrice Peltre.—First edition.
pages   cm
Includes index.
ISBN 978-1-61180-136-1 (hardcover: alk. paper)
1. Cooking, French. I. Title.
TX719.P43 2016
641.5944—dc23
2015026649

contents

introduction

introduction

WHEN OUR DAUGHTER, LULU, WAS BORN—she is now six—a new chapter opened up for me. It was my turn to become a mother and learn more about how to feed my family. I knew that I loved to cook, so cooking would not be an issue. But would I intuitively know what dishes to prepare? Would my cooking style change because of her? Would I need to simplify it? Would I have enough time to cook? And most important, would Lulu enjoy the food I made and our family meals?

Against this background, I knew one thing right away: food was going to be an essential part of her education. It was in my genes because, being French, I had been brought up to think that a healthy relationship with food is essential to happiness. And that really starts at home.

My mother showed me how to love food. She has also handed down to me one of her strongest skills—she made me see how much love and care a cook can demonstrate when he or she prepares and shares food. I don't know that she is aware of this. To be honest, for the longest time, I didn't know that she was going to influence me so strongly in both my adult life and the kitchen.

When I'm asked about my mother, I often describe her as a woman of few words, rather *réservée* (shy) in fact. She has never been comfortable sharing her feelings, unlike my father, who is the chatterbox in the family. Instead, she prefers to cook and show how much she cares through her food. *"C'est bon?"* ("Is it good?"), she invariably asked anxiously when we were children and sat down to eat a dish she'd brought to the table. *"Je t'ai gardé les premières fraises du jardin!"* ("I kept the first strawberries for you!"), she said when the season came for strawberries to ripen in her vegetable garden. Her desire to please us with food was and is heart stirring. I spent a lot of time watching and cooking with her in the kitchen. And I saw that by making sure her family and friends were happy around the dining table with her delicious foods, she was expressing her love through actions rather than words.

Hence, gathering around food was essential in my family. Part of this was setting up the table together, making sure it looked inviting for both special occasions and everyday meals. My brother and I loved our daily premeal routine of arranging plates, cutlery, and glasses on the dining table. We each had a task to accomplish, and we were extremely diligent about it. When dinner was ready, my mother would call, *"À table!"* ("Dinner is ready!") from across the room. These words worked like magic as all of us hurried to come and sit down.

Everyday foods didn't need to be elaborate. Yet as simple as they were, our meals gravitated around being *équilibrés* (balanced)—with a main course comprising vegetables and meat or fish, a salad or soup, and a dessert. As children, we ate what our parents ate. We were taught to respect food and enjoy the moments created around it, even if that meant sometimes we didn't like one food or another. The motto was *Il fallait au moins goûter* (You must at least taste it).

Good table manners and eating habits were also the norm. We ate lunch together *à midi* (at noon), which sometimes still seems fairly formal to many of my foreign friends when they come to visit; we ate *un goûter* (a snack) at 4 P.M. after school; and dinner was served around 7 P.M. Mealtime was sacrosanct—no phone calls, television, or any other distraction. Once we were seated at the dining table, what mattered was our time together enjoying food.

At first, I didn't realize that I was training Lulu to think about meals in these terms too. Then one day when she was four, she was sitting at the dining table. Neither Philip, my husband, nor I were yet ready to sit down with her. I asked her to start before her food got cold. But she protested, *"Mais non, maman, je vous attends pour manger! Je veux que tout le monde soit assis à table avec moi pour manger"* ("No, Mummy, I am waiting for you before I start! I want everyone to sit down at the table with me to eat"). On hearing those words, I must have beamed. Clearly, something magical had just happened.

When I started to think about the recipes I wanted for this book, I thought about Lulu's words. Togetherness resonated deep and strong. Essentially, what I wanted most were delicious recipes that would give enjoyment to little ones and adults alike, together as a family for everyday meals or with friends for celebrations.

The recipes here are nutritious, because I've always cared about being healthy—although I don't like to be extreme about it. They are also flexible, allowing room for simplification and personal interpretation as needed. So sometimes an everyday meal can be turned into a more dressed-up food experience—I like clothes that are that way too.

For the most part, the recipes take their inspiration from French cooking because that's what I know best and prefer. Tell me we are eating a *strawberry clafoutis* or *chocolate petits pots de crème* for dessert; a vegetable tart for lunch; or stuffed potatoes for dinner, and you will see me smile. But you will also find recipes using more exotic (for traditional French cooks) ingredients—my mother still does not use coconut milk, eat corn on the cob, or make *labneh*. My more diverse approach comes from having been lucky enough to travel globally and from living an expatriate life.

I have organized the book around the rhythm of our family meals: from morning

foods with breakfast and brunch to light dishes (soups, salads, and tarts); from children's snacks (with the traditional French after-school *goûter*) to recipes Lulu and I enjoy cooking together; and finally, from family dinners to tempting desserts that seal our meals. These are the foods I cook for Lulu and Philip, and now my young son,

Rémy. My family. Our friends. To express my care and love.

I hope you will want to go back to those recipes that appeal to you and cook them again and again for your family and friends. These foods are meant to make you happy and inspire you to cook more of them.

before you start

avant de commencer

HERE ARE A FEW TIPS for making the most of this book:

First, always read the entire recipe before you start. This will give you a much better sense of what you need, what to expect, and the steps ahead.

Second, measure *everything*, especially when you bake. A reliable kitchen scale is a necessity for successfully reproducing these recipes—French cooks never use cups to measure flour when they bake. You may perceive this to be more work, but I guarantee you will have more success and less frustration if you heed this advice.

Third, a thread runs through this book so that individual recipes can be used as part of another or to accompany another. I always approach meal planning this way;

I typically buy ingredients for one meal while also thinking about the next one. For example, I will use half a butternut squash in a soup on Tuesday and the rest in a dish of pasta on Wednesday. I avoid wasting food at all costs (which sadly still sometimes happens when ingredients are forgotten in the fridge). For example, when I prepare the Julienned Zucchini and Watermelon Radish Salad (page 138), I cannot julienne the soft center of the zucchini, so I use the leftovers to make Cocoa, Walnut, and Zucchini Muffins (page 146). When I buy radishes, I use the leaves to make Radish Leaf Soup (page 82), while the radishes go inside many of the salads you will find throughout the book.

gluten-free cooking
la cuisine sans gluten

THESE DAYS, I never think about the fact that I cook and eat gluten-free. Yet I am amazed that almost ten years have passed since I removed gluten from my diet. Those of you who own a copy of my first cookbook, *La Tartine Gourmande,* know the story behind that change. Right from the beginning, I didn't want to emphasize the absence of gluten in my food. When we were working on my first book, my publisher and I debated whether we should include "gluten-free" in the main title, and in the end, the answer was no. We didn't want the book to be limited to a specific diet because what mattered more was the focus on taste and cooking real food—ultimately, recipes that would prompt enjoyment at the dining room table regardless of whether they contained gluten or not. Because more than anything, I love to eat.

Did you know that many homemade foods are naturally gluten-free? Of course, baking is a different matter. I understood that when I wrote *La Tartine Gourmande.* At first, it was undeniably a challenge. I had failures and successes. But I loved learning new formulas for baking cakes,

madeleines and *financiers,* tart crusts, and bread. All gluten-free. It was even more exciting because my baked goods were, in fact, delicious. They were also nutritious because most of the gluten-free flours I use are made from whole grain.

The most wonderful feedback came from individual readers of the book and faithful followers of my blog who used my recipes and wrote to thank me, because they felt they were cooking normally again. They found the recipes scrumptious, prompting picky eaters in their homes to try and enjoy new foods. I loved hearing about their stories and experiences, which also built my confidence to try more new things and see where I would end up with a second book. That's why I am here with you now again.

Eating gluten-free is a natural way of being for my family. When friends come over for a meal, I don't tell them that we are following any kind of diet. There's no need. I want the focus to be on the shared experience of delicious food.

If you decide to eat and cook gluten-free, it's obvious that you will need to make a few changes, especially when it comes to stocking your pantry with flours. Here are some of my favorite tricks.

To start, I like to keep a wide selection of flours handy and use them regularly. Flours like millet, quinoa, white rice, brown rice, teff, buckwheat, oat, tapioca, and sweet rice are standards (I describe each of them in more detail in *La Tartine Gourmande*). I also use a lot of nut flours, like almond and hazelnut. I also have gluten-free baking powder—check the label on yours, because it may not be gluten-free. Do the same with oat flour and rolled oats.

I use an array of seeds, flaxseeds in particular. I've always loved to prepare vegetable and fruit tarts; I feel it's a very French thing to do. So in my first book, I used xanthan gum to create the binding agent a crust otherwise lacks without gluten. The results were great. But this time, I wanted to add more nutrition too, and I came across flaxseeds.

I was already adding flax to breads and granola, but I didn't know something important about it: by mixing ground flaxseeds with hot water, the texture becomes gelatinous (the same is true for ground chia seeds if you like to work with them). When this gel is added to gluten-free ingredients, it binds them together *comme par magie* (like magic) to form a crust. It's stunning to see how it works! My crusts are easy to roll, and the results are excellent.

Flaxseeds (also called linseeds) are one of nature's highest sources of cancer-preventing plant lignans. They are rich in dietary fiber and omega-3 oils, which are indispensable to good health. Flaxseeds come in two varieties, brown and yellow. You can purchase them as whole seeds or already ground. Since I'm lucky enough to own a heavy-duty food processor, I am able to grind my own seeds into a powder, so this is my preference. But these days, it's easy enough to buy ground flaxseeds in many places. Get whichever kind will be easiest for you to use.

You may have heard people say before that cooking and eating gluten-free is restrictive, but I don't agree with that assumption. I truly find that cooking from scratch without gluten is effortless when you like to cook. Essentially, I find it empowering. I know it's made me a more refined baker and a more knowledgeable cook, and it continues to keep two of my favorite activities—cooking and baking—more interesting.

So let's try it together, shall we? I know your family and friends will love it as much as mine do.

ingredients and equipment
les ingrédients et l'équipement

INGREDIENTS • *Ingrédients*

IF YOU CAME TO MY HOUSE, you would most likely find carrots and leeks in my fridge; potatoes and a seasonal squash of some sort in the potato room (that's really the nickname we gave to a room in our house); garlic and shallots; butter, Parmesan, and Comté cheese; eggs, yogurts, and *crème fraîche*. I find that these ingredients work as the backbone of many dishes I improvise. And I am someone who improvises with food a lot.

Take a typical spring day, for example. I might prepare a green asparagus omelet with herbs from the garden and eat it with a finely shaved (hello, mandoline!) Radish, Fennel, and Apple Salad with Truffle Salt (see recipe on page 136). You may be thinking that this lunch, as simple as it is, takes a lot of time to put together. But it doesn't if you have the basic ingredients, plus a few extras, on hand.

I spend a lot of time choosing my ingredients. Growing up in rural France, where we didn't have everything available all year round, I learned to follow the seasons and buy what was *de saison et de préférence local* (seasonal and preferably local), which for us meant produce grown in France. Whenever my mother and I visited *le marché* near my home village, I remember she always pointed to the labels that indicated where a vegetable came from. *"Je vais prendre celles-là parce qu'elles sont françaises"* ("I will buy those because they were grown in France"), she'd exclaim in front of a display of tomatoes or strawberries. Even though I was a young girl, this experience stayed with me. It wasn't about feeling French. I quickly gathered that my mother was making a point of not buying food that had been picked while it was still green and then traveled for a long time from Spain, Holland, or Morocco. And that mattered a great deal.

My ingredients are also preferably organic. At home, my parents maintained a vegetable garden that still inspires the way I shop for produce. I also have a small vegetable patch where Lulu and I like to grow salad greens, loads of fresh herbs,

chamomile, lemon verbena, radishes, carrots, peas, and tomatoes. I believe choosing food in this manner is important because it translates into high-quality, tasty ingredients that ultimately result in more tasteful dishes. It's as simple as that.

I like to plan my meals in such a way that nothing is wasted. If I use the white part of a leek in a recipe, then I keep the green part to add to a vegetable stock I will eventually make. When I roast a chicken, I purposely buy a large one so I have leftovers that I can use in a salad or to make a *hachis parmentier* or a savory *clafoutis* for the next day. One dish always paves the way for another.

With all of this in mind, I thought you might find it useful to read about some of the basic ingredients I keep in my pantry and use every day. They are in the recipes I created for this book, and they help me plan my meals. Ultimately, always choose what makes sense to you. In my mind, this means variety and moderation in everything; taste and enjoyment above everything else.

Flours • *Les Farines*

I keep many flours handy, all of them gluten-free: millet, quinoa, sweet rice, white rice, brown rice, teff, buckwheat, oat, and tapioca. They all play a different role depending on what I decide to cook. I always try to have a ratio of two-thirds whole-grain flours to one-third starch to bind the ingredients in my gluten-free baked goods. I don't use a flour mix because I feel that each flour is important for the specific flavor it imparts; for example, teff and buckwheat flours work very

well and shine with chocolate. I keep my nut flours—such as almond, hazelnut, and pistachio—in glass jars in the fridge, since they tend to have a shorter shelf life. The others are in tall glass containers—that look pretty too—lined up in the pantry.

Salt • *Le Sel*

I prefer to use sea salt, and I keep different kinds on hand. I use *du gros sel* (coarse salt) to season water for cooking pasta, quinoa, or rice or to prepare fish *en croûte de sel* (baked in salt crust); *fleur de sel* and Maldon sea salt for their delicate taste and texture to finish a dish; and pink or gray sea salts for their attractive color (in France, we use a lot of gray salt). My everyday table salt though is Herbamare, by A. Vogel, which is a blend of sea salt and organically grown herbs and vegetables like celery, leek, watercress, chives, parsley, marjoram, and kelp. I've been using it for years, and I like its subtle flavor, especially in my vinaigrettes and added to soups and roasted vegetables.

Eggs • *Les Oeufs*

Eggs are one of my true weaknesses. I always have them on hand, and I'm picky when it comes to choosing them. For that, I have to thank my grandmother Marie, who always let me collect eggs on their farm when we visited. Hence, my favorite eggs are farm fresh. It's worth mentioning that if you happen to find blue eggs from Araucana chickens, you will notice the rich yellow color and stunning taste of their yolks. I can never resist them, and since I can find them easily from a nearby farm, they are often my eggs of choice.

Oils • *Les Huiles*

I pay close attention to the quality of the oils I use, and like everything else in my kitchen, I prefer them to be organic.

The top shelf of one of my fridge doors is filled with randomly aligned bottles of nut oils (almond, hazelnut, walnut, and pistachio are staples). As with nut flours, I keep them refrigerated to prolong their shelf life and try to use them within six months if possible. Mostly, I use nut oils to prepare vinaigrettes for our salads.

I always buy extra-virgin, cold-pressed olive oil. I keep a few bottles open at a time—a less expensive one for cooking, and a few others with more body and character to add to my vinaigrettes.

Olive oil is often my oil of choice, though I also use a number of others, depending on what I decide to cook. For example, coconut oil is lovely in many baked goods (such as Every-Morning Granola, page 26, and Banana and Coconut Muffins, page 48) and for sautéing vegetables at high temperatures. Buy organic, and make sure it is extra-virgin and cold-pressed as well.

For oils that are slightly more neutral in taste, sunflower oil (cold-pressed) and grapeseed oil are other good choices. Like coconut oil, they hold high cooking temperatures, making them ideal for sautéing ingredients.

Vinegar and Wine • *Les Vinaigres et le Vin*

I use many vinegars, and I have a number of bottles on hand: red and white balsamic (aged); apple cider (for a more fruity taste); sherry (a favorite that is milder than the red wine variety); rice (mild and beautiful in delicate salads like the Mint-Flavored Cucumber Salad, page 206); and red and white wine. When I don't use vinegar in a vinaigrette, I choose lemon or lime juice.

I also cook with white wine fairly frequently to give aromas to sautéed mushrooms or a sauce or to add to a risotto. Since I don't always have a bottle of white wine open, I always keep white vermouth in my pantry; it keeps for a long time and does not need to be refrigerated.

Chocolate • *Le Chocolat*

I don't know many people who don't like chocolate, do you? In our household, it is treasured. We prefer dark chocolate especially; you will notice that numerous recipes in this book let chocolate shine.

I like to bake with Valrhona for its ease of use and rich flavor. I use different types, such as hazelnut flavored, with different cocoa contents, 70% or 64%. The taste of each one is unique and wonderful. Of course, choosing a chocolate is utterly personal. I suggest that you use the type you enjoy most and feel most comfortable with.

Sugar • *Le Sucre*

I rarely use white sugar, opting instead for blond cane sugar or raw evaporated cane sugar in many baked goods. I like their subtle taste and fine texture. But in recipes where I want to add a more pronounced molasses flavor, products like light or dark Muscovado sugar (which is a type of unrefined brown sugar with a strong molasses flavor), Turbinado, Demerara, coconut, or Rapadura work best. Keeping a variety of sugars handy helps me decide what makes sense when I need it.

Rather than buying confectioner's sugar, I often make my own using a powerful food processor. Blond cane sugar makes a more traditional confectioner's sugar, but you can also use Sucanat or Rapadura—just know that it will not be white.

I use pearl sugar (also known as nib sugar) exclusively in my *chouquettes* recipe (page 150). It can be difficult to find, though it is available online from retailers such as Amazon. I buy mine from l'Epicerie (www.lepicerie.com) or bring it back from France when I'm there for a visit.

I also use a lot of honey, preferring locally (New England) produced clover honey with a liquid texture so it's easy to use, like in my Every-Morning Granola (page 26).

Herbs and Spices •
Les Herbes et les Épices

Fresh herbs always flavor my cooking. During summer, Lulu and I enjoy maintaining a vegetable patch where we plant micro greens alongside all kinds of herbs, including marjoram, basil, oregano, thyme, parsley, cilantro, sage, and lemon balm. In addition to their delicate taste, I also use herbs as a final touch to beautify a dish before serving. It really makes a difference—even Lulu notices it!

When my basil, parsley, or tarragon goes wild and I have more than I need, I use up the surplus in several ways. In addition to preparing a large batch of pesto, I chop the herbs and put them in small bags that I store in the freezer so I can happily add them to soups, stews, and many other cooked dishes during the winter.

I also keep an extensive collection of spices (ground cumin, ground coriander, fennel seeds, and saffron being staples), because I often find them useful when thinking up new ideas for a dish. You never know where a scent or flavor may lead you.

EQUIPMENT • *L'Équipement*

Although I am able to cook with very little equipment—and do whenever I travel and stay in houses with minimal kitchen amenities—when I am at home, I enjoy using my favorite tools.

Kitchen Scale • *Balance de Cuisine*

Yes, it's a must—you know this already if you've read my first book. I give measurements in cups for convenience alongside the weight, but as I mentioned earlier (page 10), you will be much more accurate if you use a scale, especially when you bake.

Mandoline • *Mandoline*

I have a love affair with the mandoline. I use mine every day to shave radishes or slice apples or vegetables to use in a tart (like the Apple Tartlets with Cinnamon, page 166, and the Thyme-Flavored Turnip Tatin Tart, page 108). Mandolines don't need to be professional-grade or expensive to work well; I even own a travel-size mandoline that I sneak inside my bag when we travel to places where I know I will be able to cook.

Vegetable Peeler • *Épluche-légumes*

Why a vegetable peeler? To make it easier to prepare vegetables, because we eat a lot of them and because it's more efficient than peeling with a knife. I don't know about you, but I tend to waste more of the vegetable with the peel when I try to use the knife method. The peeler is also a great tool for preparing shaved vegetables for a salad or *papillote* (like the Blue Potato and Red Snapper Papillotes, page 278).

Stand Mixer • *Batteur sur Socle*

I am particularly fond of my stand mixer. It's my favorite tool when it comes to preparing a cake or cookie batter, whipping egg whites, or mixing a waffle or *crêpe* batter. I use the paddle attachment to cream and mix ingredients together and the whip to beat eggs.

Food Processor/Blender • *Robot de Cuisine*

A few years ago, I bought a Thermomix, which is a food processor and blender in one; it also allows you to weigh and cook your ingredients. And it's very powerful— so powerful that I nicknamed it the Rolls-Royce of food processors. I probably use it three or four times a day, on average. First, we prepare a smoothie every morning for breakfast—Lulu invented our favorite recipe, which consists of puréeing 1 cup frozen strawberries with ½ cup frozen raspberries, 1 banana, and about 1½ cups quality apple juice. If I am making a puréed soup, out comes the Thermomix again. Then maybe I need to grind nuts into meal so I can make bread, or I want to prepare a pastry crust for a tart. The uses are endless.

This is not to say that you need a Thermomix to make any of the recipes in this book. If, like most people, you have a regular food processor and a separate blender, do not worry. You will be well served by them.

Baking Sheets • *Plaques de Cuisson*

My baking sheets are mostly rimmed and standard in size (13 by 18 inches [33 by 46 cm]). They are a necessity in the kitchen—great for baking cookies, preparing granola, or roasting vegetables uniformly. I have four or five, though two is enough for most purposes.

Tart Molds • *Moules à Tarte*

I've collected a wide variety of tart molds over the years, from vintage ones that look beautiful in photos to pretty ones I use to serve at the table. For a large tart, my standard molds are 9 and 11 inches (23 and 28 cm) in size. I also have different sizes for tartlets: 3½-, 4-, and 4½-inch (9, 10, and 11.5 cm) varieties. What can I say? I love tarts.

Cake Pans • *Moules à Gâteau*

Food stylists love their cake pans, and being a stylist myself, I own many. When I travel, I cannot help but look for interesting cake pans to bring home. For example, Lulu has a chicken-shaped cake pan (I bought it in a local supermarket near where my parents live in France) that we love to use for our Marbled Cake (page 162), and I have a number of interesting Bundt and flower-shaped ones that we use for everyday cakes.

In my recipes, I suggest standard-size cake pans, such as an 8-inch (20 cm) square pan or a 10-inch (25.5 cm) round pan for the Buttermilk, Lemon, and Strawberry Brunch Cake (page 53). If you have an adventurous soul, you may want to use your favorites, which could be slightly different in size. Remember never to fill the cake pan to the top, since most cakes will rise while baking. You may also need to adjust the cooking time if a cake pan is bigger or smaller than the one called for in the recipe. In my case, I sometimes use one cake batter recipe to prepare a large cake, as well as a few smaller ones for Lulu. Since you will find recipes for *madeleines* and *financiers* in the book, I also have special molds for those—although you can easily substitute more common molds (like a mini muffin tin) that are similar in size for the latter. Make sure you always grease the pan well to ensure that you can easily unmold your cakes.

Silicone Pastry Mat • *Toile de Cuisson Anti-adhésive*

I am very attached to my Silpat silicone pastry mat, which I find makes rolling crusts, cookies, and gnocchi really easy. Its surface is nonstick, so the bonus is that you can also use it instead of parchment paper when you bake a sheet of cookies. Although I would not say that you *must* own one, it's still a nice piece of equipment to have.

Kitchen Thermometer • *Thermomètre de Cuisine*

I use a kitchen thermometer to check the doneness of meat or, more particularly, when I need to reach a precise temperature during a baking preparation. For example, use your thermometer to check the temperature of milk before mixing it with yeast when you are making Brioche-Like Bread (page 28).

morning foods

le matin

WHEN I WAS A CHILD, my day typically started with *un grand bol de chocolat chaud* (a large bowl of hot chocolate) and *une ou deux tartines de confiture* (one or two pieces of toast with jam) while *croissants, pains au chocolat,* and *brioché* were kept as special treats for Sunday. I enjoyed these foods and still have fond memories of this more classic French-style breakfast.

Over time, my breakfast habits have changed a lot. These days, you will likely see me having a more nutritious breakfast. It might be a fresh-fruit smoothie, granola with plain yogurt and fresh berries, toast topped with avocado and cheese, or a muffin or slice of cake baked the night before. The breakfast table is a happy place, and my family's day starts there, together.

This chapter presents our best-loved breakfast foods. Some are simple and suitable for every day. Others are a tad more time-consuming, to be saved for days when we don't have to go anywhere. There are also wonderful recipes for brunch, some of which I like to use as nibbles to share with friends when they come over for a drink. I hope you will find new favorites among them that you want to cook over and over for your own family to begin the day on a happy note. We all deserve that kind of start to the day.

bread and cereals
pains et céréales

Every-morning granola • *Granola du matin*   26

Brioche-like bread • *Pain brioché*   28

Quinoa and oat bread rolls with poppy and sesame seeds • *Petits pains au
quinoa et à l'avoine avec graines de pavot et de sésame*   31

Pecan, almond, and buckwheat breakfast bread • *Pain aux pécanes, aux amandes,
et au sarrasin*   35

Basil-flavored peach jam with vanilla and lime • *Confiture aux
pêches et au basilic avec vanille et citron vert*   39

Waffles with stewed apples and cardamom custard • *Gaufres avec
sa compotée de pommes et crème anglaise à la cardamome*   40

breakfast cakes and muffins
gâteaux du petit déjeuner et muffins

Apple pudding cake • *Flognarde aux pommes*   46

Banana and coconut muffins • *Muffins aux bananes et à la noix de coco*   48

Blackberry and raspberry bread puddings • *Puddings aux mûres et aux framboises*   50

Buttermilk, lemon, and strawberry brunch cake • *Gâteau aux fraises,
au citron, et au lait ribot*   53

savory dishes
plats salés

Kale and smoked salmon quiche • *Quiche au chou frisé et au saumon fumé*   56

Tomato and fennel tart • *Tarte aux tomates et au fenouil*   59

Radish, yogurt cream, and buckwheat bread *verrines* with chives • *Verrines de
radis au yaourt avec ciboulette et miettes de pain au sarrasin*   62

Apple, avocado, and crab *verrines* • *Verrines de pommes, d'avocat, et de crabe*   65

Sautéed broccoli, avocado, and black quinoa salad • *Salade au broccoli grillé,
à l'avocat, et au quinoa noir*   66

Coppa-wrapped mushroom and pepper breakfast frittata • *Frittata aux champignons,
à la coppa, et aux poivrons rouges*   68

Salmon and poppy seed spread • *Rillettes de saumon au pavot noir*   71

Savory cake with sun-dried tomatoes, nuts, and olives • *Cake salé aux
tomates séchées, aux noix, et aux olives*   72

breads and cereals
pains et céréales

Every-morning granola
Granola du matin

At my house, most days start with a bowl of granola. I bake a big batch every weekend and store it in a large glass container within easy reach for breakfast or to fulfill *une fringale* (a craving). My granola recipes change often according to my mood, but they consistently include a medley of protein-packed nuts and seeds, and I sometimes add dried fruit like cherries, strawberries, or raspberries.

Makes 15 cups

6 cups (1 lb, 5¼ oz; 600 g) rolled oats

3 cups (10½ oz; 300 g) whole pecans, coarsely chopped

1 cup (4¼ oz; 120 g) pumpkin seeds

1 cup (2¾ oz; 80 g) sliced almonds

1 cup (4 oz; 120 g) sunflower seeds

⅓ cup (1 oz; 30 g) flax meal

1 cup (4 oz; 120 g) unsweetened coconut flakes or grated coconut

½ cup (120 ml) grapeseed oil or melted coconut oil

½ cup (120 ml) clover honey

½ cup (2¾ oz; 80 g) light Muscovado sugar or coconut palm raw sugar

½ teaspoon sea salt

2 tablespoons pure vanilla extract

Preheat the oven to 320°F (160°C). Line two rimmed baking sheets with parchment paper; set aside.

In a large bowl, combine the rolled oats, pecans, pumpkin seeds, sliced almonds, sunflower seeds, flax meal, and coconut; set aside. In a pot, combine the grapeseed or coconut oil with the honey, sugar, and sea salt. Warm and stir until the sugar is dissolved. Remove from the heat and add the vanilla extract. Pour the wet ingredients over the dry ones and toss until combined. Divide between the two baking sheets and spread evenly. Bake for 20 minutes. Stir the granola and rotate the baking sheets. Continue to bake for 10 minutes, checking occasionally to be sure the granola does not burn. Stir, rotate the sheets again, and bake for another 10 minutes, or until the granola has a nice golden color. Remove from the oven and let cool completely. When the granola is cooled, store it in a large airtight container for two to three weeks. Serve with your favorite milk or yogurt (both Lulu and I love kefir with ours), a dash of maple syrup or honey, and fresh berries.

Brioche-like bread
Pain brioché

Preparing this delectable bread makes the house smell sweet and delicious. It's most enjoyable on the day you make it, but if you are lucky enough to have some left—we rarely do—slice it into thick pieces and toast them the next day. Or use leftovers to prepare the Blackberry and Raspberry Bread Puddings (page 50) or to make croutons for a soup or a salad like the French Green Bean Salad (page 126).

You will need: a 5½-by-10¼-inch (14 by 26 cm) loaf pan.

Makes one 10-inch loaf

Unsalted butter, for the pan, plus 4 tablespoons (2 oz; 60 g), melted

1 tablespoon (⅓ oz; 10 g) active dry yeast

2 teaspoons blond cane sugar

¾ cup (180 ml) whole or 2% milk, heated to 110°F (43°C)

1 cup (5½ oz; 160 g) brown rice flour

1 cup (3½ oz; 100 g) gluten-free oat flour

1 cup (4¼ oz; 120 g) cornstarch

⅓ cup (1½ oz; 40 g) tapioca starch

1 teaspoon sea salt

1 batch Flax Gel (see sidebar)

¼ cup (60 ml) honey

3 large eggs, at room temperature

Butter the loaf pan; set aside.

In a small bowl, combine the yeast with the sugar. Stir in the warm milk until the yeast is dissolved. Let it rest for 10 to 15 minutes—the yeast will become active and frothy.

In the bowl of a stand mixer fitted with the paddle blade, mix together the brown rice flour, oat flour, cornstarch, tapioca starch, and sea salt. Leaving the machine on, add the flax gel and mix on medium speed until incorporated. Pour in the yeast mixture and continue to blend until incorporated. Add the melted butter and honey; continue to mix. Add the eggs, one at a time, waiting until the first one is well incorporated before adding the next. The dough will be wet and runny. Pour the batter into the buttered bread pan and cover with a clean kitchen towel. Let rise in a warm, nondrafty part of the house, between 75°F and 85°F (24°C–29°C), for 60 to 90 minutes, or until the dough fills the pan. If the dough touches the towel, remove it.

Preheat the oven to 400°F (200°C). Bake the bread for 10 minutes. Reduce the heat to 350°F (180°C) and bake for another 30 minutes, or until a skewer inserted in the middle of the *pain brioché* comes out dry and the top is golden brown in color. Remove from the oven and let rest for 5 minutes. Run the blade of a knife around the edge of the pan, then flip the pan onto a working surface. Place the *pain brioché* on a cooling rack and leave to cool for at least 20 minutes before slicing. The bread is best on the day it is baked, of course, but it also keeps well for two to three days when wrapped in a kitchen towel.

Flax gel
Gel aux graines de lin

I like to call this *gel* the "magic bind." I use it to prepare my tart crusts as it makes them easy to roll (besides the addition of welcoming nutrients), and I also add it inside recipes such as the Kale and Pea Pancakes (page 200).

2 tablespoons golden flax meal	⅓ cup (80 ml) hot water

Put the flax meal in a small bowl and whisk in the hot water. Let rest for 15 minutes; the mixture will become gelatinous; set aside.

(I don't recommend making this ahead and storing it; it's really simple and fast to make as needed.)

Quinoa and oat bread rolls

WITH POPPY AND SESAME SEEDS

Petits pains au quinoa et à l'avoine avec graines de pavot et de sésame

I remember the morning I baked these rolls for the first time. I woke up unexpectedly at 4 A.M. and could not go back to sleep, so I decided to bake. When Lulu came downstairs at 7 A.M., hungry for breakfast, she exclaimed, *"Mm, ça sent bon, maman. Comme à la boulangerie."* ("Yum, that smells good, Mummy. Just like in a bakery.") She grabbed a roll and began to nibble the seeds off the top. Then she tore the roll open and drizzled honey on one half. After her first bite, her face started to beam with delight; she looked so happy! *"Je t'en referrai d'autres"* ("I will bake you some more"), I told her, feeling tired but smiling as I watched my little girl enjoying the bread.

Serve these rolls with butter and jam or honey. They also make a wonderful companion for soup. Of course, there's no need to wake up at 4 A.M. to bake them!

You will need: twelve 3½-inch brioche molds, a muffin pan lined with 12 paper liners, or silicone muffin molds.

Makes twelve 3½-inch (9 cm) petits pains

Unsalted butter, for the molds, plus 4 tablespoons (2 oz; 60 g), melted

1 tablespoon (⅓ oz; 10 g) active dry yeast

2 teaspoons blond cane sugar

¾ cup (180 ml) water, heated to 110°F (43°C)

⅔ cup (2¾ oz; 80 g) quinoa flour

⅓ cup (1½ oz; 40 g) quinoa flakes

⅔ cup (2¼ oz; 65 g) oat flour

⅔ cup (2¾ oz; 80 g) cornstarch

⅓ cup (1½ oz; 40 g) tapioca starch

1 teaspoon sea salt

1 batch Flax Gel (page 30)

2 large eggs, at room temperature

FOR THE GARNISH:

1½ to 2 oz (45 to 60 g) of your favorite seeds, like poppy seeds, sunflower seeds, sesame seeds, or pumpkin seeds

Butter the brioche molds; set aside.

In a small bowl, combine the yeast with the sugar. Whisk in the hot water until the yeast is dissolved. Let it rest for 10 to 15 minutes—the yeast will become active and frothy.

In the bowl of a stand mixer fitted with the paddle blade, mix together the quinoa flour, quinoa flakes, oat flour, cornstarch, tapioca starch, and sea salt. Leaving the machine on, add the flax gel and mix on medium speed until incorporated. Pour in the yeast mixture and continue to blend until incorporated. Add the melted butter; continue to mix. Add the eggs, one at a time, waiting until the first one is well incorporated before adding the next. The dough will be wet. Fill the molds two-thirds full and cover with a kitchen towel. Let rise in a warm, nondrafty part of the

continued

house, between 75°F (24°C) and 85°F (29°C), for about 60 to 90 minutes, or until the dough fills the molds. If the dough touches the towel, remove it.

Preheat the oven to 420°F (215°C). Just before baking, sprinkle the *petits pains* with your choice of seeds. Bake the rolls for 10 minutes. Reduce the heat to 350°F (180°C) and bake for another 15 to 20 minutes, or until a skewer inserted in the middle of a roll comes out dry and the tops are golden brown in color. Remove from the oven and let rest for 5 minutes. Run the blade of a knife around the edge of the molds and slide the rolls out. Place them on a rack to cool before slicing. They are best on the day they are baked, but they also keep for a few days when wrapped in a kitchen towel.

Pecan, almond, and buckwheat breakfast bread

Pain aux pécanes, aux amandes, et au sarrasin

This recipe is inspired by a family picnic we shared with my brother and his wife at *l'abbaye d'Autrey,* a beautiful twelfth-century abbey tucked away in the French countryside near where my parents live. I had baked Lulu's favorite chocolate cake, while my sister-in-law, Geneviève, brought a loaf of bread similar to this one. Feeling curious, I immediately asked her how she had made it, knowing that I would want to bake my own. *"Oh, tu sais,"* she said. *"Je l'ai fait un peu au pif!"* ("Oh, you know. I bake it without really measuring.") If you ever ask, that is often how the French cook. But I still took mental notes, and a few breads later, I settled on this version. Friends and family love it and always ask for the recipe; they love it even more when I tell them how quick and easy it is to make.

Enjoy this bread plain or toasted, with the topping of your choice—cheese, butter, jam, or tapenade; the options are endless as the bread goes well with so many things. I use it in the Radish, Yogurt Cream, and Buckwheat Bread *Verrines* (page 62). I also love to serve it with homemade Labneh (see page 36), olive oil, or honey, and micro greens and *fleur de sel.*

You will need: a 7¾-by-4-inch (19.5 by 10 cm) loaf pan (I like to use a silicone pan).

Makes one 8-inch (20.5 cm) loaf

Coconut or safflower oil, for the pan

1 cup (3½ oz; 100 g) whole pecans

½ cup (2 oz; 60 g) almond meal

¼ cup (1¼ oz; 38 g) buckwheat flour

1 tablespoon golden flax meal

¼ teaspoon sea salt

½ tablespoon baking powder

1 tablespoon Turbinado, Rapadura, or coconut sugar

3 large eggs

¼ cup (60 ml) buttermilk

Preheat the oven to 350°F (180°C). Brush the pan with oil (I use a spray bottle).

Using your food processor, grind the pecans finely. In a mixing bowl, combine the pecan meal, almond meal, buckwheat flour, flax meal, sea salt, baking powder, and sugar. Whisk to combine. Beat in the eggs. Stir in the buttermilk. Transfer the batter to the oiled loaf pan and bake for about 30 minutes or until the blade of a sharp knife inserted in the middle comes out clean. Remove from the oven, and let cool for 5 minutes before unmolding.

Labneh

Labneh is yogurt that has been strained to remove its whey. It has a thicker consistency than yogurt and a distinctive sour taste. If you use Greek yogurt to make labneh, the texture will be thicker than if you use regular yogurt, so choose whichever you prefer. Labneh is versatile and goes well with both sweet and savory foods. For a savory version, stir the labneh, drizzle with olive oil, and top with ground red peppercorns. Spread it on bread, or serve it as a side with grilled fish and salad.

Makes 1¾ cups

4 cups (32 oz; 900 g) whole plain yogurt

½ teaspoon fine sea salt

In a large bowl, combine the yogurt and sea salt. Line a strainer with 3 to 4 layers of cheesecloth. Pour the yogurt into the lined strainer, and cover with the edges of the cheesecloth. Tie a knot at the top and place the strainer over a bowl so the whey can drain into the bowl. (Be sure the strainer doesn't touch the bottom of the bowl.) Place in the fridge overnight. The next day, open the cheesecloth and transfer the labneh (without the whey) into a fresh bowl. Enjoy plain or drizzle with a plain or flavored oil like parsley oil (page 88) as an accompaniment.

Basil-flavored peach jam

WITH VANILLA AND LIME

Confiture aux pêches et au basilic avec vanille et citron vert

Jam tastes like summer for me. Perhaps because summer is the season when I learned to make jam with my mother. The jams we prepared the most used strawberries, cherries, rhubarb, and red currants, because these were the fruits we had in the garden. But every summer, we also brought crates of apricots and peaches back from local *marchés* in the south of France near where we used to vacation as a family. I remember the sweet aroma filling the kitchen and my mother letting me stir the pot of hot fruit that simmered on the stove. To do that with her felt so special. Today it's Lulu and I who share the same tradition. We drive to nearby orchards where we pick strawberries, apples—and the peaches for this jam. Choose peaches that are ripe and juicy so the jam is packed with flavor.

You will need: five sterilized 6-oz (175 ml) Mason jars (or recycled glass jars with lids).

Serves 6

3⅓ lb (1½ kg) ripe yellow peaches

1 lb, 5¼ oz (600 g) blond cane sugar

Juice and zest of 2 limes

1 vanilla bean, split lengthwise and seeds scraped out

12 basil leaves, finely chopped

Bring a large pot of water to a boil. Poach the peaches for 1 minute, then transfer them to an ice water bath. Once they are cool, peel, core, and dice them. Transfer peaches to a large sauté pan or jam pot. Add the sugar, lime juice, lime zest, vanilla bean and seeds, and basil; stir and cover. Place in the fridge for 24 hours.

The next day, bring the peaches to a simmer and cook for 20 minutes, stirring occasionally. Using a slotted spoon, skim the foam that forms on the surface regularly. To test whether your jam is ready, scoop out a little with a wooden spoon and place it on a small plate. Using a clean, dry finger, draw a line through the middle of the jam to create a "channel." If the channel remains intact, the jam has set; if the jam oozes back toward the center, more cooking time is needed.

Divide the hot jam between the jars. Close the lids tightly while the jam is still hot, and flip the jars upside down. This helps to create an airtight seal. Let cool completely. Flip the jars upright to store. Enjoy for months to come at breakfast with slices of your favorite bread. (I keep mine in the pantry for up to twelve months.)

Waffles with stewed apples and cardamom custard

Gaufres avec sa compotée de pommes et crème anglaise à la cardamome

As a child in France, I enjoyed my *gaufres* (waffles) for *le goûter* (afternoon snack) dusted with a cloud of confectioner's sugar. Now I also like to serve waffles for breakfast, as is more common in the States. I make this recipe at least once a week, especially on weekends when we have more time for leisurely mornings. The waffles are delicious drizzled with maple syrup or served with *compotée de pommes* and *crème anglaise*, as I suggest here.

Note: When apples are very sweet, at the peak of their season, I stew them without adding any extra sugar.

Makes six 6½-inch (16.5 cm) waffles, 2 cups stewed apples, and 1¼ cups (295 ml) custard (for us this serves 4)

FOR THE WAFFLES:

Sunflower or grapeseed oil, to brush lightly on the waffle iron

1 cup (4½ oz; 125 g) millet flour

½ cup (1¾ oz; 50 g) oat flour or light buckwheat flour

¼ cup (1 oz; 30 g) cornstarch or tapioca starch

1 tablespoon coconut sugar or blond cane sugar

¼ teaspoon fine sea salt

1 teaspoon baking powder

1 tablespoon poppy seeds (optional)

2 large eggs, separated

1¼ cups (300 ml) whole or 2% milk

1 tablespoon pure vanilla extract

4 tablespoons (2 oz; 56 g) unsalted butter, melted, or ¼ cup (60 ml) grapeseed oil

Pinch of sea salt

FOR THE STEWED APPLES:

3 lb (1.4 kg) Macoun or McIntosh apples, peeled, cored, and cut in quarters (see Note)

3 tablespoons blond cane sugar, to taste (optional)

1 vanilla bean, split lengthwise and seeds scraped out

¼ cup (60 ml) water

FOR THE CARDAMOM-FLAVORED CUSTARD:

1 cup (236 ml) whole milk

4 cardamom pods, crushed

1 vanilla bean, split lengthwise and seeds scraped out

3 large egg yolks

2 tablespoons blond cane sugar

To prepare the waffles: Preheat the oven to 250°F (120°C). Line a rimmed baking sheet with parchment paper. Preheat the waffle iron and brush it with oil.

In a bowl, combine the millet flour, oat flour, cornstarch, and sugar. Add the sea salt, baking powder, and poppy seeds, if using; set aside. In another bowl, beat the egg yolks with the milk to combine. Stir in the vanilla. Beat the wet ingredients into the dry ones. Stir in the melted butter or oil. Whisk the egg whites with a pinch of sea salt until soft peaks form. Fold into the batter.

Fill the waffle iron three-fourths full with batter; the waffles will rise. Cook the waffles for a few minutes, following the instructions for your machine—I like to

continued

keep mine on the lighter side. Keep waffles warm in the oven as you make more. Serve the waffles with stewed apples and cardamom custard.

To prepare the stewed apples: In a pot, combine all the ingredients. Cover and simmer over low to medium heat, stirring occasionally, until the apples are soft. This usually takes about 20 minutes, but the time varies depending on the type of apples you use. Discard the vanilla bean, and transfer the apples and their juice to the bowl of a food processor. Purée to the texture you prefer; I generally like a fine texture. Refrigerate or, if you are making them for future use, pour into 6-ounce (175 ml) Mason jars and freeze.

To prepare the cardamom-flavored custard: In a pot, combine the milk with the cardamom pods and seeds, and the vanilla bean and seeds. Bring to a simmer over medium heat, making sure the milk does not overflow. Just before it reaches the boiling point, remove from the heat, cover, and let infuse for 30 minutes to 1 hour. Using a fine sieve or *chinois,* strain the milk and discard the cardamom pods and seeds and the vanilla bean. Keep the milk warm over low heat.

Meanwhile, in a bowl or stand mixer fitted with a whisk, beat the egg yolks with the sugar until light and pale in color. Pour the warm milk in slowly, stirring continuously. Transfer the custard back to the pot and cook over low to medium heat, stirring constantly, until the cream thickens—it should *never* boil. Cook the custard until it coats the spoon, between 7 to 10 minutes. Once the custard is ready, transfer it to a bowl and let cool, stirring occasionally to keep it smooth. Cover with plastic wrap and refrigerate until ready to use. The custard keeps for 2 to 3 days in the fridge.

Sometimes, we also enjoy savory waffles. Use the same waffle batter but omit the sugar and vanilla, substitute ½ cup oat flour instead of ¼ cup, and reduce the millet flour to ¾ cup. Serve the waffles with wild-caught smoked salmon and *crème fraîche,* and add a side salad. This makes an excellent lunch.

breakfast cakes
and muffins
gâteaux du petit déjeuner et muffins

Apple pudding cake
Flognarde aux pommes

A *flognarde* is nothing more than an autumnal version of a sweet *clafoutis*, made with apples in place of cherries. The flavors are wonderful when the apples are sautéed in butter and vanilla is used to infuse the milk and cream. Use your favorite apples—I love Fuji in mine. At home, we enjoy a *flognarde* for breakfast, but we also love it to finish a meal with something slightly sweet.

You will need: a 10-inch (25.5 cm) rimmed baking dish.

Makes one 10-inch (25.5 cm) cake

½ cup (120 ml) whole milk

½ cup (120 ml) heavy cream or *crème fraîche*

1 vanilla bean, split lengthwise and seeds scraped out

3 tablespoons unsalted butter, plus more for the mold

3 organic red apples, cored and sliced in ⅓-inch pieces

⅓ cup (2½ oz; 70 g) blond cane sugar, plus 3 tablespoons

Juice of ½ lime (about 1 tablespoon)

¼ cup (1 oz; 30 g) almond meal

¼ cup (1 oz; 30 g) quinoa flour

2 tablespoons cornstarch or tapioca starch

Pinch of fine sea salt

3 large eggs

Coarse raw cane sugar, to serve

Crème fraîche, to serve (optional)

In a pot, combine the milk, heavy cream, and vanilla bean and seeds. Bring to a simmer over medium heat. Remove from the heat and cover. Let infuse for an hour (or overnight in the fridge). Strain and discard the vanilla bean; set aside.

In a frying pan, melt 1 tablespoon butter over medium heat. Add the apples and 2 tablespoons blond cane sugar. Cook for 5 minutes, until the apples have softened. Drizzle with lime juice and set aside. Melt the remaining 2 tablespoons butter; set aside.

Preheat the oven to 375°F (190°C). Butter the baking dish. Coat it with 1 tablespoon sugar and tap out excess; set aside.

In a bowl, combine the almond meal, quinoa flour, cornstarch, and sea salt; set aside. In a large bowl, beat the eggs with ⅓ cup blond cane sugar just to combine. Stir in the dry ingredients until incorporated. Stir in the melted butter, then the infused milk and cream. Pour into the buttered dish and stud with the apple slices. (It's OK if they float; they will settle once the batter cooks.) Bake the *flognarde* for 30 to 35 minutes, or until the flan is set and the top is lightly browned. Serve lukewarm or at room temperature with a sprinkle of raw cane sugar and *crème fraîche* on the side.

Banana and coconut muffins

Muffins aux bananes et à la noix de coco

Lulu does not eat bananas, yet she likes them in a smoothie or a muffin, so this recipe is for her. I use a blend of wholesome flours, along with coconut and orange flavors, to welcome the morning. The breakfast table always looks more inviting with these muffins in the center.

Makes 12 muffins

½ cup (2¼ oz; 62.5 g) millet flour

½ cup (2 oz; 60 g) almond meal

¼ cup (1½ oz; 40 g) brown rice flour

¼ cup (1 oz; 30 g) cornstarch or tapioca starch

¼ cup (1 oz; 30 g) grated unsweetened coconut

1 tablespoon golden flax meal

¼ cup (1¾ oz; 50 g) blond cane sugar

¼ cup (1¼ oz; 35 g) light Muscovado sugar

¼ teaspoon sea salt

1 teaspoon baking powder

½ teaspoon baking soda

3 ripe bananas, mashed with a fork into a fine purée, plus ½ banana, sliced, to finish

2 large eggs

⅓ cup (80 ml) melted coconut oil

1 tablespoon pure vanilla extract

1 teaspoon organic orange zest, finely grated

Confectioner's sugar, to serve

Preheat the oven to 350°F (180°C). Line a muffin pan with 12 paper liners, or use silicone muffin molds if you prefer.

In a bowl, combine the millet flour, almond meal, brown rice flour, cornstarch, grated coconut, flax meal, blond cane sugar, light Muscovado sugar, sea salt, baking powder, and baking soda; set aside. In another bowl, beat together the banana purée, eggs, oil, vanilla, and orange zest. Stir the wet ingredients into the dry ones until well combined.

Divide the batter between the muffin cups, filling them only three-fourths full. Add a few slices of bananas on top and bake for 25 to 30 minutes. Remove from the oven and let cool. To serve, dust with confectioner's sugar.

Blackberry and raspberry bread puddings

Puddings aux mûres et aux framboises

In Philip's Irish family, say "bread pudding," and you can sense happiness throughout the house. So I thought there should be a recipe for it in my book, just to please them. I use leftovers of the Brioche-Like Bread (page 28) to prepare the puddings, adding whatever berries are seasonal. I am fond of pairing blackberries with raspberries and adding hints of vanilla and cardamom.

You will need: four 1-cup (2½-by-3½-inch [6.5 by 9 cm]) ramekins.

Serves 4

Unsalted butter, for ramekins, plus 3½ tablespoons (1¾ oz; 50 g), melted

⅔ cup (160 ml) whole or 2% milk

⅓ cup (60 ml) heavy cream

1 vanilla bean, split lengthwise and seeds scraped out

3 green cardamom pods, crushed

Four ⅓-inch (1 cm) slices of Brioche-Like Bread (page 28)

3½ oz (100 g) blackberries

1 oz (30 g) raspberries

2 large eggs

¼ cup (1¾ oz; 50 g) blond cane sugar

Confectioner's sugar, to serve

Preheat the oven at 350°F (180°C). Butter the ramekins; set aside.

In a pot, combine the milk and cream with the vanilla bean and seeds and the cardamom pods and seeds. Bring to a simmer over medium heat. Remove from the heat and cover. Set aside to infuse for 30 minutes. Strain and discard the vanilla and cardamom; set aside.

In the meantime, slice the bread into 12 triangular pieces that are identical in size. Arrange them inside the ramekins, alternating the angle with each piece—you should have 4 pieces in each ramekin. Drizzle with the melted butter and tuck the blackberries and raspberries between the slices.

In a bowl, beat together the eggs and sugar to combine. Stir in the infused milk and cream. Divide the batter between the ramekins and let rest for 10 minutes.

Bake the puddings for 30 minutes, or until the flan is set and the bread is lightly browned. Remove from the oven and let cool. Serve lukewarm and dusted with confectioner's sugar.

Buttermilk, lemon, and strawberry brunch cake

Gâteau aux fraises, au citron, et au lait ribot

You will generally find a cake on our table, although for breakfast, I tend to make my cakes less sweet and studded with fruit inside. This strawberry cake is a perfect example, with its beautiful accents of lemon and almond. Prepare it at the peak of strawberry season when the fruit is small and packed with flavor. I love to eat it with whole milk plain yogurt on the side.

You will need: a 9- or 10-inch (23 or 25.5 cm) round cake pan.

Makes one 9- or 10-inch (23 or 25.5 cm) cake

8 tablespoons (4 oz; 113 g) unsalted butter, softened and diced, plus more for the mold

½ cup (2¾ oz; 80 g) brown rice flour, plus more to dust

½ cup (2 oz; 60 g) almond meal

½ cup (2 oz; 60 g) quinoa flour

1½ teaspoons baking powder

¼ teaspoon baking soda

¼ teaspoon sea salt

½ cup (3½ oz; 100 g) blond cane sugar

1 teaspoon finely grated lemon zest

3 large eggs

⅓ cup applesauce (see stewed apples on page 40)

¼ teaspoon lemon oil

¾ cup (175 ml) buttermilk

4½ oz (125 g) strawberries, sliced

Confectioner's sugar, to dust

Preheat the oven to 350°F (180°C). Butter the cake pan, coat with rice flour, and tap out the excess; set aside.

In a bowl, combine the rice flour, almond meal, quinoa flour, baking powder, baking soda, and sea salt; set aside.

In the bowl of a stand mixer fitted with the paddle blade, cream the butter with the sugar and lemon zest. Add the eggs, one at a time, waiting until the first one is well incorporated before adding the next. Scrape the sides of the bowl frequently. Add the flour mixture to the wet ingredients, and beat until combined. Add the applesauce, lemon oil, and buttermilk; stir to combine.

Pour the batter into the buttered pan and bake for 10 minutes. Remove the cake from the oven and arrange the strawberries on top. Continue to bake for 20 to 30 minutes, or until the blade of a sharp knife inserted in the middle comes out clean. Remove from the oven and let cool for at least 20 to 30 minutes before slicing. Dust with confectioner's sugar to serve.

savory dishes
plats salés

Kale and smoked salmon quiche

Quiche au chou frisé et au saumon fumé

In the Lorraine region of France, where I come from, we eat the traditional quiche that uses *lardons* (bits of bacon) with the eggs, cheese, and cream, but I prefer mine with leafy greens like young kale, spinach, or chard instead. Quiche is wonderful for its flexibility—you can prepare the crust ahead of time or even bake the quiche the day before, as the dish reheats beautifully. Serve it with a generous green mesclun salad to complete the meal.

Note: Spinach or chard greens (I like baby chard or Swiss chard) are also wonderful green vegetable substitutes for the kale in this quiche.

You will need: an 11-inch (28 cm) quiche mold.

Serves 4 (2 slices each)

Savory Crust with Hazelnut (see page 58)

3 tablespoons olive oil

5¼ oz (150 g) kale leaves, destemmed and finely chopped

1 shallot, finely chopped

1 leek, finely chopped

3 large eggs

⅓ cup (80 ml) whole or 2% milk

⅓ cup (2½ oz; 75 g) *crème fraîche*

3½ oz (1½ cups; 100 g) finely grated Emmentaler cheese

2 oz (60 g) wild smoked salmon

1½ tablespoons finely chopped parsley

Pepper and sea salt

¼ cup (1 oz.; 30 g) finely grated Parmesan cheese

Dash of finely grated nutmeg

Preheat the oven to 400°F (200°C).

Roll and cut the dough to fit inside the mold. Arrange the dough inside the mold and, using a fork, make small holes in the bottom. Place in the fridge while you prepare the filling.

In a frying pan, heat 1 tablespoon olive oil over medium heat. Sauté the kale for 2 to 3 minutes, or until wilted; set aside. In the same pan, heat the remaining 2 tablespoons of olive oil. Add the shallot and leek. Cook on low heat for 5 minutes, stirring frequently, until soft but not browned; set aside. Add to the bowl containing the kale.

In another bowl, beat the eggs with the milk and *crème fraîche*. Stir in the Emmentaler cheese, smoked salmon, and parsley, followed by the kale and leek preparation. Season with pepper and just a little sea salt—the cheese and salmon are already salty. Fill the crust with the custard. Sprinkle the Parmesan cheese on top and add a dash of grated nutmeg.

Bake the tart for 30 to 35 minutes, or until the top is lightly golden in color. Remove from the oven and let cool for 10 minutes before slicing.

Savory crust with hazelnut
Pâte salée aux noisettes

I bake a lot of *tartes salées* (savory tarts), so I keep a number of favorite crusts handy to complement various wholesome vegetables-based fillings. I like the crusts to be nutritious and original, hence the use of flours like quinoa and brown rice with hints of hazelnuts for this nourishing quiche.

Note: You can also make this crust by hand, following the same instructions.

Makes one 11-inch (28 cm) tart or six 4½-inch (11.5 cm) tartlets

⅔ cup (2¾ oz; 80 g) quinoa flour

½ cup (2¾ oz; 80 g) brown rice flour or white rice flour, plus more to dust

½ cup (1¾ oz; 50 g) hazelnut meal

⅓ cup (1¼ oz; 40 g) cornstarch

½ teaspoon sea salt

1 batch Flax Gel (page 30)

8 tablespoons (4 oz; 113 g) unsalted butter, diced

3 tablespoons cold water

In the bowl of a stand mixer fitted with the paddle blade, combine the quinoa flour, brown rice flour, hazelnut meal, cornstarch, and sea salt. Add the flax gel and beat until incorporated. Add the butter and beat on medium speed until crumbles form. Gradually add the water while beating until the dough detaches from the bowl and forms a ball—it will be sticky. Dust the dough with brown rice flour and shape into a 6-inch (15 cm) circle. Place on a plate, cover, and refrigerate for at least 1 hour. Remove from the fridge at least 10 minutes before using if it's too cold.

Tomato and fennel tart

Tarte aux tomates et au fenouil

While I enjoy the clean fresh bite of fennel when it's raw and thinly sliced in a salad, I also like to cook with it, like in this tart where it's simmered until it is softened and tender. In this tart, it pairs beautifully with the more vibrant flavor of summery sun-filled tomatoes.

You will need: an 11-inch (28 cm) tart mold with a removable bottom.

Serves 4 (2 slices each)

Rustic Crust with Teff Flour (page 60)

FOR THE TOPPING:

4 to 5 small tomatoes (1 lb; 450 g), cut in ¼-inch slices

Sea salt and pepper

4 lemon thyme sprigs

Olive oil, to drizzle on tomatoes, plus 2 tablespoons

1 fennel bulb (12¼ oz; 350 g), cleaned and thinly sliced with a mandoline

2 thyme sprigs

1 bay leaf

1 teaspoon light Muscovado sugar

1 teaspoon balsamic vinegar

FOR THE BATTER:

2 large eggs

½ cup (120 ml) heavy cream, unsweetened coconut milk, or *crème fraîche*

1½ oz (40 g; ⅓ cup) finely grated manchego cheese or Parmesan cheese

2 tablespoons mixed chopped herbs (such as dill, parsley, chives, cilantro)

Sea salt and pepper

Roll the crust to a ⅕-inch (0.5 cm) thickness (patch it with your hands if it breaks in places). Arrange the dough inside the mold and, using a fork, make small holes in the bottom. Place in the fridge while you prepare the filling.

Preheat the oven to 325°F (160°C).

Line a rimmed baking sheet with a large piece of parchment paper. Arrange the tomato slices on the sheet and season with sea salt and pepper. Sprinkle with the chopped lemon thyme and drizzle with olive oil. Bake for 30 minutes. Remove from the oven and let cool.

In the meantime, heat 2 tablespoons olive oil in a sauté pan over medium heat. Add the fennel and whole thyme sprigs and cook for a few minutes. Add the bay leaf and sugar, then season with sea salt and pepper. Cover and reduce the heat. Simmer, stirring occasionally, for about 10 to 15 minutes. Add the balsamic vinegar and continue to cook, uncovered, for 5 more minutes, or until the fennel is tender. Discard the bay leaf and thyme.

Turn the oven up to 400°F (200°C). In a bowl, beat the eggs with the heavy cream. Stir in the cheese and fresh herbs, then season with sea salt and pepper. Layer the fennel in the bottom of the tart crust, then cover evenly with the batter. Arrange the tomatoes on top.

Bake for about 30 minutes, or until the filling is set and a light golden brown. Remove from the oven and let cool for 5 to 10 minutes before slicing.

Rustic crust with teff flour
Pâte salée à la farine de teff

Teff flour is pleasantly light and slightly gritty, which makes it a great addition to a crust with a rustic flavor.

Note: You can also make this crust by hand following the same instructions.

Makes one 11-inch (28 cm) tart or six 4½-inch (11.5 cm) tartlets

1 cup (4½ oz; 125 g) millet flour

¼ cup (1½ oz; 35 g) teff flour

⅓ cup (1¾ oz; 54 g) brown rice flour or white rice flour, plus more to dust

⅓ cup (1½ oz; 40 g) tapioca starch or cornstarch

½ teaspoon sea salt

1 batch Flax Gel (page 30)

8 tablespoons (4 oz; 113 g) unsalted butter, cold and diced

3 to 4 tablespoons cold water

In the bowl of a stand mixer fitted with the paddle blade, combine the flours, tapioca starch, and sea salt. Add the flax gel and beat on medium speed. Add the butter and continue to beat until crumbles form. Gradually add the water while beating until the dough detaches from the bowl and forms a ball—it will be sticky.

Dust the dough with brown rice flour and shape it into a 6-inch (15 cm) circle. Place on a plate, and cover. If using for tartlets, divide the dough into smaller balls (one for each tartlet) and wrap in plastic wrap. Refrigerate for at least 1 hour. Remove from the fridge at least 10 minutes before using if it's too cold.

Radish, yogurt cream, and buckwheat bread *verrines*
WITH CHIVES
Verrines de radis au yaourt avec ciboulette et miettes de pain au sarrasin

Lulu is always excited when spring arrives, because she knows we will head to the garden to plant radishes together. In this recipe, I especially like the French breakfast variety—the most common in France—because of their pretty color, small size, and sweet spiciness, but multicolored radishes are also beautiful if that's what you have. The contrast of texture, taste, and color here is delightful; from the delicate heat of the radishes to the smoothness of the cream and the crunch of the crumbs, the last spoonful will leave you wanting more. Serve as part of a brunch or as an *amuse-bouche* to start a meal.

The inspiration for this recipe comes from the Danish restaurant Noma, where Philip and I were lucky enough to eat many years ago.

Serves 8

22 small French breakfast radishes or 12 medium-size colored radishes

2 tablespoons chopped chives

8 oz (227 g) quark, Greek yogurt, or *fromage blanc*

Sea salt and pepper

2 tablespoons olive oil

2 thin slices Pecan, Almond, and Buckwheat Breakfast Bread (page 35)

1 tablespoon (½ oz; 15 g) walnuts, toasted and coarsely chopped

Fleur de sel

Coarsely chop 4 small radishes (or 2 colored ones, if that's what you're using). In a bowl, stir the chopped radishes and chives into the quark. Season with sea salt and pepper, then stir in 1 tablespoon olive oil. Spoon the mixture evenly into eight ⅓-cup (80 ml) glasses; set aside.

In a frying pan, heat the remaining tablespoon of olive oil over medium heat.

Add the slices of bread and fry for 1 to 2 minutes on each side, or until crispy. Transfer the bread to a clean working surface and leave to cool, then chop into fine breadcrumbs; set aside.

Stud the quark cream in each glass with the remaining radishes, and top with walnuts and breadcrumbs. Sprinkle with *fleur de sel*.

Fromage blanc, a cross between yogurt and sour cream, is popular in France. While it has a thicker texture than yogurt, it is often used like yogurt in many sweet and savory preparations. *Quark* (German for "fresh curd") is a fresh and lightly drained cow's milk cheese, very similar to yogurt cheeses like *fromage blanc.*

Apple, avocado, and crab *verrines*

Verrines de pommes, d'avocat, et de crabe

I find this *verrine* irresistible because it uses some of my best-loved flavors and ingredients. I pay particular attention to the quality of the crabmeat. If I can find them, I buy frozen Alaskan king crab legs and break them open to remove the meat (making sure to wear gloves, as the legs are prickly).

Prepare this dish as close to serving time as you can; you want the apple and avocado to stay as fresh and bright as possible.

Note: Gomasio is also known as sesame salt.

Serves 6

1 large Pink Lady apple or another flavorful apple

1 avocado (not too ripe but ready to eat)

3 tablespoons lime juice

Sea salt and pepper

1 teaspoon finely grated fresh ginger

1 tablespoon almond or avocado oil

2 tablespoons olive oil, plus more to drizzle

1 teaspoon chopped chives

1 teaspoon chopped cilantro

4½ oz (125 g) fresh crabmeat, diced

Micro greens (beetroot or radish), to serve

2 tablespoons black gomasio or black sesame seeds with a dash of *fleur de sel*, to serve

Core the apple and dice. Pit the avocado and dice the same size as apple pieces. Combine the apple and avocado in a bowl, and toss gently with 2 tablespoons lime juice.

Place a pinch of sea salt and pepper in a small bowl. Stir in the ginger and 1 tablespoon lime juice. Add the oils and emulsify with a small whisk. Stir in the fresh herbs; set aside.

Add three-fourths of the crab to the apple and avocado. Pour the dressing over the crab mixture and toss gently. Divide the mixture between six 1-cup glasses and top with the remaining crabmeat. Garnish with micro greens, gomasio, and a drizzle of olive oil. Serve as part of a brunch or as an *amuse-bouche* to start a meal.

Sautéed broccoli, avocado, and black quinoa salad

Salade au broccoli grillé, à l'avocat, et au quinoa noir

Whenever I cook quinoa, Lulu invariably asks, *"Quelle couleur il a?"* ("What color is it?") At home, we like to eat all the varieties: white, red, and black. I love black quinoa more for its dramatic color and welcoming al dente texture; you can feel each bite with your teeth. Its color also makes this zesty, green vegetable–filled salad stand out—just what your body needs to start the day on the right foot.

Note: Collect and use the grapefruit juice released when you slice it.

Serves 4

FOR THE DRESSING:

Sea salt and pepper

2 tablespoons grapefruit juice

1 tablespoon tahini

2 tablespoons whole plain yogurt

2 tablespoons olive oil

2 tablespoons water

1 tablespoon chopped chives

1 tablespoon chopped cilantro or parsley

FOR THE SALAD:

2 pink grapefruit

2 tablespoons (10 oz; 30 g) pine nuts

½ cup (3½ oz; 100 g) dry black quinoa

Sea salt

2 tablespoons olive oil

1 lb, 2 oz (500 g) broccoli heads, well separated

Pepper

2 avocados, pitted and diced

With a sharp serrated knife, peel the skin and pith from the grapefruit. Cut the fruit into segments, discarding the membrane and collecting the juice for the dressing; set aside.

To prepare the dressing: In a bowl, whisk together sea salt, pepper, grapefruit juice, and tahini; combine well. Stir in the yogurt and olive oil. Add the water and emulsify with a small whisk. Stir in the fresh herbs; set aside.

To prepare the salad: In a frying pan, roast the pine nuts for 1 to 2 minutes over low to medium heat, or until lightly golden in color (watch carefully as the color turns quickly); set aside.

Place the quinoa in a pot with ¾ cup (175 ml) water and a pinch of sea salt. Bring to a boil and cover. Simmer for about 20 minutes, or until the quinoa has absorbed the water. Remove from the heat, leave covered, and set aside.

In a large frying pan, heat the olive oil over medium heat. Add the broccoli and cook for 2 minutes, stirring frequently. Season with sea salt and cook for 3 to 4 more minutes, or until the broccoli starts to brown lightly but retains its crunch; season with pepper. In a large bowl, combine the broccoli, cooked quinoa, avocado, grapefruit, and pine nuts. Toss with the dressing and serve.

Coppa-wrapped mushroom and pepper breakfast frittata

Frittata aux champignons, à la coppa, et aux poivrons rouges

Aside from *un oeuf à la coque et des mouillettes* (eggs and soldiers), the French are not notorious for including eggs on their breakfast menu. I'm still French, but I've lived abroad long enough that I've grown to find eggs indispensable. Individually baked frittatas like these frequently find their way to our table. I like to use ramekins to give them their nest-like shape and favor herbs freshly picked in the garden when possible. I suggest marjoram and parsley because I always grow some, but you can really choose whatever herbs you prefer.

You will need: four ¾-cup (180 ml), 4-by-2-inch (10 by 5 cm) ramekins.

Serves 4

2 tablespoons olive oil, plus more for the ramekins

16 slices (2¾ oz; 80 g) *coppa*

4½ oz (125 g) crimini mushrooms, cleaned or peeled, and thinly sliced

1 garlic clove, peeled and minced

¼ cup diced red bell pepper

1 tablespoon white vermouth or dry white wine

Sea salt and pepper

4 large eggs

2 tablespoons *crème fraîche*

1 teaspoon finely chopped parsley

1 teaspoon finely chopped marjoram

1 oz (30 g; ½ cup) cheddar cheese, finely grated

Brush the insides of the ramekins with oil, and line each with 4 slices of *coppa*, making sure the sides and bottoms are well covered, like a nest. Set aside.

Preheat the oven to 350°F (180°C).

In a frying pan, heat 2 tablespoons olive oil over medium heat. Add the mushrooms. Cook for 3 to 4 minutes, stirring frequently, until they are soft. Add the garlic and bell pepper; continue cooking and stirring for 3 minutes. Add 1 tablespoon vermouth and season with sea salt and pepper. Cook for 1 minute more, or until all juice has evaporated. Transfer to a small bowl to cool.

In a large bowl, beat the eggs until uniform in consistency. Stir in the *crème fraîche*, parsley, marjoram, and cheese. Season with pepper (the cheese and *coppa* provide enough salt). Stir in the mushroom mixture. Divide the batter evenly between the ramekins. Bake the frittatas for 25 minutes until golden brown. Serve with a simple green salad on the side.

Salmon and poppy seed spread

Rillettes de saumon au pavot noir

One of my mother's weaknesses is eating a piece of *baguette* with creamy *rillettes* (rustic *pâté*) spread on top. Unlike her, I never cared much for *rillettes*, until I started to make my own with salmon instead of the traditional pork. I find it much more lively with a hint of mustard, a lot of fresh herbs, and crunchy bits inside. Here, I combine smoked salmon with freshly cooked salmon to deepen the flavor even more, but trout would be a great stand-in too. You can serve them *nature* (plain) with toast, or for a more sophisticated look, use the garnish of apple and lime I suggest—it's a burst of flavors in one bite.

Makes 2¼ cups

7 oz (200 g) skinned wild salmon

2 tablespoons olive oil

Sea salt and pepper

3 tablespoons (1½ oz; 40 g) unsalted butter, softened

2¾ oz (80 g) smoked salmon, finely chopped

3 tablespoons *crème fraîche*

1 teaspoon *moutarde forte de Dijon* (Dijon mustard)

1 tablespoon dill, finely chopped

1 tablespoon chives, finely chopped

1 celery branch, finely chopped

1 tablespoon poppy seeds

Crushed red peppercorns

2 tablespoons lime juice

FOR THE GARNISH:

2 limes, one to slice and one juiced

1 apple, cored

Slices of gluten-free country bread or Pecan, Almond, and Buckwheat Breakfast Bread (page 35), to taste

Chives or dill, finely chopped

Preheat the oven to 375°F (190°C).

Brush the salmon with 1 tablespoon olive oil on both sides, and season with sea salt and pepper. Place in an ovenproof dish and bake for about 10 minutes, or until just cooked through. Remove from the oven and transfer to a bowl to cool.

In a small bowl, mash the butter with a fork; set aside.

Add the smoked salmon, *crème fraîche*, mustard, dill, chives, celery, and poppy seeds to the bowl with the cooled salmon. Season with crushed red peppercorns to taste. Work with a fork or the tips of your fingers until everything is combined. Add the butter and continue to mix. Stir in the lime juice and remaining tablespoon of olive oil. The texture should be slightly chunky. Cover and place in the fridge until ready to use. If making ahead of time, it will keep for 1 to 2 days.

To prepare the garnish: Peel the skin and pith from one lime and slice thin; set aside. Slice the apple very thin with a mandoline, and drizzle with lime juice to prevent oxidation; set aside.

Toast the bread and spread the smoked salmon mixture on top. Add a slice of apple and a slice of lime to each toast. Top with chopped chives.

Savory cake

WITH SUN-DRIED TOMATOES, NUTS, AND OLIVES

Cake salé aux tomates séchées, aux noix, et aux olives

Despite what the name *cake* suggests, this is savory food, not sweet. I love the versatility of the cake and serve it on many different occasions, including brunch, a picnic, or *l'heure de l'apéro* (or *apéritif*), when the French like to gather to unwind before dinner. Cut the cake in slices or in strips; enjoy it plain or spread with soft goat cheese. However you serve it, it's irresistible finger food!

Serves 6 to 8

⅓ cup (80 ml) olive oil, plus more for the pan

⅔ cup (2¾ oz; 80 g) millet flour

¼ cup (1½ oz; 40 g) buckwheat flour

⅓ cup (1¼ oz; 35 g) hazelnut meal

⅓ cup (1½ oz; 40 g) cornstarch or tapioca starch

1 teaspoon baking powder

½ teaspoon baking soda

½ teaspoon light Muscovado sugar

¼ teaspoon sea salt

Dash of pepper

3 large eggs

½ cup (120 ml) buttermilk

3 tablespoons vermouth or dry white wine

¾ cup (3 oz; 90 g) finely grated Parmesan cheese or crumbled goat cheese

2 oz (60 g) sun-dried tomatoes, chopped

⅓ cup (1½ oz; 40 g) coarsely chopped pine nuts or walnuts

⅓ cup (1¾ oz; 50 g) pitted Kalamata olives, finely chopped

1 tablespoon finely chopped parsley

1 tablespoon finely chopped basil

1 tablespoon finely chopped oregano

3 slices prosciutto, finely diced

Preheat the oven to 400°F (200°C).

Oil a 9-by-4½-inch (23 by 11.5 cm) bread pan and set aside.

In a bowl, combine the flours, hazelnut meal, cornstarch, baking powder, baking soda, sugar, salt, and pepper; set aside. In a separate bowl, beat the eggs with a whisk; add to the dry ingredients and stir well. Stir in the buttermilk, olive oil, and vermouth. Add the cheese, sun-dried tomatoes, nuts, olives, herbs, and prosciutto and stir.

Transfer the cake batter to the pan and bake for 10 minutes. Reduce the heat to 350°F (180°C) and bake for 35 minutes, or until the blade of a sharp knife inserted in the middle comes out clean. Let it cool slightly before unmolding. Place on a rack to cool completely.

Slice to serve.

soups, savory tarts, and salads

les soupes, les tartes salées, et les salades

SOUPS, SAVORY TARTS, AND SALADS—these are the foods I often crave for lunch. I never ignore a craving.

When I was studying languages at the university, I remember my Dutch teacher telling me in her thickly accented but impeccable French, *"Vous verrez Béatrice, une fois que vous travaillerez et que vous aurez une famille, vous n'aurez plus le temps de cuisiner"* ("You will see, Béatrice. Once you have a family and work, you won't have time to cook"). I don't remember why we were talking about this, but I recall secretly thinking that she was crazy and clearly didn't know what she was talking about. I didn't set out to prove her wrong, but I was convinced that what she was telling me would never happen. Impossible!

With a family, children, or none of it, I knew that I would continue to cook—breakfast, lunch, dinner, and whatever goes in between. I enjoyed homemade food too much to sacrifice it. Perhaps my cooking would simplify when the circumstances required it (and it did when Lulu, and now Rémy, was a baby and I was sleep-deprived), but it would never stop. In fact, becoming a mother made cooking even more meaningful—and necessary. Eating well meant that I would be able to take better care of my family.

C'est tout simple, non? (Straightforward, isn't it?)

"Tu es la reine des soupes" ("You are the queen of soups"), my sister-in-law, Geneviève, once told me when she and my brother came for lunch. For some reason, those words were music to my ears, even more than when she told me she liked my roasted chicken recipe. Perhaps it's because I've always believed that a soup, a mixed salad, or a vegetable tart reveals a lot about who I am and my style of cooking. It may be silly to think that way, but the fact is that, above any others, these are the foods I will always go back to should I have to choose. (I should mention that I will also gladly reach for a slice of hazelnut, chocolate, and olive oil cake or a berry crumble.) These foods are simple to execute; loaded with vegetables, legumes, and good grains; visually stimulating; fun to transport and share; and keep well if I see the need for it.

Sometimes my soups are hearty and a meal in themselves, like the Hearty Fish Soup (page 92) and the Minestrone Soup with Cilantro Pesto (page 89). Other times they start off a meal; I've often served the Tomato and Watermelon Gazpacho (page 85) as part of a more generous summer lunch in the garden with friends. My vegetable tarts are nutritious and have personality—and they are also oh so French. My salads adapt to whatever the occasion and what I feel like adding to them (you will notice radishes appear in many of them).

These recipes are suitable for many meals too: a simple family lunch or one shared with a friend when Lulu and Philip are gone for the day; a casual dinner at home or one shared with a crowd of friends; a potluck at someone's house or a picnic at the beach. Remember these dishes when you are short on ideas about what to cook for such occasions. That's what I do, and it makes my family happy every time.

soups, savory tarts, and salads

soups
les soupes

Radish leaf soup • *Soupe de fanes de radis*   82

Tomato and watermelon gazpacho with fresh crabmeat and *crème fraîche* •
Gazpacho de tomates et de pastèque avec crabe et crème fraîche   85

Corn and fennel soup with sage, steamed clams, chorizo, and parsley oil • *Soupe au maïs et
au fenouil à la sauge avec praires, chorizo, et huile au persil*   86

Minestrone soup with cilantro pesto • *Minestrone et pesto de coriandre*   89

Hearty fish soup • *Soupe de poisson complète*   92

Sweet potato and orange soup with smoked trout and pumpkin oil • *Soupe à la patate douce
et à l'orange avec truite fumée et huile de courge*   95

Parsnip, potato, and pear soup with goat cheese, and hazelnut and tarragon pesto •
*Soupe aux panais, aux pommes de terre, et aux poires avec fromage de chèvre et
pesto à l'estragon et aux noisettes*   97

tartine and vegetable tarts
tartine et les tartes aux légumes

Fava bean and pea spread with roasted almond and herbs • *Tartinade de petits pois et
de fèves aux herbes et aux amandes grillées*   102

Tomato tart with mustard and honey • *Tarte aux tomates à la moutarde au miel*   104

Thyme-flavored turnip tatin tart • *Tarte tatin aux navets et au thym*   108

Red kuri squash and celeriac tart • *Tarte au potimarron et au céléri rave*   111

Vegetable tart with pear and Roquefort, and an endive salad • *Tarte fine aux légumes,
aux poires et au Roquefort avec salade d'endives*   112

mixed salads
les salades composées

Potato, cucumber, and asparagus salad with goat cheese • *Salade de pommes de terre, de concombre et d'asperges avec fromage de chèvre*   118

Shaved vegetable salad with sunchokes • *Salade de pluches de légumes aux topinambours*   120

Warm salmon and spring vegetable salad with soft-boiled eggs and vanilla-flavored vinaigrette • *Salade tiède de saumon et de légumes printaniers avec oeuf mollet et vinaigrette à la vanille*   123

Cranberry bean and watercress salad with anchovies and grapes • *Salade aux haricots coco et au cresson avec anchois et raisins*   124

French green bean salad with *croûtons*, olives, and ricotta salata • *Salade de haricots verts avec croûtons, olives, et ricotta salata*   126

Fava beans and cherry salad with ginger-flavored vinaigrette • *Salade de fèves et de cerises avec vinaigrette au gingembre*   129

Red lentil salad with citrus, fennel, and smoked salmon with tahini vinaigrette • *Salade de lentilles corail aux agrumes et au fenouil avec saumon fumé et vinaigrette au tahini*   130

Avocado and melon salad with dill, mozzarella, and prosciutto • *Salade d'avocat et de melon avec aneth, mozzarella, et prosciutto*   132

Spring green quinoa salad • *Salade de quinoa aux légumes verts printaniers*   135

Radish, fennel, and apple salad with truffle salt • *Salade de radis, de fenouil, et de pommes au sel parfumé à la truffe*   136

Julienned zucchini and watermelon radish salad • *Salade de julienne de courgettes et de pastèque radis*   138

soups

les soupes

Radish leaf soup

Soupe de fanes de radis

Radish greens are what bring the cheerful spring color and delightful peppery flavor to this simple soup. (This soup is also an excellent way to use the greens of root vegetables too often forgotten.) Choose superfresh radishes for their vibrant leaves—maybe those from your garden if you keep one, or the farmers' market—and enjoy the soup *nature* (plain) as we do, with thinly sliced radishes and a dash of *fleur de sel* sprinkled on top.

Serves 6

2 tablespoons butter

1 large shallot, finely chopped

1 celery stalk, diced

1 garlic clove, minced

3 potatoes (400 g), peeled and diced

1 ripe Bartlett pear, peeled, cored, and diced

3 cups (710 ml) water

2 cilantro sprigs, plus more for garnish

Sea salt and pepper

4½ oz (125 g) radish leaves (from 2 bunches radishes)

6 small pink radishes, thinly sliced

Fleur de sel, to serve

Olive oil or herb-flavored oil, to drizzle

In a large pot, melt the butter over medium heat. Add the shallot and celery. Cook for 3 minutes, stirring occasionally; do not let the mixture brown. Add the garlic and cook for 1 minute. Add the potatoes and pear, and continue to cook for 5 minutes. Add the water and cilantro, and season with sea salt and pepper. Cover and simmer for 17 minutes. Add the radish leaves and cook for 5 more minutes.

Transfer the soup, a few cups at a time, to the bowl of a food processor and purée until smooth. Check the seasoning, and ladle into shallow bowls or soup plates. Top with slices of radish and a sprinkle of *fleur de sel*. You can add a little cream for richness, if you like, or flavored oil such as cilantro or parsley oil (page 88).

Tomato and watermelon gazpacho
WITH FRESH CRABMEAT AND *CRÈME FRAÎCHE*

Gazpacho de tomates et de pastèque avec crabe et crème fraîche

A chilled gazpacho soup makes summer sing. In mine, I use watermelon to mellow the taste and serve it with a dollop of silky *crème fraîche* and some crab for added sweetness. If you can, make the soup the day before so the flavors have time to develop—they will improve. Also, use the best watermelon, tomatoes, and crab you can find, because fresh ingredients make all the difference in the taste of a cold soup. People at the table applaud when they see me arrive with bowls of this bright gazpacho for them to enjoy.

Serves 6

FOR THE GAZPACHO:

1 lb, 5¼ oz (600 g) ripe seedless watermelon flesh, diced

1 lb, 5¼ oz (600 g) tomatoes, diced (about 4 tomatoes)

1 English cucumber, peeled, seeded, and diced (makes 7 oz, 200 g)

1 red bell pepper, seeds and pith removed (makes 7 oz, 200 g)

1 large shallot, coarsely chopped

1 garlic clove, minced

Sea salt and pepper

⅓ cup (80 ml) olive oil

2 tablespoons sherry vinegar

FOR THE GARNISH:

1 avocado, pitted

1 teaspoon lime juice

4½ oz (125 g) fresh crabmeat

1 cup cucumber cut in ⅓-inch (1 cm) pieces

1 cup seedless watermelon cut in ⅓-inch (1 cm) pieces

1 cup tomatoes cut in ⅓-inch (1 cm) pieces

A few leaves of basil, finely chopped

1 tablespoon chopped chives

6 teaspoons *crème fraîche*

Fleur de sel, to serve

Olive oil, to drizzle

To prepare the gazpacho: In the bowl of your food processor, combine the watermelon, tomatoes, cucumber, bell pepper, shallot, and garlic. Purée until smooth, using batches if necessary. Transfer to a large bowl. Season with sea salt and pepper. Stir in the olive oil and vinegar. Place in the fridge for a few hours, or preferably overnight.

To prepare the garnish: Dice the avocado into ⅓-inch (1 cm) cubes and drizzle with the lime juice; set aside.

When ready to serve, divide the gazpacho between bowls. Top each with fresh crabmeat; diced cucumber, watermelon, avocado, and tomatoes; and chopped herbs. Add a dollop of *crème fraîche*, sprinkle with *fleur de sel*, and drizzle with olive oil.

Corn and fennel soup

WITH SAGE, STEAMED CLAMS, CHORIZO, AND PARSLEY OIL

Soupe au maïs et au fenouil à la sauge avec praires, chorizo, et huile au persil

Being French, I did not know that corn soup had such flavorful potential (in France, you rarely find or eat fresh corn). Once I had a taste, though, I could see I had been missing out. I've tried my hand at many corn soups, and while I liked them all, I think this one is the best. It is especially good when, to add more body, I top it with steamed clams and aromatic parsley oil. This makes the soup a bridge between *terre et mer* (earth and ocean), a beloved theme in my cooking.

Serves 4

FOR THE GARNISH:

2 tablespoons olive oil

1 potato, peeled and finely diced

¼ cup red bell pepper, finely diced

¼ cup orange pepper, finely diced

Kernels cut from 1 ear of corn

Sea salt and pepper

FOR THE SOUP:

16 slices of spicy Spanish chorizo

16 littleneck clams

4 ears corn, husks and silks removed

2 cups (473 ml) whole milk

3 cups (710 ml) Homemade Vegetable Stock (page 96)

6 sage leaves

Sea salt and pepper

2 tablespoons olive oil

¼ red onion, finely chopped

¼ teaspoon fennel seeds, crushed

1 teaspoon ground coriander

1 leek, white part only, finely chopped

2 celery stalks, diced

1 fennel bulb, diced

2 bay leaves

Parsley Oil (see page 88), for serving

Fresh parsley, finely chopped

To prepare the garnish: In a frying pan, heat the olive oil over medium heat. Add the potato and bell peppers. Sauté for 5 minutes, or until the vegetables are cooked through (test by piercing them with a sharp knife). Add the corn kernels and cook for another minute. Season with sea salt and pepper; set aside.

To prepare the soup: In a nonstick frying pan, cook the sliced chorizo for a few minutes on each side, until browned. Transfer to paper towels to absorb the excess oil; set aside.

Heat a pot of water and place the clams in a steamer basket on top. Cover and cook until the clams open (about 5 minutes). Remove from the heat, and discard the clams that don't open. Cover the pot to keep the clams warm; set aside.

Using a sharp knife, cut the kernels off the ears of corn over a large bowl; set aside.

In a pot wide enough to hold the corncobs, combine the milk, stock, corn kernels and cobs, and sage. Season with sea salt and pepper, and bring to a simmer. Cook for 10 minutes, then remove from the heat. Keep covered and let rest for 10 minutes.

continued

soups, savory tarts, and salads

In the meantime, in a large pot, heat the olive oil over medium heat. Add the onion, fennel seeds, and ground coriander. Cook for 2 minutes, stirring occasionally, until soft but not browned. Add the leek and celery, and cook for 5 more minutes, stirring occasionally. Add the diced fennel and continue cooking for 5 minutes, stirring occasionally. Add the milk and corn mixture (with the corncobs still in it) and bay leaves. Simmer the soup, covered, for 15 minutes, or until the vegetables are soft. Discard the corncobs and bay leaves.

Transfer the soup to the bowl of a food processor, a few cups at a time, and purée until smooth. Pour the soup back into the pot. To serve, ladle the soup into bowls. Add a few steamed clams, slices of chorizo, and some of the garnish. Drizzle with Parsley Oil (see below), and finish with chopped parsley.

Parsley oil
Huile au persil

In addition to its scrumptious earthy taste, I love the constrast of the vibrant green of this oil against muted colors like the one in this corn soup.

Makes ⅔ cup (160 ml) parsley oil

2 cups packed parsley leaves

Sea salt

1 cup (236 ml) olive oil

Blanch the parsley for 10 seconds in salted boiling water (page 386). Transfer to an ice water bath to cool. Drain and dry between towels. Place the parsley leaves in the bowl of your food processor with the oil, and blend until the texture is fine. Pass the oil through a *chinois* or fine sieve. Pour into a glass jar and store in the fridge. The oil keeps for 1 week in the refrigerator. In addition to a garnish for the Corn and Fennel Soup, it's also lovely in a vinaigrette and as a garnish for a risotto or fish.

Minestrone soup

WITH CILANTRO PESTO

Minestrone et pesto de coriandre

I prepared this wholesome vegetable soup for the first time during a blizzard, when Philip, Lulu, and I were stuck inside. I happened to have a full fridge, including all the ingredients you see listed, and assuredly a lot of time on my hands. Preparing minestrone requires careful attention to timing; you need to add each ingredient at the right moment and in the proper order to ensure the vegetables don't become mushy. Now I make a minestrone like this one even when the weather is nice and we can go outside and play. It's a stunning soup to repeat again and again!

Notes: If you cannot find Romanesco, substitute colored cauliflower or broccoli florets. If you are using dry beans, soak them overnight before using.

Serves 6;
makes 1 cup pesto

FOR THE CILANTRO PESTO:

¼ cup (1 oz; 30 g) pine nuts or pecans

Sea salt and pepper, to taste

2 garlic cloves

¾ cup (1 oz; 30 g) packed cilantro leaves

¼ cup (1 oz; 30 g) finely grated Parmesan cheese

½ cup (120 ml) olive oil, or more to taste

FOR THE SOUP:

2 tablespoons olive oil, plus more to serve

1 large shallot or ¼ cup red onion, finely chopped

3 thyme sprigs

3 garlic cloves, minced

2 tomatoes, blanched (page 386), peeled, seeded, and diced

2 cups (7 oz; 200 g) celeriac cut in ½-inch (1.25 cm) pieces (see page 90)

2 celery stalks, diced

1 cup (3½ oz; 100 g) carrot cut in ½-inch (1.25 cm) pieces

1 cup (4½ oz; 125 g) shelled cranberry beans (see Note)

1 tablespoon finely chopped tarragon

2 bay leaves

6½ cups (1½ liters) Homemade Vegetable Stock (page 96)

½ cup (2 oz; 60 g) elbow pasta

2 cups (7 oz; 200 g) Romanesco florets

2 cups (8¾ oz; 250 g) peas (fresh or frozen)

Shaved Parmesan cheese, to serve

1 tablespoon finely chopped cilantro, to serve

To prepare the cilantro pesto: In a frying pan, toast the pine nuts over medium heat for 1 to 2 minutes, until they are slightly golden. Remove from the heat and let cool.

In the bowl of a food processor, combine sea salt and pepper, pine nuts, garlic, cilantro, and cheese; pulse to finely chop. Add the olive oil and continue to work to obtain a paste. Transfer to a glass jar and keep refrigerated until ready to use.

This pesto keeps for 1 week in the fridge. You can also freeze what you don't need.

To prepare the soup: In a large pot, heat the olive oil over medium heat. Add the shallot and thyme. Cook for 3 minutes, stirring occasionally; do not let the mixture brown. Add the garlic and continue to cook for another minute. Add the tomatoes and cook, stirring occasionally, for

continued

3 to 4 minutes, until the tomatoes soften. Add the celeriac, celery, and carrot pieces; cook for 4 minutes, stirring occasionally. Add the cranberry beans, tarragon, and bay leaves. Pour in the stock and bring to a simmer. Cook for 20 minutes, or until the vegetables are just cooked through. Add the pasta and cook for another 5 minutes. Add the Romanesco; cook for 2 more minutes. Add the peas and cook for another minute. Taste for salt and pepper, and season if necessary. Remove from the heat, and discard the thyme and bay leaves.

Ladle the soup into bowls. Add a heaped teaspoon of cilantro pesto, shaved Parmesan, and chopped cilantro, to taste. Drizzle with olive oil and serve.

To prepare celeriac for cooking, peel off the thick outer skin and remove the soft hollow part in the middle. Dice and place in a water bath with lemon juice until ready to use.

soups, savory tarts, and salads

Hearty fish soup

Soupe de poisson complète

When I was young, we often ate a *soupe de poissons* for dinner during the cold winter months. My mother didn't always make hers from scratch, as our local fishmonger sold a high-quality fish soup preserved fresh in tall *bocaux* (glass jars). This was the beginning of my love for fish soup.

While many of the soups we enjoy at home have a smooth texture, I like my fish soups richly flavored with chunky bits in them. This one has vegetables and pieces of aromatic smoked trout, fresh salmon, and cod. I am always reminded that it is Philip's Irish grandfather's favorite dish! It's an all-in-one kind of dish that I particularly love to cook on a frosty day when nothing feels more comforting than a nourishing soup in our tummies.

Serves 4

1 tablespoon olive oil

1 tablespoon butter

1 shallot, finely chopped

2 celery stalks, diced

1 tomato, peeled, cored, seeded, and finely chopped

3 garlic cloves, minced

14 oz (400 g) russet potatoes, peeled and diced

2 bay leaves

Sea salt and pepper

3 cups (710 ml) fish stock or clam juice

2 cups (473 ml) whole or 2% milk

¼ cup (60 ml) white vermouth or dry white wine

1 oregano sprig

2 thyme sprigs

3 oz (85 g) skinned smoked trout, coarsely shredded

½ lb (225 g) wild salmon, skinned and cut in 1-inch (2.5 cm) pieces

½ lb (225 g) cod, cut in 1-inch (2.5 cm) pieces

1 carrot, peeled and thinly sliced

1 cup (4½ oz; 125 g) peas (fresh or frozen)

¼ cup (60 ml) unsweetened heavy cream

2 tablespoons finely chopped parsley

In a large saucepan, heat the olive oil with the butter over medium heat until the butter melts. Add the shallot and celery. Cook for about 5 minutes, stirring occasionally, until the vegetables are soft but not brown. Add the tomato and garlic and cook for 2 more minutes. Stir in the potatoes and bay leaves, and season with sea salt and pepper. Cook for 3 minutes. Stir in the stock, milk, and vermouth, and bring to a simmer. Add the oregano and thyme. Cover and simmer for 20 minutes, stirring occasionally, until the potatoes are tender. Stir in the smoked trout, salmon, and cod. Add the sliced carrot, and simmer for 5 minutes. Add the peas and cream; cook for 5 more minutes. Remove from the heat, and discard the bay leaves, oregano, and thyme.

Ladle the soup into deep bowls. Garnish with fresh parsley and serve immediately.

Sweet potato and orange soup

WITH SMOKED TROUT AND PUMPKIN OIL

Soupe à la patate douce et à l'orange avec truite fumée et huile de courge

I feel the day is off to a good start when I find myself preparing a large pot of soup early in the morning. This sweet potato and orange soup is gorgeous and easy to make while you are doing something else. What's not to love about that?

It's a beautiful soup to cook in large batches to serve a crowd—I've taken it to potlucks with great success. I also often like to freeze some in Mason jars for future use; it comes in really handy when I feel like eating a nutritious soup and don't have the time to prepare one.

Serves 6 to 8

FOR THE SOUP:

2 tablespoons olive oil

1 teaspoon ground coriander

Zest of 1 orange, finely grated

1 red onion, finely chopped

1 leek, finely chopped

1-inch (2.5 cm) piece fresh ginger, finely chopped

2 garlic cloves, peeled and minced

2 sweet potatoes (1 kg), peeled and diced

3 carrots (7¾ oz [220 g] unpeeled), peeled and diced

A few stems of fresh cilantro

2 bay leaves

5 cups (1.2 liters) Homemade Vegetable Stock (see page 96) or chicken stock

Sea salt and pepper

Juice of 2 oranges (⅔ cup; 160 ml)

1 cup (236 ml) unsweetened coconut milk

FOR THE GARNISH:

Shredded smoked trout (½ oz; 15 g, per serving)

Chopped cilantro

Pumpkin oil

In a large pot, heat the olive oil over medium heat. Add the ground coriander and orange zest; cook for 1 minute, until fragrant. Add the onion, leek, and ginger. Cook for 5 minutes, without browning, stirring occasionally. Add the garlic and cook for 1 minute. Add the potatoes, carrots, cilantro, and bay leaves; cook for 5 minutes, stirring occasionally. Add the stock. Cover and simmer for 20 minutes, or until the vegetables are soft.

Season with sea salt and pepper. Discard the bay leaves and cilantro stems. Transfer the soup, a few cups at a time, to the bowl of a food processor, and purée until smooth. Pour the soup back into the pot, and stir in the orange juice and coconut milk. Taste for salt and pepper, and season accordingly.

Ladle the soup into bowls. Garnish with smoked trout and chopped cilantro. Drizzle with pumpkin oil and serve.

Homemade vegetable stock
Bouillon de légumes fait maison

I like to make my own stock because I can then flavor it with my preferred spices and fresh herbs. I always prepare large batches, as in this recipe, and freeze leftovers for future needs. Use it in risotto or soups.

Makes 10 cups (2.3 liters)

3 carrots, peeled and diced

1 onion, peeled and diced

1 leek, chopped

1 turnip, peeled and diced

3 garlic cloves, peeled and minced

3 celery stalks, diced

6 mushrooms, peeled

8 fennel seeds

3 black peppercorns

2 teaspoons sea salt

1 clove

12 cups (2.75 liters) cold water

2 bay leaves

3 thyme sprigs

In a pot, combine all the ingredients and bring to a boil. Cover and simmer for 1 hour. Remove from the heat, and leave to infuse for a few hours or overnight in the fridge. Strain the broth through a fine sieve or a *chinois*.

This broth keeps in the fridge for 1 week. Freeze any you do not use right away. You can also make ice cubes with it, and use them whenever you need only a small quantity in a dish.

Parsnip, potato, and pear soup

WITH GOAT CHEESE, AND HAZELNUT AND TARRAGON PESTO

Soupe aux panais, aux pommes de terre, et aux poires avec fromage de chèvre et pesto à l'estragon et aux noisettes

Don't be fooled by the humble appearance of parsnips. These root vegetables have a distinct flavor and are full of nutrition—and what's more, I personally find them beautiful to photograph. This soup pairs parsnips with sweet, juicy pears; bits of goat cheese; and an herb-scented nut pesto to finish. These are modest additions to enhance the naturally nutty flavor of the vegetable.

Serves 6; makes 1 cup (236 ml) pesto

Hazelnut and Tarragon Pesto (see page 99)

FOR THE TOPPING:

5¼ oz (150 g) fresh goat cheese, crumbled

2–3 tablespoons dried cranberries, coarsely chopped

FOR THE SOUP:

1 lb (450 g) parsnips

1 lb, 3½ oz (550 g) red potatoes

2 tablespoons olive oil

1 shallot, finely chopped

1 large leek, white part only, chopped

2 ripe green pears, peeled, cored, and diced

5 to 5½ cups (1.2 to 1.3 liters) chicken stock or Homemade Vegetable Stock (page 96)

2 bay leaves

2 teaspoons finely chopped tarragon

Sea salt and pepper

1 cup (236 ml) heavy cream

To prepare the topping: In a small bowl, gently stir together the crumbles of goat cheese and cranberries; set aside.

To prepare the soup: Peel and dice the parsnips and potatoes. Place in a bowl filled with cold water; set aside.

In a large pot, heat olive oil over medium heat. Add the shallot and leek. Cook for 5 minutes without browning, stirring occasionally, until the vegetables are soft. Add the parsnips, potatoes, and pears; cook for 5 minutes. Add the stock, bay leaves, and tarragon. Cover and cook for 20 minutes, or until all vegetables are soft. Remove from the heat, and discard the bay leaves.

Transfer the soup, a few cups at a time, to the bowl of a food processor and purée until smooth. Return the soup to the pot, season to taste with sea salt and pepper, and stir in the cream. Heat gently until warm. To serve, ladle the soup into bowls. Add a spoonful of pesto to each and stir just enough to swirl it through. Top with crumbles of goat cheese and cranberries.

continued

Hazelnut and tarragon pesto
Pesto aux noisettes et à l'estragon

To me a pesto stands as a beautiful addition to elevate a simple recipe into a more unique and memorable one. Hence I keep a number of pesto recipes up my sleeve, like this one, which I love because it's made with tarragon—one of my favorite garden herbs—hints of orange, and protein-packed hazelnuts.

¼ cup (1 oz; 30 g) whole hazelnuts

1 garlic clove

½ teaspoon orange zest, finely grated

¼ cup tarragon leaves

½ cup parsley leaves

¼ cup (1 oz; 30 g) finely grated Parmesan cheese

Freshly ground pepper

½ cup (120 ml) olive oil, or more to taste

In a nonstick frying pan, toast the hazelnuts over medium heat for 1 to 2 minutes, until slightly golden. Remove from the heat and rub the nuts with a kitchen towel to remove the skins.

In the bowl of a food processor, combine the roasted hazelnuts, garlic, orange zest, tarragon, parsley, cheese, and pepper to taste. Add the olive oil and continue to work to obtain a paste. Transfer to a jar. This pesto keeps for a week in the fridge, and you can freeze any extra.

tartine and vegetable tarts
tartine et les tartes aux légumes

Fava bean and pea spread

WITH ROASTED ALMOND AND HERBS

Tartinade de petits pois et de fèves aux herbes et aux amandes grillées

Pairing fava beans and peas with lime and fresh herbs makes for food that is vibrant in color and clean in taste. This spread is perfect for adding enjoyment to some of the best vegetables we find in spring. Use it alone with a bowl of steaming fingerling potatoes, or make it part of this wholesome *tartine*—one of my favorite foods to enjoy when I feel like a light lunch.

Makes 4 large or 8 small tartines

1 cup (4½ oz; 125 g) shelled fresh green peas

1 lb, 9 oz (700 g) fresh fava beans

2 tablespoons whole almonds

½ tablespoon lime juice

¼ cup parsley

Sea salt and pepper

3 tablespoons olive oil, plus more to drizzle

1 tablespoon finely chopped mint

1 garlic clove, peeled and cut in half (optional)

4 slices bread of your choice (I used maple-flavored oat GF bread.)

3½ oz (100 g) soft goat cheese (like Petit Billy) or Labneh (page 36)

12 multicolored cherry tomatoes, cut in half

Shaved pecorino cheese, to taste

A few thinly sliced radishes, to serve

Pea shoots (optional)

Fleur de sel

Blanch the peas in salted boiling water for 1 minute (page 386). Transfer to an ice water bath to cool; drain and set aside.

Prepare the fava beans (see below).

In a frying pan, roast the almonds for 2 to 3 minutes over medium heat; remove from the heat and set aside to cool. In the bowl of a food processor, grind the almonds into a coarse powder; transfer to a small bowl, and set aside.

In the bowl of the food processor, add the peas, ½ cup fava beans, lime juice, and parsley; purée to a chunky texture. Transfer to a bowl, season with sea salt and pepper, and stir in 3 tablespoons olive oil. Stir in the mint and almonds. Add the garlic, if using; set aside.

To serve, toast the bread. Spread the toasts with goat cheese and top with the green mash. Divide the tomatoes and remaining beans between the toasts. Top with shaved cheese, radishes, and pea shoots. Add a dash of *fleur de sel*, and drizzle with olive oil.

Remove the fava beans from their pods. Boil them for 1 minute in a large pot of salted boiling water, then drain and transfer to an ice water bath to cool. Pinch the beans between two fingers to remove their skins. You will have about 1 cup fava beans; set aside.

soups, savory tarts, and salads

Tomato tart

WITH MUSTARD AND HONEY

Tarte aux tomates à la moutarde au miel

I find that mustard is a very French ingredient to add to a tomato tart. My mother often baked a tart similar to this one when I was a kid.

The flavor of quality tomatoes is everything in this tart—it's also one of my favorite summer vegetable tarts. I prefer to prepare it with yellow, orange, and red heirloom tomatoes for their vibrant colors. This tart is best eaten on the day you bake it, since the tomato juices may make the crust soggy if it sits too long. Not to worry; it's delicious enough that no one will want to leave leftovers.

You will need: one 11-inch (28 cm) tart mold.

Serves 4 (2 slices each)

Savory Crust with Oat (see page 106)

2 tablespoons *moutarde forte de Dijon au miel* (honey-flavored Dijon mustard)

1 tablespoon *crème fraîche*

3 oz (85 g) Comté cheese, finely grated

1 lb, 12½ oz (800 g) sun-ripened tomatoes (choose different colors)

1 teaspoon finely chopped marjoram

1 teaspoon finely chopped thyme

Olive oil to drizzle

Pepper

Arrange the crust inside the mold and, using a fork, make small holes in the bottom. Place in the fridge for 30 minutes to 1 hour.

Preheat the oven to 400°F (200°C).

In a small bowl, stir the mustard and *crème fraîche* together. Spread over the pastry. Sprinkle the cheese on top. Slice the tomatoes and arrange over the cheese in an even layer. Sprinkle the fresh herbs evenly over the tomatoes. Drizzle olive oil over the tart and season with pepper; salt should be unnecessary as it is present in the mustard. Bake the tart for 30 to 35 minutes. Remove from the oven and let cool for 15 minutes before slicing. Enjoy with a green salad on the side.

Savory crust with oat
Pâte salée à la farine d'avoine

This savory crust is more neutral in taste than the others I bake, so I like to use it to prepare savory or sweet tarts such as the Apple Tartlets on page 166.

Note: You can also make this crust by hand following the same instructions.

Makes one 11-inch (28 cm) tart or six 4½-inch (11.5 cm) tartlets.

1 cup (4½ oz; 125 g) millet flour

⅓ cup (1½ oz; 40 g) oat flour

⅓ cup (2 oz; 55 g) sweet rice flour

⅓ cup (1½ oz; 40 g) cornstarch

½ teaspoon sea salt

1 batch Flax Gel (page 30)

8 tablespoons (4 oz; 113 g) unsalted butter, diced

2 to 3 tablespoons cold water

In the bowl of a stand mixer fitted with the paddle blade, combine the millet flour, oat flour, sweet rice flour, cornstarch, and sea salt. Add the flax gel and beat on medium speed. Add the butter and continue to beat until crumbles form. Gradually add the water while beating and work until the dough detaches from the bowl and forms a ball—it will be sticky. Dust the dough with white rice flour, shape into a 6-inch (15 cm) circle, and place on a plate. Cover and refrigerate for at least 1 hour. Remove from the fridge at least 10 minutes before using if it's too cold.

Thyme-flavored turnip tatin tart

Tarte tatin aux navets et au thym

You may have tasted an apple *tarte tatin* before. But what about one made with vegetables like turnips? I love how the slightly bitter taste of this often-unsung root vegetable balances with the sweetness of the honey.

A fresh turnip should be hard and its skin should glow. Choose medium or small turnips for this dish.

You will need: one 11-inch (28 cm) tart mold.

Serves 4 (2 slices each)

4 tablespoons (2 oz; 56 g) unsalted butter

3 to 4 medium turnips (1 lb; 450 g), peeled and cut with a mandoline into ⅛-inch (3 mm) pieces

4 tablespoons clover honey

Sea salt and pepper

½ tablespoon finely chopped thyme

1 tablespoon white balsamic vinegar or white wine vinegar

Rustic Crust with Teff Flour (page 60)

Freshly cracked red peppercorns

Line a baking sheet with a piece of parchment paper; set aside.

Melt 2 tablespoons butter in a large sauté pan over low heat. Cover the bottom of the pan with one-third of the turnip slices and cook over medium-low heat for about 1 minute on each side, without browning, until they soften. Remove from the heat and transfer to the baking sheet. Add more butter to the pan between each batch of turnips, and repeat until all are cooked; set aside.

Preheat the oven to 375°F (190°C).

Line the bottom of the tart mold with a piece of parchment paper. In the same pan that you cooked the turnips, heat the honey until it becomes liquid. Cover the bottom of the tart mold evenly with the honey. Arrange the slices of turnip on the honey in concentric circles; season with sea salt and pepper. Sprinkle with thyme, and drizzle evenly with the vinegar.

Roll the crust to a ⅕-inch (0.5 cm) thickness and cut a 12-inch (30.5 cm) round. Cover the tart with it, making sure all the turnips are covered, and tuck the sides in. Using a fork, make small holes in the top of the crust. Bake the tart for 35 to 40 minutes. Remove from the oven and let cool for 2 minutes before gently flipping onto a plate to unmold. Remove the parchment paper. Finish with red peppercorns. Slice and serve with a side salad.

Red kuri squash and celeriac tart

Tarte au potimarron et au céléri rave

Potimarron (red kuri) is easily my favorite winter squash. I am fond of its chestnut-like, buttery flavor (a *marron* is a chestnut in French) and always buy organic so that I can cook and eat the skin too—which I love for its remarkable flame-bright orange color.

When I am not roasting it or using it in a soup, I also like to use this squash to top a tart, as with this humble creation that uses a cream made of ricotta, eggs, cheese, and fresh herbs.

You will need: one 9-inch (23 cm) tart mold.

Serves 4

Savory Crust with Hazelnut (page 58)

14 oz (400 g) red kuri squash (seeded but skin on), diced

3½ oz (100 g) cleaned celeriac, diced (page 90)

2 large eggs

½ cup (4½ oz; 125 g) whole milk ricotta cheese

1 tablespoon finely chopped parsley

A dash of freshly grated nutmeg

½ cup (2 oz; 60 g) grated aged cheddar cheese

1 ripe tomato, thinly sliced

Sea salt and pepper

Olive oil, to drizzle

Preheat the oven to 350°F (180°C). Butter the tart mold; set aside.

Roll and cut the crust to fit inside the mold. Arrange the dough inside the mold and, using a fork, make small holes in the bottom. Place in the fridge for 30 minutes to 1 hour before using.

In the meantime, steam the squash and celeriac for about 20 minutes, or until tender. Using a ricer or food processor, purée the vegetables; set aside. In a bowl, beat the eggs with the ricotta. Stir in the squash and celeriac purée, parsley, nutmeg, and half of the grated cheddar. Pour the filling into the crust and top with the tomato slices. Season with sea salt and pepper, then sprinkle with the rest of the grated cheese. Drizzle with olive oil. Bake the tart for about 40 minutes or until golden in color. Remove from the oven and let cool for at least 10 minutes before slicing. Serve with a green salad on the side.

Vegetable tart

WITH PEAR AND ROQUEFORT AND AN ENDIVE SALAD

*Tarte fine aux légumes, aux poires et au Roquefort avec
une salade aux endives*

This autumnal vegetable tart beckons with thin slices of potatoes, celeriac, and zucchini finely layered with pear and pieces of Roquefort. I use perfectly ripe pears to add extra sweetness to contrast with the sharp and tangy flavor of the cheese. The endive salad on the side is a perfect choice to complete your meal; if you prefer a more basic salad, simply toss 4 cups of arugula with 4 tablespoons of Everyday Salad Dressing with Shallot (see page 115).

You will need: one 11-inch (28 cm) tart mold.

Serves 4 (2 slices each)

FOR THE TART:

1 tablespoon (½ oz.; 14 g) whole hazelnuts

2 red potatoes (7 oz; 200 g), thinly sliced with a mandoline

3½ oz (100 g) cleaned celeriac (page 90), thinly sliced with a mandoline

Rustic Crust with Teff Flour (page 60) or Savory Crust with Hazelnut (page 58)

3 large eggs, lightly beaten

¼ cup (2 oz; 60 g) crème fraîche

1 tablespoon whole or 2% milk

1 teaspoon finely chopped thyme

1 tablespoon finely chopped parsley

1½ oz (40 g) manchego cheese or Comté cheese, grated

Sea salt and pepper

5¼ oz (150 g) zucchini, thinly sliced with a mandoline

1 ripe red pear, cored, and thinly sliced

1½ oz (40 g) Roquefort cheese or Gorgonzola cheese, crumbled

Drizzle of honey (optional)

FOR THE ENDIVE SALAD:

2 tablespoons butter

½ cup (1¾ oz; 50 g) whole pecans

1 tablespoon clover honey

A dash of ground paprika

A dash of *fleur de sel*

2 red Anjou pears

A dash of cinnamon

2 heads of endive

2 cups green salad leaves or *mâche* (lamb's lettuce)

¼ cup (60 ml) Everyday Salad Dressing with Shallot (see page 115)

2¾ oz (80 g) crumbled Roquefort cheese (You can also use cranberry and crumbled goat cheese; see recipe on page 97.)

To make the tart: In a nonstick frying pan, roast the hazelnuts over medium heat for 1 to 2 minutes, until fragrant. Remove from the heat and transfer to a kitchen towel; rub the nuts with the towel until the skins come off. Chop coarsely; set aside.

Preheat the oven to 375°F (190°C).

Blanch the potato and celeriac slices in salted boiling water for 3 minutes (page 386). Transfer to an ice water bath to cool; drain and set aside.

Roll and cut the crust to fit the mold. Arrange the dough inside the mold and, using a fork, make small holes in the

continued

bottom. Blind bake the crust for 10 minutes (page 386). Remove from the oven, and take out the parchment paper and weights; set aside.

Meanwhile, in a bowl, beat together the eggs, *crème fraîche*, and milk. Stir in the thyme, parsley, and manchego cheese. Season with sea salt and pepper.

Arrange the sliced vegetables and fruit in the crust in alternating layers, following this order: potato, celeriac, zucchini, and pear. Repeat until you run out of

ingredients. Pour the egg mixture over the vegetables, and scatter the Roquefort cheese on top. Drizzle a little honey (if using) on top, to taste. Bake the tart for 25 to 30 minutes.

Top the tart with the chopped roasted hazelnuts. Let cool slightly before slicing, and serve with the endive salad on the side.

To prepare the endive salad: Preheat the oven to 375°F (190°C). Line a baking sheet with parchment paper; set aside.

In a nonstick frying pan, melt 1 tablespoon butter over medium heat. Add the pecans and honey. Cook, stirring occasionally, for 1 to 2 minutes. Remove from the heat and transfer the pecans to the baking sheet; and sprinkle with paprika and *fleur de sel*. Bake for about 10 minutes, checking that the nuts do not burn. Remove from the oven and transfer to a plate to cool; set aside.

Wash, peel, and core the pears. Quarter them, then cut them in half again. Toss lightly with cinnamon to coat. Heat the remaining tablespoon butter in the same pan you used for the nuts, and add the pears to the pan. Cook on medium to high heat for 2 minutes on each side until tender but not brown. Remove from the heat and set aside.

Cut the yellow leaves from the base of the endive heads. Place the endive leaves in a large bowl (you can slices them in sticks if you prefer). Add the mixed greens or *mâche,* and toss with the dressing. Divide the salad between plates and add slices of pears, the caramelized pecans, and cheese to each plate.

soups, savory tarts, and salads

Everyday salad dressing with shallot
Vinaigrette de tous les jours à l'échalote

This incredibly versatile dressing is easy to make and pairs well with most any salad vegetable. I prefer to prepare a vinaigrette for each salad I make (my ratio is 1 teaspoon mustard, 1 teaspoon honey, and 1 tablespoon vinegar to 3 tablespoons oil) rather than prepare a larger batch and have some left over. However, this is handy for those of you who prefer to save a little time on making the vinaigrette each time.

Makes 1½ cups (356 ml)

1 tablespoon *moutarde forte de Dijon* (Dijon mustard)

1 tablespoon honey

⅓ cup (80 ml) red wine vinegar or sherry vinegar

1 cup (236 ml) olive oil

1 shallot, finely chopped

In a bowl, combine the mustard and honey. Stir in the vinegar. Pour in the oil and whisk to emulsify. Add the shallot. The dressing can be used immediately or transferred to a glass jar and kept in the fridge for 5 days. Season just the quantity you need with sea salt and pepper each time you use it on a salad.

mixed salads
les salades composées

Potato, cucumber, and asparagus salad

WITH GOAT CHEESE

Salade de pommes de terre, de concombre et d'asperges avec fromage de chèvre

To this day, my mother's potato salad remains one of the best I've ever eaten. Warm chunks of potato are dressed in a yogurt-based vinaigrette with strong accents of shallot and chives. Mine is even more piquant than hers. I like to use fingerling potatoes for their firm texture and buttery taste, and I pair them with young asparagus lightly sautéed in cumin and olive oil. Add a few radishes for extra spiciness, cucumber for crunch, and soft goat cheese to round out the taste, and you're sure to go back for seconds.

Serves 4

FOR THE
VINAIGRETTE:

Sea salt and pepper

1 teaspoon *moutarde forte de Dijon* (Dijon mustard)

1 teaspoon honey

Juice of 1 lemon (about 2 tablespoons)

7 to 8 tablespoons olive oil

1 shallot, finely chopped

1 tablespoon chopped mint

1 tablespoon chopped chives

1 tablespoon chopped basil

FOR THE SALAD:

½ English cucumber, peeled and thinly sliced with a mandoline

Sea salt

2 lb (90 g) fingerling potatoes

1 tablespoon olive oil

1 teaspoon ground cumin

1 bunch green or purple asparagus, cut diagonally in ½-inch (1.25 cm) pieces

Pepper

1 garlic clove, crushed

1 bunch French breakfast pink radishes, thinly sliced with a mandoline

2 tablespoons capers

⅔ cup (3½ oz; 100 g) soft goat cheese crumbles

To prepare the vinaigrette: In a small bowl, combine the sea salt, pepper, and mustard. Stir in the honey and lemon juice. Add the olive oil and whisk to emulsify. Stir in the shallot and fresh herbs; set aside.

To prepare the salad: Place the slices of cucumber in a colander and season with sea salt. Let rest for 30 minutes so the cucumber softens and releases water.

In the meantime, place the potatoes in a large pot. Cover with water and bring to a boil. Cook for about 20 minutes, or until fork-tender. Drain and let cool slightly before removing the skins. Slice the potatoes into ½-inch (1.5 cm) pieces, and

put them in a large bowl. Toss with three-fourths of the dressing while still warm; set aside.

In a frying pan, heat 1 tablespoon olive oil over medium heat. Add the cumin and cook for 1 minute. Add the asparagus. Season with sea salt and pepper, and cook for 1 minute, stirring frequently. Stir in the garlic, and cook for another minute. Set aside to cool.

When cooled slightly, add the asparagus to the potatoes. Add the radishes, cucumber, capers, and goat cheese. Toss gently with the rest of the vinaigrette and serve.

Shaved vegetable salad
WITH SUNCHOKES
Salade de pluches de légumes aux topinambours

You will often come across stew, gratin, or soup recipes using sunchokes. They are surprisingly good raw in a salad as well. In this salad, I combine an array of finely shaved vegetables and, for something more exotic, dress the salad with a gingery sauce with a definite Asian touch.

Note: Slice the zucchini until you reach the soft center of the vegetable. Use the leftovers to make Cocoa, Walnut, and Zucchini Muffins (page 146) or to prepare the stuffing for the Oven-Roasted Monkfish (page 288).

Serves 4

FOR THE
VINAIGRETTE:

1 teaspoon minced fresh ginger

1 garlic clove, peeled and finely grated

Pepper

3 to 4 tablespoons lime juice, to taste

2 teaspoons brown sugar

2 teaspoons fish sauce

6 tablespoons olive oil

2 teaspoons finely chopped cilantro

FOR THE SALAD:

8 small sunchokes, peeled and thinly sliced with a mandoline

3 cups arugula

2 carrots, peeled and thinly sliced lengthwise with a vegetable peeler

1 zucchini, thinly sliced lengthwise with a vegetable peeler (see Note)

4 pink radishes, thinly sliced with a mandoline

2 tablespoons pomegranate seeds

1 red apple, cored and thinly sliced with a mandoline

To prepare the vinaigrette: In a small bowl, combine the ginger and garlic. Season with pepper and add the lime juice. Stir in the brown sugar and fish sauce. Add the olive oil and whisk to emulsify. Stir in the chopped cilantro; set aside.

To prepare the salad: In a salad bowl, gently toss the sunchokes, arugula, carrots, and zucchini. Add the radishes, pomegranate seeds, and apple. Drizzle with the vinaigrette and toss gently. Serve immediately.

Warm salmon and spring vegetable salad

WITH SOFT-BOILED EGGS AND VANILLA-FLAVORED VINAIGRETTE

Salade tiède de saumon et de légumes printaniers avec oeuf mollet et vinaigrette à la vanille

A vinaigrette gains an extraordinary perfume when you add vanilla seeds. It's stunning used to dress a salad of warm, chunky salmon and crunchy green vegetables, with a rich, runny egg yolk on top—a perfect light meal but easy to adapt into a more substantial dish.

Serves 4

FOR THE VANILLA-FLAVORED VINAIGRETTE:

Pinch of sea salt

2 tablespoons sherry vinegar

1 teaspoon honey

6 tablespoons olive oil

1 vanilla bean, sliced lengthwise and seeds scraped out

1 tablespoon chopped parsley

1 tablespoon chopped mint, plus some small leaves to garnish

Crushed red peppercorns

FOR THE FISH AND VEGETABLES:

1 lb (450 g) wild salmon fillet or Arctic char fillet, with its skin

Sea salt and pepper

Olive oil

6 medium Yukon gold or blue potatoes, brushed and cut in quarters

1 tablespoon white wine vinegar

4 large eggs

2 cups (5¼ oz; 150 g) snow peas or sugar snap peas

4 young leeks, white part only

16 green asparagus spears, cleaned

To prepare the vinaigrette: In a bowl, combine sea salt and vinegar. Stir in honey. Pour in the olive oil and whisk to emulsify. Stir in the vanilla seeds, parsley, and mint. Add crushed red pepper, to taste; set aside.

To prepare the fish and vegetables: Preheat the oven to 375°F (190°C). Line a baking sheet with parchment paper. Place the fish on it, season with sea salt and pepper, and drizzle olive oil. Bake for about 12 to 15 minutes. Remove from the oven. Skin the salmon and break into chunky, bite-size pieces; keep warm on the side.

Meanwhile, steam the potatoes for 10 minutes, or until fork-tender; remove from the heat and keep warm on the side.

Bring a large pot of water with the white wine vinegar and a pinch of sea salt to a boil. Carefully place the eggs in the water with a spoon. Cook for 5 minutes. Lift the eggs out and place them on a plate on the side.

While the eggs are cooking, blanch the peas, leeks, and asparagus in boiling salted water for 5 minutes (page 386), then transfer to an ice water bath. Drain, then pat dry with a towel. Place the vegetables in a large bowl, and dress them with the vinaigrette. Divide the vegetables and potatoes between four plates. Add pieces of salmon on top of each. Holding an egg in one hand, tap with a knife to crack the shell; remove the shell carefully. Repeat for all eggs. Place an egg on top of the salmon and vegetables on each plate. Run a knife through the eggs to slit them open. Serve immediately with crusty bread on the side.

Cranberry bean and watercress salad
WITH ANCHOVIES AND GRAPES
Salade aux haricots coco et au cresson avec anchois et raisins

Cranberry beans are called *haricots cocos* (or *cocos rouges*) in French; they prevail especially in markets in the south of France. Every summer I eagerly wait for their appearance at my neighborhood farmers' market; I can't resist their gorgeous red speckled color (even if they lose it once they are cooked). Their soft, nutty consistency makes them attractive in a salad, like this Mediterranean-style one in which I like to add a medley of crunchy vegetables, fruit, and protein. As such, it's filled with nutrients, and I like to serve it as a meal on its own.

Serves 4

FOR THE
VINAIGRETTE:

Sea salt and pepper

1 teaspoon *moutarde forte de Dijon* (Dijon mustard)

1 tablespoon honey

2 tablespoons apple cider vinegar or sherry vinegar

2 tablespoons olive oil

4 tablespoons hazelnut oil

1 small red spring onion, finely chopped

1 tablespoon chopped tarragon

1 tablespoon chopped parsley

1 tablespoon chopped chives

FOR THE SALAD:

1 lb, 7 oz (650 g) cranberry beans in their pods (yields about 10½ oz [300 g], once cleaned)

1 thyme sprig

1 bay leaf

Sea salt and pepper

3 cups fresh watercress

24 small cherry tomatoes, cut in quarters (use different colors)

⅓ cup Kalamata olives, pitted

16 Spanish white anchovies preserved in vinegar

6 radishes, thinly sliced with a mandoline

1 cup red grapes, cut in half

To prepare the vinaigrette: In a small bowl, combine the sea salt, pepper, and mustard. Stir in the honey and vinegar. Add the oils and whisk to emulsify. Stir the onion and fresh herbs; set aside.

To prepare the salad: Remove the cranberry beans from their pods. Place them in a pot and cover with water. Add the thyme, bay leaf, and sea salt; cook for about 40 minutes, or until tender. Strain and let cool—the salad is best when the beans are lukewarm or cooled through.

In a large bowl, combine the watercress, *cocos rouges*, tomatoes, olives, anchovies, radishes, and grapes. Add the vinaigrette and toss gently, then serve.

French green bean salad

WITH *CROÛTONS*, OLIVES, AND RICOTTA SALATA

Salade de haricots verts avec croûtons, olives, et ricotta salata

Since my mother grew a lot of *haricots verts* in her garden, we always ate a lot of them in mixed sautéed vegetables and salads. She showed me how to select the small ones, as they are more tender and delicate. *Haricots verts* should be only slightly cooked so they stay green and crunchy. Lulu likes *haricots verts* just fine, but she thinks everything tastes better with *croûtons,* so this salad is for her. Somehow, I always think of it as a close cousin to a *salade niçoise,* especially when I am able to find *petite niçoise* olives—so cute and delicate—at my local gourmet shop.

Serves 4

FOR THE *CROÛTONS*:

Two ¾-inch (2 cm) slices Brioche-Like Bread (page 28), or your preferred type of country bread, toasted and cut in 1-inch (2.5 cm) pieces

1 garlic clove, minced

2 tablespoons olive oil

1 tablespoon finely chopped cilantro

Sea salt and pepper

FOR THE VINAIGRETTE:

1½ teaspoons *moutarde à l'ancienne* (grainy mustard)

1½ teaspoons honey

Sea salt and pepper

1½ tablespoons apple cider vinegar

3 tablespoons olive oil

1½ tablespoons hazelnut oil

1 tablespoon finely chopped shallot

1 tablespoon chopped cilantro

1 tablespoon chopped chives

FOR THE SALAD:

¼ cup (1¼ oz; 35 g) pine nuts

1 lb (450 g) *haricots verts fins* (fine French green beans)

11¼ oz (320 g) cherry tomatoes (yellow and red), cut in half

⅔ cup (3½ oz; 100 g) black olives cured in olive oil or *petite niçoise* olives

7¼ oz (175 g) ricotta salata cheese, cut in ½-inch (1.5 cm) pieces

2 cups mixed salad greens

To prepare the *croûtons*: Preheat the oven to 400°F (200°C).

In a bowl, combine the bread pieces with the garlic, olive oil, and cilantro. Season with sea salt and pepper, and toss gently. Transfer to a baking sheet and bake for 10 minutes, or until crispy and golden in color. Remove from the oven and let cool.

To prepare the vinaigrette: In a small bowl, stir together the mustard and honey with a pinch of sea salt and pepper. Whisk in the vinegar. Add the oils and whisk to emulsify. Stir in the shallot and fresh herbs; set aside.

To prepare the salad: Toast the pine nuts in a nonstick frying pan over medium heat for 1 to 2 minutes, or until fragrant and light brown. Remove from the heat and set aside.

Steam (or boil in salted water) the *haricots verts* for 10 minutes; they should still be green and slightly crunchy. Transfer to an ice water bath to cool. Drain and transfer to a salad bowl. Add the cherry tomatoes, olives, and cheese. Toss with the vinaigrette, *croûtons,* and mixed greens. Serve topped with the pine nuts.

Fava beans and cherry salad
WITH GINGER-FLAVORED VINAIGRETTE
Salade de fèves et de cerises avec vinaigrette au gingembre

The sweet-sharp accent of bright red cherries lifts the gentler taste of fava beans, so that you have a salad full of vigor. Choose your favorite herbs, as any will go well here.

Serves 4

FOR THE GINGER-FLAVORED VINAIGRETTE:

Sea salt and pepper

2 tablespoons lime juice

1-inch (2.5 cm) piece fresh ginger, finely grated

1 teaspoon honey

4 tablespoons olive oil

2 tablespoons pistachio oil

2 tablespoons blend of fresh chopped herbs (dill, parsley, oregano, basil, mint, cilantro)

FOR THE SALAD:

3 teaspoons black sesame seeds

5 lb (2¼ kg) fresh fava beans

4 tablespoons (2 oz; 60 g) pine nuts

12 pink radishes, thinly sliced

24 Rainier or Bing cherries, pitted and cut in half

4 oz (115 g) fresh soft goat cheese

To prepare the vinaigrette: In a bowl, combine the sea salt, pepper, lime juice, and ginger. Stir in the honey. Pour in the oils and whisk to emulsify. Add the fresh herbs; set aside.

To prepare the salad: Toast the sesame seeds in a nonstick frying pan over medium heat for 1 to 2 minutes, or until fragrant. Remove from the heat and set aside.

Prepare the fava beans (page 102); set aside.

Toast the pine nuts in a nonstick frying pan over medium heat for 1 to 2 minutes, or until fragrant and light brown; set aside.

In a large bowl, combine the fava beans, radishes, cherries, and goat cheese. Drizzle the vinaigrette over the mixture and toss gently. Add the toasted nuts and seeds, and toss again. Serve immediately.

Red lentil salad

WITH CITRUS, FENNEL, AND SMOKED SALMON WITH TAHINI VINAIGRETTE

Salade de lentilles corail aux agrumes et au fenouil avec saumon fumé et vinaigrette au tahini

I often cook lentils with the idea of a salad in the back of my mind. Then I add whatever ingredients I have handy to turn my mellow bowl of lentils into something bubbling with life—like here. This zesty fruit-loaded salad has everything you need to brighten your day.

Serves 4

FOR THE VINAIGRETTE:

1 tablespoon tahini

3 tablespoons water

2 tablespoons heavy cream

2 tablespoons lemon juice

1 tablespoon hazelnut oil

1 garlic clove, crushed

Sea salt and pepper

1 tablespoon finely chopped chives

1 tablespoon finely chopped parsley

1 tablespoon finely chopped fennel greens

FOR THE SALAD:

⅔ cup (4¾ oz; 135 g) red lentils, sorted and rinsed

2 tablespoons black sesame seeds

4 slices of smoked salmon, cut in long strips

2 fennel bulbs, thinly sliced with a mandoline

2 oranges, peel and pith removed, and sectioned

2 pink grapefruit, peel and pith removed, and sectioned

8 pink radishes, thinly sliced with a mandoline

¼ small red onion, thinly sliced

4½ oz (125 g) goat milk feta cheese, crumbled

To prepare the vinaigrette: In a small bowl, beat the tahini and water together with a fork. Stir in the heavy cream, lemon juice, and hazelnut oil, and whisk to emulsify. Add the garlic, season with sea salt and pepper, and stir in the fresh herbs; set aside. If you want the sauce a little thinner, simply add more water (and lemon juice); taste for seasoning again.

To prepare the salad: Bring a large pot of water to boil. Add the lentils and cook for 7 to 8 minutes over medium heat. Drain and rinse under cold water. Transfer to a large bowl and set aside.

In a frying pan, toast the sesame seeds for 2 minutes over medium heat; set aside.

Add the smoked salmon, fennel, oranges, grapefruit, radishes, and onion to the bowl with the lentils. Drizzle with the tahini dressing and toss gently. Add the crumbled cheese and sesame seeds, and toss gently before serving.

Avocado and melon salad
WITH DILL, MOZZARELLA, AND PROSCIUTTO
Salade d'avocat et de melon avec aneth, mozzarella, et prosciutto

The sweet perfume of a *Charentais* melon takes me back to my grandmother's house on a hot summer day in August, when the family traditionally gathered for a meal. She liked to serve hers simply paired with homemade *jambon fumé* (smoked ham) and porto; it's the fine quality of the ingredients chosen that made her salad outstanding.

I thought to use my grandmother's classically French recipe as a base for a more complex and nourishing salad. Bite-size pieces of avocado, cherry tomatoes, and mozzarella all come together to make this happen.

Serves 4

FOR THE DILL
AND MUSTARD
VINAIGRETTE:

2 teaspoons
moutarde à l'ancienne
(grainy mustard)

2 tablespoons apple
cider vinegar

4 tablespoons olive oil

2 tablespoons
hazelnut oil

Sea salt and pepper

1 small shallot, finely
chopped

1 tablespoon finely
chopped dill

FOR THE SALAD:

2 tablespoons
pumpkin seeds

2 avocados, pitted

1 tablespoon
lemon juice

1 *Charentais* melon or
½ cantaloupe, seeded

4 cups mixed
spring greens

8½ oz (240 g)
mozzarella cheese
(about 2 balls)

8 slices prosciutto

20 yellow cherry
tomatoes, cut in
half (if small, keep
them whole)

To prepare the vinaigrette: In a small bowl, stir the mustard and vinegar together. Pour in the oils and whisk to emulsify. Season with sea salt and pepper. Stir in the shallot and dill; set aside.

To prepare the salad: Toast the pumpkin seeds in a frying pan over medium heat for a few minutes, until fragrant; set aside.

Using a melon baller, make small avocado balls. Drizzle with lemon juice as you go; set aside. Do the same with the melon.

Cut or tear the mozzarella into bite-size pieces.

Place the greens in a salad bowl. Add the avocado and melon balls, cheese, prosciutto, and tomatoes. Drizzle with the vinaigrette and toss gently. Add the pumpkin seeds on top and serve.

Spring green quinoa salad

Salade de quinoa aux légumes verts printaniers

When preparing a picnic or a summer garden party, I unfailingly include a quinoa salad because not only does a quinoa salad travel well, but it also adds a healthy kick to any meal. This one is dressed with a medley of wonderful spring greens flavored with an extra lemony dressing—if you have a weakness for fresh herbs in a salad, this is your chance to add as many as you like, as it will always enhance the salad.

Note: Use asparagus stems for Asparagus and Pistachio Pesto (page 294).

Serves 4

FOR THE LEMON AND HERB VINAIGRETTE:

Sea salt and pepper

Zest of 1 lemon, plus 1 teaspoon to serve

1 garlic clove, crushed

Juice of 1 lemon (about 2 tablespoons)

6 tablespoons olive oil

4 tablespoons chopped chives

2 tablespoons chopped mint, plus a few more whole leaves

1 tablespoon chopped basil, plus a few more whole leaves

1 tablespoon chopped cilantro, plus a few more whole leaves

FOR THE SALAD:

2 tablespoons black sesame seeds

⅔ cup (3¾ oz; 105 g) dry quinoa, rinsed and drained

1⅓ cups (315 ml) water

Sea salt

1 lb (450 g) fresh fava beans

1 lb (450 g) fresh English peas

1 tablespoon olive oil

½ teaspoon ground coriander

4¾ oz (135 g) asparagus tips, diced diagonally in ½-inch (1.25 cm) pieces

1 garlic clove

Pepper

3½ oz (100 g) goat or sheep milk feta cheese

To prepare the vinaigrette: In a small bowl, mix the sea salt, pepper, lemon zest, and garlic. Add the lemon juice and olive oil, and whisk to emulsify. Add the fresh herbs; set aside.

To prepare the salad: Toast the sesame seeds in a frying pan over medium heat for 1 to 2 minutes, or until fragrant. Remove from the heat and set aside.

Add the quinoa, water, and a pinch of sea salt to a pot. Bring to a boil, then turn down the heat, cover, and simmer for 12 to 14 minutes, or until the water is absorbed. Remove from the heat and keep covered for 5 minutes. Transfer the quinoa to a bowl, fluff with a fork, and let cool.

Prepare the fava beans (page 102); set aside.

Blanch the peas in salted boiling water for 1 minute (page 386). Transfer to an ice water bath to cool; drain and set aside.

In a frying pan, heat 1 tablespoon olive oil over medium heat. Add the coriander and cook for 1 minute. Add the asparagus and cook, stirring for 2 minutes. Add the garlic and cook for another minute. Season with sea salt and pepper; set aside.

Add the fava beans, peas, and asparagus to the bowl of quinoa and sprinkle with the feta cheese. Toss gently with the vinaigrette. Top with the sesame seeds and serve garnished with small leaves of fresh herbs and lemon zest.

Radish, fennel, and apple salad

WITH TRUFFLE SALT

Salade de radis, de fenouil, et de pommes au sel parfumé à la truffe

I often make a variant of this refreshing salad because fennel, apple, and radishes are staple vegetables in my fridge. In this version, the truffle salt gives it a distinct earthy flavor. You can decide to serve it as part of a buffet or as a side, with grilled fish or meat for example, which is what I do when I want to serve a fresh salad with a great crunch.

Serves 4

2 bunches pink radishes (about 12¼ oz; 350 g), thinly sliced with a mandoline

1 fennel bulb, white part only, thinly sliced with a mandoline

1 Pink Lady apple, cored and thinly sliced with a mandoline

3 to 4 tablespoons lime juice

Olive oil, to drizzle

1 tablespoon chopped cilantro

2 teaspoons chopped mint

Truffle salt, to taste

In a large dish, gently toss the radishes, fennel, and apple together. Drizzle with the lime juice and olive oil to taste. Top with fresh herbs, and add a dash of truffle salt just before serving.

Julienned zucchini and watermelon radish salad

Salade de julienne de courgettes et de pastèque radis

Colorful salads like this one always make my friends who discover them for the first time smile. I am a big fan of the taste and vibrant hue of watermelon radishes, so I always look for ways to sneak them in my salad recipes. Slicing the vegetables thin is also what makes this salad scrumptious and distinctive. Remember it when you find the radishes at your market.

Serves 4

FOR THE DRESSING:

Sea salt and pepper

3 tablespoons rice vinegar

¾ tablespoon blond cane sugar

1 tablespoon chopped mint

1 tablespoon chopped chives

FOR THE SALAD:

3 tablespoons (1½ oz.; 45 g) pine nuts

8¾ oz (250 g) zucchini

2 watermelon radishes, peeled and thinly sliced with a mandoline

1½ cups pea shoots, baby arugula leaves, or mesclun

Finely shaved cheddar, Comté, or manchego cheese, for garnish

Olive oil, to drizzle

To prepare the dressing: In a bowl, stir together the sea salt, pepper, rice vinegar, and sugar until the sugar dissolves. Add the fresh herbs; set aside.

To prepare the salad: In a frying pan, toast the pine nuts over medium heat for 1 to 2 minutes, until slightly golden. Remove from the heat and set aside to cool.

Using your mandoline or a julienne cutter, cut the zucchini into thin slices, stopping when you get to the core, which is softer and not as easy to slice. Use the leftover zucchini for something else, like the Cocoa, Walnut, and Zucchini Muffins (page 146) or the stuffing for the Oven-Roasted Monkfish with Clams and Herb Ricotta Stuffing (page 288).

Transfer the zucchini to a bowl and toss with three-fourths of the dressing. Place in the middle of four plates. Add the slices of watermelon radish. Divide the greens between the plates, and top with shaved cheese and pine nuts. Drizzle with the rest of the dressing and olive oil, and serve.

snack time

l'heure du goûter

IF YOU EVER HAD A CONVERSATION with my father, at some time he'd make a point of saying, *"Chez nous on ne mange pas entre les repas"* ("At home, we don't snack"), and for the most part, he'd be right. French people do not like to snack between meals, except when the hour for the *goûter* strikes around four in the afternoon. The French, however, do not consider this *grignotage* (snacking).

Le goûter (you pronounce it "luh goo-tay") is a food tradition as deeply woven into the French culture as afternoon tea is for the British. Many years ago, it used to be a real meal, when workers came back from the fields and needed to have substantial food to replenish their strength. Now, *le goûter* has become a somewhat more sophisticated—mostly sweet—afternoon nibble that is meant to keep you going until dinner, assuredly much later in the evening for the French.

L'heure du goûter happens every day at around 4 P.M., starting when children are getting out of school and people are almost finished with their workday. At this time, children usually rush home or to a neighbor-hood *pâtisserie* (pastry shop) in search of a tasty treat, enough to satisfy a craving but not enough to spoil their appetite for dinner. Many adults like to join in too. In cities, they generally visit their favorite cafés and *salons de thé*, looking for something delicious to eat with coffee or tea—and a great amount of conversation to go along it.

In its simplest form, our *goûters* at home in France typically included a piece of bread with butter, a few *carreaux* (squares) of chocolate, or jam. I loved Nutella the best, *naturellement*. There were also afternoons when we'd enjoy almond or chocolate-filled croissants, *petits pains au lait* (one of my favorite treats), *chaussons aux pommes* (apple turnovers), thick slices of brioche, cherry *clafoutis* or rhubarb tart, or plump *madeleines* baked right before we headed home.

It may not make as much sense for me to follow the *goûter* tradition now that I no longer live in France. But the truth is that I've always been very attached to it and to the lovely moments it creates. Besides, knowing that Lulu and soon Rémy will learn about this slice of my culture from me is important. So we make it happen every day when Lulu comes back from school or when her friends come over to play. I take pleasure in setting up an inviting table with pretty plates, cups, straws, spoons, and forks for them, and Lulu loves to be involved. She tells me who is going to sit where and which plate to give to each of her friends—of course, hers always has flowers on it. They sit down to share a piece of apple tart, a warm *crêpe* filled with melted chocolate, or perhaps *madeleines* that Lulu helped me bake, before they go off to play, happy to have their tummies full of a tasty treat. Often I call my friends and ask them to join in, as I feel a good-looking cake should always be shared with a large group.

I find that something unique and magical happens at *l'heure du goûter*. I am not sure why, but I can definitely see that we all get a great deal of enjoyment out of it, so that alone is an excellent reason to keep the tradition going. I created the following recipes for those times. I hope you'll make them for your favorite little ones and friends.

Cocoa, walnut, and zucchini muffins

Muffins au cacao, aux noix, et aux courgettes

A chocolate muffin can be decadent and rich, but for something we like to enjoy every day, I prefer to think about nutrition first. So instead of chocolate, I use cocoa, then add nuts, protein-filled flours, and zucchini.

The zucchini mellows down the taste of the muffins and, along with walnuts, keeps the muffins extremely moist for days—another reason why we love them. When your little one asks for more, you really know you have a keeper.

Note: This is a good place to use zucchini left over from the Julienned Zucchini and Watermelon Radish Salad (page 138).

Makes ten ½-cup muffins or fifteen ⅓-cup muffins

7 oz (200 g) zucchini

3½ oz (100 g) walnut kernels

½ cup (1¾ oz; 50 g) oat flour

½ cup (2 oz; 60 g) quinoa flour

⅓ cup (1½ oz; 40 g) tapioca starch

2 teaspoons baking powder

½ teaspoon baking soda

¼ cup (1 oz; 25 g) unsweetened cocoa powder, sifted, plus more to serve

3 large eggs

¾ cup (3½ oz; 100 g) light Muscovado sugar

Pinch of sea salt

½ cup (120 ml) grapeseed oil

¼ cup (60 ml) buttermilk

1 tablespoon pure vanilla extract

Place the zucchini in the bowl of a food processor and purée. Transfer to a plate and set aside.

Preheat the oven to 350°F (180°C). Line a muffin pan with 10 (or 15) paper liners, or use silicone muffin molds if you prefer. (I use hard-shelled muffin cases that are stiff enough to be used without a muffin pan.)

Add the walnuts to the bowl of a food processor and pulse into a meal. Add the walnut meal to a large bowl with the flours, tapioca starch, baking powder, baking soda, and cocoa powder; set aside.

In the bowl of a stand mixer fitted with the whisk, beat the eggs with the sugar and a pinch of sea salt for 1 minute. Add the grapeseed oil and whisk until it is a uniform consistency. Stir in the buttermilk and vanilla. Beat in the zucchini purée. Add the dry ingredients and beat until well combined. Fill the muffin cups three-fourths full. Bake for 30 minutes (25 minutes for smaller muffins), or until the blade of a sharp knife inserted in the middle comes out clean. Dust with cocoa powder to serve.

Vanilla and orange *cannelés*

Cannelés à la vanille et à l'orange

Cannelés—pastries traditionally from the Bordeaux region of France—are the perfect size for little hands to grab; these are especially good since they are baked in mini *cannelé* molds. It's best to prepare the batter the night before and bake the *cannelés* the following day. Don't forget the rum, since this is what gives a *cannelé* its unique flavor.

You will need: one 30-capacity mini *cannelé* mold (see note below).

Makes 30 mini **cannelés**

1 cup plus 1 tablespoon (250 ml) whole milk

1 vanilla bean, split lengthwise and seeds scraped out

2 tablespoons (1 oz; 30 g) unsalted butter

Zest of 1 large orange

½ cup (3½ oz; 100 g) blond cane sugar

¼ cup (1 oz; 30 g) quinoa flour

3 tablespoons (¾ oz; 25 g) cornstarch or tapioca starch

Pinch of sea salt

1 large egg plus 1 large egg yolk

1 tablespoon plus 1 teaspoon rum

In a small pot, heat the milk with the vanilla bean and seeds. Remove from the heat when it starts to boil. Stir in the butter until it melts, and add the orange zest. Cover and let infuse for 30 minutes. Strain and discard the vanilla bean and orange zest.

In a bowl, combine the sugar, quinoa flour, cornstarch, and sea salt. Make a well in the middle, and add the egg and egg yolk. While beating with a whisk, add the milk gradually. Stir in the rum and beat just until consistency is uniform. Pour the batter into a pitcher. Cover and place in the fridge for a minimum of 12 hours or overnight.

The next day, preheat the oven to 410°F (210°C). Stir the batter before using. Fill each *cannelé* mold to ⅕ inch (0.5 cm) from the top. Bake the *cannelés* for 40 to 45 minutes, or until brown. Unmold while they are still warm. Let cool slightly and enjoy! They are best eaten when they are still slightly warm. You can reheat them in a preheated oven at 400°F (200°C) for 5 minutes.

Cannelé molds are specially designed to give the pastries a thick, caramelized crust with a tender pudding-like inside. Purists often prefer copper molds, but I find that sicilone molds work just fine, and they're cheaper.

Chouquettes with pearl sugar and quinoa
Chouquettes au sucre et au quinoa

Lulu's teacher, Jeannette, tells me she loves it when Lulu brings *chouquettes* to school and exclaims, "*J'ai des chouquettes pour le goûter*" ("I have chouquettes for my snack"). The melody of Lulu's pronunciation—"Shoo ket"—is irresistible to me.

Prepare them as you would cream puffs with pearl sugar sprinkled on top. We prefer ours plain, but they can also be filled with pastry cream like a *petit choux,* as noted on page 152.

You will need: a pastry bag fitted with a ⅝-inch (1.6 cm) (Ateco 808) tip.

***Makes about thirty-two 1½-inch* chouquettes**	¼ cup (1½ oz; 40 g) white rice flour	4 tablespoons (2 oz; 55 g) unsalted butter	2 oz (75 g) eggs (a little less than 2 large eggs)
¼ cup (1 oz; 30 g) quinoa or millet flour	¼ cup (60 ml) whole milk	Pinch of sea salt	Pearl sugar, for garnish
	¼ cup (60 ml) water	½ tablespoon blond cane sugar	

Preheat the oven to 400°F (200°C). Line a baking sheet with parchment paper; set aside.

In a small bowl, combine and sift the quinoa flour and rice flour; set aside.

In a small pot, combine the milk, water, butter, sea salt, and sugar. Cook over low heat, stirring occasionally, until the sugar dissolves. Once the butter is melted and the liquid is just starting to boil, remove from the heat and immediately add the flour mixture, stirring vigorously with a wooden spoon until it's elastic. Place on the stove over low heat and continue to beat for 1 to 2 minutes, until the dough pulls away from the sides of the pot and forms a ball. Remove from the heat and place the dough in a clean bowl to cool for 5 minutes. Beat in 1 egg, stirring quickly until the dough is a uniform consistency (it should be fairly sticky). In a small bowl, beat the second egg; add about one-quarter of the egg to the dough, stirring quickly. Add more egg if necessary—the dough should fall slowly from the spoon in thick ribbons; it should not be runny.

These pastries are also delicious filled with pastry cream. Prepare the cream per the recipe (page 152), then beat again just before using. Make a small hole in the bottom of each *chouquette* and then, using a pastry bag, fill each with a little of the pastry cream.

continued

snack time

Scrape the dough into the pastry bag, and pipe into 1½-inch (3.8 cm) mounds on the baking sheets, leaving 1 inch between them. Brush the *chouquettes* lightly with the remaining egg, and sprinkle with pearl sugar. Bake for 20 to 22 minutes, or until golden brown in color—do not open the oven before they are done, or your *chouquettes* will deflate. Remove from the oven and transfer to a rack to cool completely. The *chouquettes* are best eaten on the day you make them, although they will still be nice the next day.

Pastry cream
Crème pâtissière

This *crème pâtissière* is a true classic that can be used to fill *choux, éclairs,* or a tart crust. It's usually flavored with vanilla, but I like to add pods of cardamom for extra flavor (and because I love anything with cardamom).

Makes 1 cup pastry cream

1 cup (236 ml) whole milk

1 vanilla bean, split lengthwise and seeds scraped out

3 green cardamom pods, crushed

3 large egg yolks

¼ cup (1¾ oz; 50 g) blond cane sugar

2½ tablespoons cornstarch

2 tablespoons (1 oz; 30 g) unsalted butter, cold and diced

In a small pot, combine the milk, vanilla bean and seeds, and crushed cardamom pods. Bring to a simmer over medium heat. Remove from the heat, cover, and let infuse for 30 minutes to 1 hour. Strain the milk to remove the vanilla bean and cardamom pods and seeds, then return the milk to the stove to keep warm over low heat.

In a bowl, beat the egg yolks with the sugar and cornstarch. While beating, pour the warm milk in slowly. Return the cream to the pot and bring to a simmer, stirring constantly. Once small bubbles form, cook for 1 minute, still stirring constantly—the cream should be thick. Remove from the heat and pour into a clean bowl; stir in the butter until melted and well incorporated. Let cool, stirring occasionally. Cover and place in the fridge until ready to use.

Chestnut flour *crêpes* with chocolate

Crêpes à la farine de chataîgne et au chocolat

I couldn't be completely French if I didn't cook and like to eat *crêpes*. I like to prepare the batter in the morning (or the night before), and keep it refrigerated in a clean glass bottle so I can easily make a *crêpe* when a craving hits me. This is one of my most beloved recipes. I actually have a stack of *crêpe* recipes, but this one uses chestnut flour, giving it a sweet, nutty taste that pairs beautifully with oozing melted dark chocolate. Seconds are a must.

Makes ten 9-inch (23 cm) crêpes

⅓ cup (1½ oz; 40 g) chestnut flour (or almond meal or oat flour)

⅓ cup (1½ oz; 42 g) millet flour

⅓ cup (1½ oz; 40 g) cornstarch or tapioca starch

1½ tablespoons blond cane sugar or coconut sugar

Pinch of sea salt

2 large eggs

1¼ cups (295 ml) whole or 2% milk

½ tablespoon pure vanilla extract

1½ tablespoons (20 g) melted butter or safflower oil, plus more to cook

FOR THE TOPPING:

⅓ cup (2¼ oz; 65 g) blond cane sugar

¼ cup plus 2 tablespoons finely chopped chocolate (70% cocoa)

In a bowl, combine the chestnut flour, millet flour, cornstarch, sugar, and a pinch of sea salt. Make a well in the middle and break the eggs into it. Start beating the eggs into the dry ingredients, adding the milk gradually as you beat. Stir in the vanilla and melted butter until well incorporated. Cover and place in the fridge for at least 1 hour.

To cook the *crêpes*, stir the batter again so it's of uniform consistency. In a *crêpe* pan, melt about ½ teaspoon butter or oil over medium heat; wipe off the excess with a paper towel. When the pan is hot, pour in enough batter to cover the bottom (about ¼ cup). Swirl quickly to coat the bottom of the pan, and cook for 1 to 2 minutes, until the edges are brown and the *crêpe* can be easily handled. Using a spatula, flip the *crêpe* and cook on the other side for about 1 minute, or until cooked. Transfer the *crêpe* to a plate and cover with a large piece of foil to keep warm. Add butter to the pan

and stir the batter between each *crêpe,* and repeat until you run out of batter, stirring the batter each time between the *crêpes.*

To prepare the topping: Sprinkle 1½ teaspoons sugar in the *crêpe* pan, and put it over low to medium heat. Place a *crêpe* in the bottom of the pan. Cover one half of the *crêpe* with 1½ teaspoons finely chopped chocolate, then fold the other half over to close. Cook for 1 minute, or until the chocolate melts. Fold again to form a triangle and cook for 30 seconds, or until the sugar starts to ooze and caramelize lightly. Transfer to a plate and repeat until you run out of *crêpes.*

Alternatively, you can omit this topping and serve the *crêpes* sprinkled with sugar and lemon juice, which is how we often enjoy them. Or sprinkle cocoa powder with a dash of sugar on each *crêpe* after you've flipped it in the pan during cooking. I often do this when I serve *crêpes* at breakfast, and we all love it.

Rice pudding

Riz au lait

There is something extraordinarily comforting about a simple bowl of ivory rice pudding. You may prefer to eat yours cold, but we like ours best when the rice is still warm and deliciously creamy. The nutty coconut and apricot topping is Philip's favorite, but you can leave it out if you enjoy the purity of rice pudding *au naturel* (plain) as I do.

Serves 4

1 tablespoon (1/2 oz.; 14 g) pine nuts

2 cups plus 2 tablespoons (500 ml) whole or 2% milk

½ cup (118 ml) unsweetened coconut milk

6 cardamom pods, slightly crushed

1 vanilla bean, split lengthwise and seeds scraped out

Pinch of sea salt

½ cup (3½ oz; 100 g) Arborio rice or pearl rice

¼ cup (1¾ oz; 50 g) blond cane sugar

2 tablespoons grated coconut

2 to 3 dried apricots, diced

1 tablespoon (½ oz; 14 g) shelled unsalted green pistachios, coarsely chopped

In a frying pan, toast the pine nuts over medium heat for 2 minutes, or until lightly golden in color. Remove from the heat and set aside.

In a pot, combine the milk, coconut milk, cardamom pods, and vanilla bean and seeds. Add a pinch of sea salt, and cook over medium heat until the mixture simmers. Remove from the heat, cover, and set aside to infuse for 1 hour. Strain, reserving the vanilla bean. Return the milk to the heat.

Rinse and drain the rice. Once the milk comes to a simmer again, add the rice and vanilla bean. Cook over medium to low heat, stirring occasionally, until the rice is creamy but al dente. Stir in ¼ cup sugar. Discard the vanilla bean.

Serve in small bowls, garnishing with grated coconut, dried apricots, pine nuts, and pistachios.

Quinoa pudding with stewed fruit

Pudding au quinoa avec compote de fruits

This pudding is very pretty served in glasses that allow the layers to show. It is similar to a rice pudding except that in place of rice, I use quinoa. The stewed summer fruit are packed with flavor and complement beautifully the more mellow taste of the milk-based pudding.

Serves 6

FOR THE STEWED FRUIT:

8 apricots, pitted and diced

3 peaches, peeled, pitted, and diced

1 lemongrass stalk, cut in 1-inch (2.5 cm) pieces

1 lemon thyme sprig

¼ cup (1¾ oz; 50 g) blond cane sugar

1 vanilla bean, split lengthwise and seeds scraped out

1-inch (2.5 cm) piece of fresh ginger

Zest of ½ organic lime or lemon, finely grated

FOR THE QUINOA PUDDING:

2 cups (475 ml) whole milk

2 cups (475 ml) unsweetened coconut milk

1 vanilla bean, split lengthwise and seeds scraped out

1 lemon thyme sprig

¼ teaspoon sea salt

1 cup (5 oz; 140 g) white quinoa, rinsed and drained

¼ cup (1¾ oz; 50 g) blond cane sugar

Toasted sliced almonds, to serve

To prepare the stewed fruit: Combine all ingredients in a pot, and stew for 15 minutes over low heat, stirring occasionally. Remove from the heat and discard the vanilla bean, lemongrass, ginger, and lemon thyme. Cover and set aside.

To prepare the quinoa pudding: In a medium pot, combine the milk, coconut milk, vanilla bean and seeds, lemon thyme, and sea salt. Bring to a simmer over medium-high heat. Add the quinoa and simmer, stirring often, about 30 minutes, or until the quinoa is cooked, most of the liquid is absorbed, and the consistency is creamy. Remove from the heat and transfer to a bowl to cool slightly. Stir in the sugar. Divide the quinoa between six glasses or bowls, and top with the stewed fruit and toasted almonds.

Apricot and pistachio teacakes
WITH OLIVE OIL

Petits gâteaux aux abricots et aux pistaches à l'huile d'olive

I came rather late to the enjoyment of the rich, sweet taste of pistachio. Now I like to buy varieties that are as green as possible and grind them into meal to use in my baked goods. The result here is delicious olive oil–flavored teacakes, colored bright green from the pistachios, studded with a slice of apricot, and, if you like, a cherry on its stem to make them more adorable. Everyone who has tried these always asks for more, and the recipe!

You will need: ⅓-cup molds or *financier* molds; I use individual molds, but a muffin pan of that size works too.

Makes 12 teacakes

½ cup (120 ml) olive oil, plus more for molds

½ cup (3½ oz; 100 g) blond cane sugar

¾ cup (2¾ oz; 80 g) ground pistachio meal

⅓ cup (2 oz; 53 g) white rice flour

Pinch of sea salt

4 large egg whites, beaten with a fork until frothy

2 teaspoons pure vanilla extract

1 large apricot, pitted and sliced in 12 pieces

12 cherries with their stems

Confectioner's sugar, to dust

Preheat the oven to 350°F (180°C). Brush the molds with olive oil; set aside.

In the bowl of a food processor, pulse the sugar into a fine powder. Transfer to a bowl and add the pistachio meal, flour, and a pinch of sea salt; stir to combine. Beat in the egg whites. Stir in the olive oil and vanilla extract. Using a spoon or an ice cream scoop (which is easier for scooping batter), divide the batter between the 12 molds. Stud each cake with a slice of apricot and a cherry. Bake for 20 minutes. Remove from the oven, unmold immediately, and let cool. Dust with confectioner's sugar to serve.

Marbled cake

Marbré vanille et chocolat

My mother always baked two loaves of marbled cake on Saturdays so we'd have a slice or two for our *goûter* during the week. This is a classic recipe that I wanted to revisit with more nutritious flours. I dress it up by baking it in pans with more interesting shapes too, just as Lulu likes.

You will need: a 4-cup cake pan. (Mine is a 6-by-4-inch [15 by 10 cm] Bundt pan, but Lulu likes animal-shaped pans, such as her rooster.)

Vegetable oil, for the pan

½ cup (2 oz; 60 g) quinoa flour or millet flour

½ cup (2¾ oz; 80 g) brown rice flour

¼ cup (1 oz; 30 g) cornstarch or tapioca starch

½ cup (1¾ oz; 50 g) hazelnut meal

1 tablespoon golden flax meal

1½ teaspoons baking powder

¼ teaspoon sea salt

3 large eggs

¼ cup (1¾ oz; 50 g) blond cane sugar

¼ cup (1¾ oz; 50 g) Demerara sugar or brown sugar

7 tablespoons (3½ oz; 100 g) unsalted butter, melted

¼ cup (60 ml) heavy cream or buttermilk

1 tablespoon pure vanilla extract

1 tablespoon unsweetened cocoa, sifted

Preheat the oven to 350°F (180°C). Oil the pan; set aside.

In a bowl, combine the flours, cornstarch, hazelnut meal, flax meal, baking powder, and sea salt; set aside.

In another bowl, beat the eggs with the sugars until light and pale in color. Stir in the melted butter, cream, and vanilla. Beat in the mixture of dry ingredients. Pour one-third of the batter into a clean bowl, and beat in the cocoa powder—this is your chocolate batter. Pour half of the vanilla batter into the cake pan. Pour in all of the chocolate batter, and finish with the rest of the vanilla batter. Stir with a fork to create swirls in the combined batters. Bake the cake for about 40 to 45 minutes (35 minutes for smaller cakes), or until the blade of a sharp knife inserted in the middle comes out clean. Remove from the oven and let cool for 10 minutes before unmolding. Slice and serve. Wrap any leftover cake in a kitchen towel to keep it fresh.

Rhubarb *verrines*

WITH YOGURT AND GRANOLA

Verrines au yaourt, à la compote de rhubarbe, et au granola

We eat a lot of yogurt and granola at home—and not only at the breakfast table. Simple, healthy snacks like this one can be enjoyed at any time of day. They are irresistible when prepared so the layers show through the glass—Lulu always notices. When we go out, I like to prepare them in 6-oz (175 ml) Mason jars that are easily transportable to the park or wherever we are heading. *Chez nous* (at home), we cannot resist the crunchy and subtly tart taste of cocoa nibs, so they invariably go in the jars as well.

I have purposely omitted ingredient quantities for the *verrines* since you may want to adjust them depending on the glasses you use and your appetite.

Makes 1⅓ cups (315 ml) stewed rhubarb

FOR THE RHUBARB:

14 oz (400 g) organic red rhubarb

⅓ cup (2¼ oz; 65 g) blond cane sugar

1 vanilla bean, split lengthwise and seeds scraped out

FOR THE *VERRINES*:

Whole milk Greek yogurt, stirred with a fork to soften

Every-Morning Granola (page 26)

Fresh seasonal fruit, diced

Clover honey

Cocoa nibs

To prepare the rhubarb: Wash the rhubarb thoroughly, dry, and cut into a fine dice. Add to a bowl with the sugar. Let sit for 1 hour so the rhubarb releases its juice.

Transfer the rhubarb and juice to a pot; add the vanilla bean and seeds. Bring to a simmer over low heat until the fruit softens. Remove from the heat, take out the vanilla bean, and let cool. Use this stewed rhubarb in these *verrines* or add to a rice pudding. It keeps refrigerated in a jar for 1 week.

To prepare the *verrines*: Spoon a layer of the rhubarb into small glasses. Add one layer each of yogurt, granola, and fruit. Finish with a drizzle of honey and cocoa nibs to taste.

Apple tartlets

WITH CINNAMON

Tartelettes aux pommes à la cannelle

These rustic tartlets are baked in an unsweetened crust that allows the taste of the apples to shine—nothing complex here. Make sure to choose beautifully scented apples, and eat the tarts fresh on the day they are made.

You will need: ten 4-inch (10 cm) tartlet molds.

Makes ten 4-inch (10 cm) tartlets

Savory Crust with Oat (see page 106)

10 tablespoons applesauce (see stewed apples recipe on page 40)

4 small red apples, cored, sliced in ¼-inch (0.5 cm) pieces, and drizzled with lime juice

3 tablespoons honey

2 tablespoons (1 oz; 30 g) unsalted butter, diced

Ground cinnamon, to finish

Roll and cut the dough ⅕-inch (0.5 cm) thick to fit inside the tartlet molds. Arrange the dough inside the molds and, using a fork, make small holes in the bottom. Place in the fridge for 30 minutes.

Preheat the oven to 400°F (200°C).

Spread 1 tablespoon applesauce in the bottom of each crust. Arrange the slices of apples on top. Drizzle with honey and top with small pieces of butter. Bake the tartlets for 25 to 30 minutes. Remove from the oven and let cool to room temperature. Sift a dash of cinnamon on top of each tart to serve.

Lulu's brown butter *madeleines*

WITH BUCKWHEAT AND CHOCOLATE CHIPS

Les madeleines au beurre noisette, au sarrasin, et au chocolat de Lulu

When Lulu and I bake *madeleines*, she likes to keep her nose pressed up against the oven door in the hope of seeing their little bump form. She adores these, and she always goes after the pieces of oozing melted chocolate right after I take them out of the oven.

This recipe is unique because the butter is browned to deepen the hazelnut flavor present in the flour. *Madeleines* taste better on the day they are baked, but you can keep them for a few days in an airtight box. I often freeze them. You can also make the *madeleines* without the chocolate chips if you wish, although Lulu is right: that oozing chocolate is truly irresistible.

You will need: a *madeleine* pan with 12 molds.

Makes 20 madeleines

½ cup (1¾ oz; 50 g) hazelnut meal

⅓ cup (1¾ oz; 50 g) buckwheat flour

¼ cup (1 oz; 30 g) millet flour

1 tablespoon golden flax meal

¼ teaspoon sea salt

1½ teaspoons baking powder

7 tablespoons (3½ oz; 100 g) unsalted butter, plus more for the mold

1 vanilla bean, split lengthwise and seeds scraped out, or ½ tablespoon pure vanilla extract

2 large eggs, at room temperature

⅓ cup (2¼ oz; 65 g) blond cane sugar

1 tablespoon clover honey

2 oz (⅓ cup; 60 g) chocolate chips

Rice flour, to dust the mold

In a bowl, combine the hazelnut meal, flours, flax meal, sea salt, and baking powder; set aside.

In a pot, melt the butter. Cook over medium heat until slightly golden and with a nutty aroma. Remove from the heat; add the vanilla bean and seeds. Cover and let infuse for 30 minutes. Strain and discard the vanilla bean and seeds.

In the bowl of a stand mixer fitted with the whisk, beat the eggs, sugar, and honey until light in color. Beat in the melted butter (and vanilla extract, if using). Stir in the flours. Stop the machine and fold in the chocolate chips. Cover the bowl and refrigerate for at least 2 hours.

When you are ready to bake the *madeleines*, preheat the oven to 420°F (215°C). Generously butter the *madeleine* molds. Coat with rice flour and tap out the excess. Using a spoon, fill each madeleine mold two-thirds full (not more or the madeleines will overflow as they bake). Bake for 6 minutes. Reduce the temperature to 350°F (180°C) and bake for 3 more minutes, or until lightly browned at the edges. Remove from the oven and let cool for 1 minute. Tap the molds firmly on the countertop to help release the *madeleines* from the pan and unmold. Let cool completely before eating.

Cereal bars

Barres de céréales

I imagined these as a delicious everyday treat filled with nuts—the kind you can wrap easily and have on hand wherever you go if someone feels hungry. If you like dried fruit, feel free to add some to the preparation before adding the liquid and baking the bars. I typically prepare them in the evening so the chocolate has time to cool and set, and they can be ready to go the next day.

You will need: a 7-by-11-inch (18 by 28 cm) baking dish.

Makes sixteen 3½-by-1½-inch (9 by 4 cm) bars

1 tablespoon (½ oz; 14 g) unsalted butter, plus more for the pan

3 tablespoons coconut oil, melted

¼ teaspoon sea salt

2 cups (7 oz; 200 g) rolled oats

1½ cups (1¾ oz; 50 g) puffed rice

½ cup (1¾ oz; 50 g) whole pecans

½ cup (2½ oz; 75 g) whole almonds

¼ cup (1 oz; 30 g) golden flax meal

¼ cup (1 oz; 30 g) pumpkin seeds

¼ cup (1¼ oz; 35 g) light Muscovado sugar or raw coconut sugar

¼ cup (60 ml) clover honey

¼ cup (60 ml) brown rice syrup

1 tablespoon pure vanilla extract

2 tablespoons tahini sauce or almond butter

2 oz (⅓ cup; 60 g) dark chocolate (70% cocoa), melted

Preheat the oven to 350°F (180°C). Butter the bottom and sides of the baking dish. Line with parchment paper and set aside.

In a pot, melt the butter with the oil and sea salt. Transfer to a large bowl, stir in the oats, and spread on a baking sheet lined with parchment paper. Bake for 15 minutes, or until the oats start to color slightly. Transfer to a large, clean bowl. Add the puffed rice, pecans, almonds, golden flax meal, and pumpkin seeds; set aside.

In a pot, combine the sugar with the honey, brown rice syrup, vanilla, and tahini. Cook over low heat, stirring frequently, until the sugar is dissolved. Pour into the dry ingredients and mix well. Transfer the mixture to the prepared baking dish.

Spray or rub the bottom of a small cup with coconut oil and use it to press the cereal mixture into the dish; continue until the mixture looks tight and compact. Bake for 25 minutes, or until golden in color.

Remove from the oven. Dip a fork in the melted chocolate and drizzle it over the baked cereal. Leave to cool for 10 minutes, then gently lift the parchment paper out of the dish. Let cool completely.

Using a sharp knife, slice the bars in whatever shape you like, peeling off the parchment paper as you go. (I slice them into 8 sticks and then slice each stick in half.) Don't worry if the slices are uneven.

Store in an airtight container for up to 2 weeks.

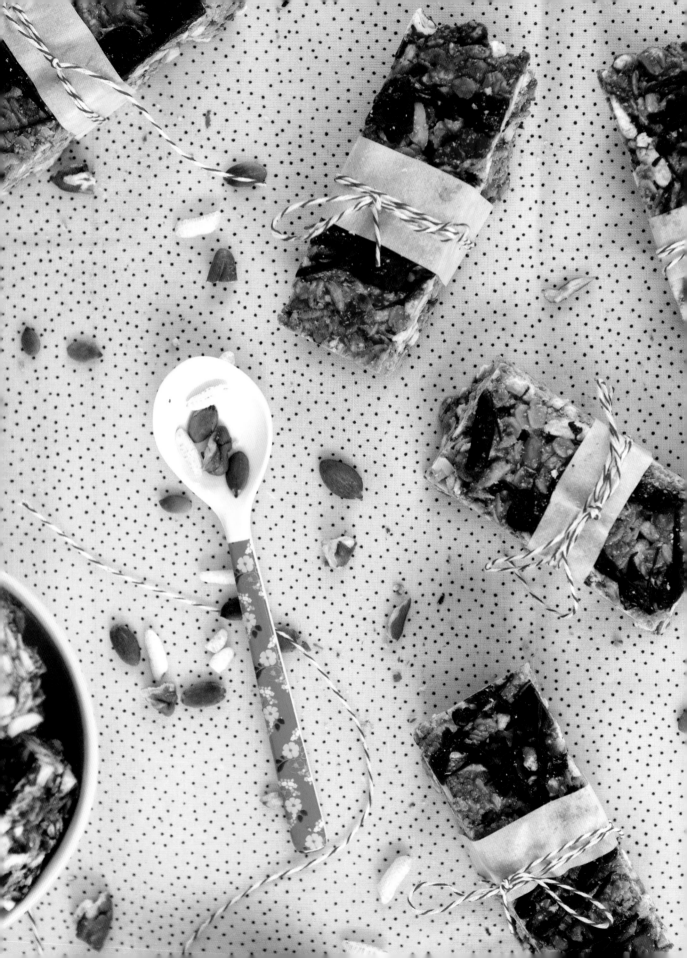

The nice cake, or the olive oil cake

Le bon gâteau , ou le gâteau à l'huile d'olive

I know it sounds strange to give a cake this name, but Philip did it when he walked into the kitchen one day and asked, "Where did you put the nice cake?" I remember I looked at him, perplexed. But now I see he is right; this is, indeed, a perfect kind of cake. It is really quick to bake, is appropriate for many occasions, and has a simple taste with a subtle touch of olive oil—it's always a crowd-pleaser. Hence, it never lasts *chez nous* (at home).

You will need: one 9-inch (23 cm) round cake pan.

Makes one 9-inch (23 cm) round or one 11½-by-5½-inch (29 by 14 cm) cake

½ cup (120 ml) olive oil, plus more for the mold

½ cup (2 oz; 60 g) quinoa flour or millet flour

¼ cup (40 g) white rice flour

¼ cup (1½ oz; 40 g) sweet rice flour or cornstarch

½ cup (2 oz; 60 g) almond meal

1½ teaspoons baking powder

¼ teaspoon sea salt

3 large eggs

½ cup (3½ oz; 100 g) blond cane sugar

1 tablespoon pure vanilla extract

Preheat the oven to 350°F (180°C). Oil the cake pan with a brush; set aside.

In a bowl, combine the flours, almond meal, baking powder, and sea salt; set aside.

In another bowl, beat the eggs with the sugar until fluffy (you can use your stand mixer fitted with the whisk, if you like).

Stir in the olive oil and vanilla. Mix in the dry ingredients until well combined. Pour the batter into the prepared pan. Bake for 25 to 30 minutes, or until the blade of a sharp knife inserted in the middle comes out clean. Remove from the oven and let cool for 5 to 8 minutes before unmolding. Transfer to a rack to cool completely.

French *macarons*

Les macarons parisiens

I took Lulu to Paris for the first time to visit friends during the summer when she was four. After spending a hot afternoon at the Jardin du Luxembourg, we stopped at the Dalloyau tea parlor for sorbet. We were preparing to leave when an elegant and impeccably dressed young man behind the cashier's desk smiled at Lulu and gently placed a chocolate *macaron* in her hand. *"Tiens, c'est pour toi"* ("This is for you"), he said. Her eyes opened wide with delight after the first bite. *"Encore, encore!"* ("More, more!"), she demanded. After that, I developed this wonderful recipe and promised her that I would include it in this book for you to enjoy—she asked me to.

While these *macarons* are not complicated, they do take some time to prepare. You will feel a deep sense of accomplishment when you master them.

Note: The egg whites make a better meringue when they have been separated for a few days or up to a week and kept in a container in the fridge. Bring them to room temperature when ready to use.

You will need: a pastry bag fitted with a ½-inch (1.25 cm) (809 Ateco) tip.

Makes about 10 macarons

FOR THE CHOCOLATE *MACARONS*:

½ cup (2 oz; 60 g) almond meal

1 cup (3¾ oz; 110 g) confectioner's sugar

1½ tablespoons unsweetened cocoa powder

2 large egg whites (2 oz; 60 g), at room temperature (see Note)

Pinch of sea salt

⅛ teaspoon cream of tartar

2 tablespoons (1 oz; 30 g) blond cane sugar

FOR THE CHOCOLATE GANACHE:

¼ cup (1¾ oz; 50 g) heavy cream

4 green cardamom pods, crushed

1¾ oz (50 g) dark chocolate (70% cocoa), finely chopped

½ tablespoon unsalted butter, diced

To prepare the chocolate *macarons*: Preheat the oven to 320°F (160°C). Line a baking sheet with parchment paper; set aside.

In the bowl of a food processor, pulse the almond meal, confectioner's sugar, and cocoa powder into a fine powder; set aside.

In the bowl of a stand mixer fitted with the whisk, beat the egg whites with a pinch of sea salt on medium speed for 30 seconds. Add the cream of tartar and continue to beat for 10 seconds. Increase the speed. When the egg whites start to form stiff peaks, add 1 tablespoon sugar and beat until all the sugar is dissolved. Add the second tablespoon and beat again until dissolved. The meringue should be stiff and glossy, which takes about 3 minutes total. Remove the bowl from the stand mixer, and gently fold in the cocoa mixture.

continued

Spoon the dough into the pastry bag. Pipe 1¼-inch (3 cm) rounds onto the baking sheet, spacing them 1 inch apart. Tap the sheet on the countertop a few times to smooth the surface. Let rest at room temperature for 15 to 30 minutes. Bake the *macarons* for 7 minutes (this is when they form their "feet"—which means a ruffle around the edges forms and the *macarons* won't rise). Reduce the oven temperature to 300°F (150°C) and use a wooden spoon to keep the oven door cracked open. Bake for 6 to 7 more minutes. Remove from the oven and slide the parchment paper directly onto the countertop. Let cool for 5 minutes. Carefully remove the shells from the paper and place them on a cooling rack. (If all goes well, you should not need a spatula to get them off the paper.) Let cool completely. Clean the pastry bag.

To prepare the chocolate ganache: In a pot, bring the heavy cream and cardamom pods to a simmer over medium heat. Remove from the heat and set aside to infuse for 30 minutes. Strain and reheat until warm to the touch. Place the chocolate in a mixing bowl and pour in the hot cream. Let sit for 10 seconds, then stir vigorously to dissolve the chocolate. Stir in the butter until the ganache is a uniform consistency. Spoon into the pastry bag, and pipe some ganache to cover the surface on the flat side of half the *macarons*. Top each with another *macaron*, flat side down. Refrigerate. The *macarons* are actually better the next day, once the flavors have had time to set. They will keep for a week in the fridge.

Hazelnut *macarons*

FOR THE HAZELNUT *MACARONS*:

¾ cup (2½ oz; 75 g) hazelnut meal

1 cup (3¾ oz; 110 g) confectioner's sugar

2 large egg whites (2 oz; 60 g), at room temperature (see Note above for French *macarons*)

Pinch of sea salt

⅛ teaspoon cream of tartar

2 tablespoons (1 oz; 30 g) blond cane sugar

1 vanilla bean, split lengthwise and seeds scraped out

Finely chopped unsalted green pistachios, to top

FOR THE HAZELNUT GANACHE:

¼ cup (1¾ oz; 50 g) heavy cream

¾ oz (25 g) dark chocolate (70% cocoa), finely chopped

¾ oz (25 g) hazelnut-flavored chocolate, finely chopped

½ tablespoon unsalted butter, diced

To prepare the hazelnut *macarons*: Follow the same instructions as for the chocolate *macarons*, but replace the almond meal, confectioner's sugar, and cocoa powder mixture with hazelnut meal and confectioner's sugar alone. Once you've piped the *macarons* onto the sheet, dust half of the shells with pistachios while they rest before baking.

To prepare the hazelnut ganache: Follow the instructions for chocolate ganache above.

Mini *clafoutis*

WITH PEACHES AND LEMON BALM

Petits clafoutis aux pêches à la mélisse

When peaches are ripe and ready to eat, they release their juices when they are cut open. This luscious fruit flavor fills my individual *clafoutis*, which are infused with the complementary aromas of vanilla and lemon balm. Serve them lukewarm, dusted with a cloud of sugar, as this is when the flavors are at their best. Feel free to try plums or apricots in this dessert, if you prefer (with these fruits, you don't need to remove the skins).

You will need: four 4¾-by-1½-inch (12 by 4 cm), ¾-cup ramekins.

Makes 4 mini clafoutis

2 large yellow peaches (about 12¼ oz; 350 g)

¼ cup (60 ml) whole milk

6 lemon balm or lemon verbena leaves

1 vanilla bean, split lengthwise and seeds scraped out, or 1 teaspoon pure vanilla extract

2 tablespoons unsalted butter, melted, plus more for the ramekins

¼ cup (1¾ oz; 50 g) blond cane sugar, plus 2 tablespoons

1 large egg plus 1 egg yolk

¼ cup (1 oz; 30 g) almond meal

2 tablespoons cornstarch or tapioca starch

2½ tablespoons *crème fraîche*

Confectioner's sugar, to serve

Blanch the peaches for 1 minute in a large pot of boiling water (page 386). Transfer to an ice water bath and peel. Cut the peaches into ¾-inch (2 cm) slices; set aside.

In a pot, combine the milk with the lemon balm and vanilla bean and seeds. Bring to a simmer. Remove from the heat, cover, and let infuse for 30 minutes. Strain and set aside.

Preheat the oven to 400°F (200°C). Butter the ramekins and coat with ½ tablespoon sugar each; tap out the excess. Arrange the peach slices in the ramekins; set aside.

In a bowl, beat the egg and egg yolk with the rest of the sugar. Beat in the almond meal, and cornstarch. Stir in the *crème fraîche*, infused milk, and melted butter. Divide the batter between the ramekins, and bake the *clafoutis* for 20 minutes, or until set and lightly golden in color. Remove from the oven and let cool slightly. Dust with confectioner's sugar and serve lukewarm.

Carrot spice cake

Gâteau aux carottes et aux épices

This carrot cake, and its orange-flavored cream cheese frosting, deserves a spotlight in your kitchen. It's moist and flavorful while remaining light. You will probably go back for a second serving once you try it—we always do.

You will need: one 9-inch (23 cm) round cake pan.

Makes one 9-inch (23 cm) cake

½ cup (120 ml) grapeseed oil, plus more for the mold

6 oz (175 g) carrots (about 3 carrots)

1 cup (3½ oz; 100 g) hazelnut meal

⅔ cup (3 oz; 85 g) millet flour

⅓ cup (1 oz; 33 g) oat flour

2 teaspoons baking powder

1 teaspoon ground cinnamon

¼ teaspoon ground nutmeg

¼ teaspoon ground ginger

¼ teaspoon sea salt

3 large eggs

¾ cup (3½ oz; 100 g) light Muscovado sugar

1 tablespoon pure vanilla extract

FOR THE CREAM CHEESE AND ORANGE FROSTING:

2 tablespoons (10 oz.; 30 g) whole hazelnuts

8 oz (227 g) cream cheese

3 tablespoons orange juice

2 teaspoons maple syrup

1 teaspoon finely grated orange zest

2 tablespoons (1 oz; 30 g) coarsely chopped unsalted green pistachios

Preheat the oven to 350°F (180°C). Spray or brush the baking pan with grapeseed oil; set aside.

Peel and dice the carrots. Transfer to the bowl of a food processor and chop finely; set aside.

In a large bowl, combine the hazelnut meal, flours, baking powder, cinnamon, nutmeg, ginger, and sea salt; set aside.

In the bowl of a stand mixer fitted with the whisk, beat the eggs with the sugar until light in color and fluffy. Stir in the grapeseed oil and vanilla. Beat in the dry ingredients; stir in the carrots until just combined. Pour the batter into the pan and bake for 35 minutes, or until the blade of a sharp knife comes out clean. Remove from the oven and let cool for 5 minutes before unmolding. Cool completely on a rack.

To serve, dust with confectioner's sugar or ice with the cream cheese frosting.

To prepare the frosting: Preheat the oven to 350°F (180°C). Toast the hazelnuts on a baking sheet for 5 minutes, or until fragrant. Remove from the oven and let cool for 5 minutes; chop coarsely.

In a bowl, beat the cream cheese with the orange juice, maple syrup, and orange zest until smooth. Frost the cake and top with the hazelnuts and pistachios, adding extra orange zest for decoration. Refrigerate until ready to serve. Cover any leftovers and keep in the fridge.

Rhubarb and strawberry cakes in a glass

Gâteaux à la rhubarbe et aux fraises cuits dans des verres

Little ones delight in these cute early summer, fruit-filled cakes eaten with a spoon directly in the glasses in which they are baked. I like to bake them close to the time they will be served and use the youngest rhubarb I can find. The juice released by the classic yet beautiful strawberry-rhubarb pairing keeps the cakes really moist.

You will need: four 1-cup heat-resistant glass jars.

Makes 4 cakes

FOR THE STEWED RHUBARB:

Butter, for the ramekins

1 tablespoon white rice flour, for the ramekins

8¾ oz (250 g) rhubarb, cut in ½-inch (1.25 cm) pieces

2 tablespoons water

2 teaspoons cornstarch

1 teaspoon pure vanilla extract

¼ cup (1¾ oz; 50 g) blond cane sugar

1 cup (5¼ oz; 150 g) strawberries, hulled and diced

FOR THE CAKES:

⅓ cup (1½ oz; 40 g) quinoa flour

⅓ cup (1¼ oz; 33 g) oat flour

1 tablespoon golden flax meal

½ tablespoon baking powder

Pinch of sea salt

1 large egg

⅓ cup plus 1 tablespoon (2¾ oz; 80 g) blond cane sugar

4¼ tablespoons (2 oz; 60 g) butter, melted

1 tablespoon *crème fraîche*

½ tablespoon pure vanilla extract

Confectioner's sugar, to serve

To prepare the rhubarb: Butter the glass jars. Coat them with rice flour and tap out the excess; set aside.

In a pot, combine the rhubarb with the water, cornstarch, vanilla, and sugar. Bring to a simmer and cook over low heat for 5 minutes, or until soft. Remove from the heat and stir in the strawberries. Divide the fruit between the jars; set aside.

To prepare the cakes: Preheat the oven to 350°F (180°C).

In a bowl, combine the flours, flax meal, baking powder, and sea salt; set aside.

In another bowl, beat the egg with the sugar for 1 minute. Stir in the melted butter, *crème fraîche*, and vanilla. Stir in the dry ingredients. Pour the batter over the fruit in the jars. Bake for 25 minutes, or until the blade of a sharp knife comes out clean when inserted into the cake. Remove from the oven and let stand until the jars are cool enough to handle.

Dust with confectioner's sugar to serve. Enjoy lukewarm or at room temperature, with plain yogurt on the side.

cooking with lulu
la cuisine avec lulu

LULU TELLS ME, "You are a good kitchener, Mummy," "You could work in a restaurant," or "You could teach my friends how to cook at school." (They have a cooking club in the school she attends.) It makes me smile when I hear those words.

My daughter has always loved working with me in the kitchen. At her age, I also watched my mother cook every day and grow vegetables in the garden. Together, we picked berries and made jam. She let me bake cakes. I learned about food instinctively. When I became a mother, I knew I would make it a priority to instill and nurture a love for and curiosity about food in Lulu and now my baby son, Rémy.

When Lulu was almost two, I let her add salt and pepper to a soup and hold the wooden spoon as we stirred it. In the garden, we collected peas, and I showed her how to pop the little green balls out of their pods. We visited orchards to pick apples, which we turned into comforting *compote de pommes* (stewed apples) and delectable tarts. I wanted to plant a seed in her little head so that she'd gradually build awareness about what we eat and where our foods come from.

Lulu is six now, and I can see that these simple gestures have already affected her in a positive way: she enjoys food and has an endless interest in it. Whenever she sees me start a *mise en place* with flours, sugar, butter, and eggs, she grabs her flowered apron and commands, *"Attends-moi maman. Je veux t'aider!"* ("Wait for me, Mummy. I want to help you!"). It's more work for me, and the kitchen gets messier than when I cook alone, but I don't mind because she is learning something valuable. Mainly, we are having a lot of fun.

We often bake a cake or whisk a *crêpe* batter together. When chocolate is involved in our culinary adventures, her eyes light up because she knows that along the way, her face, nose, and fingers will end up covered with it. She tells me she is a *gourmande,* then she laughs. She is eager to grab the rolling pin to roll out a crust—and oh, how my girl likes a crust (*la croûte*)—or to garnish a vegetable tart. When a task is more challenging, such as grating a carrot or peeling a potato, I guide her hands in mine so that she understands the movements involved.

When we carry a dish to the table for dinner, she proclaims, *"C'est maman et moi qui l'avons cuisiné ensemble"* ("Mummy and I cooked it together"). Her tone indicates that she is proud of her accomplishments in the kitchen. To me, that matters a great deal. Above all, I want to bring her happiness when we cook and share the foods we prepare. Clearly, something special happens in the kitchen each time we are busy touching and transforming food together.

These are sweet and savory recipes Lulu and I enjoy preparing together. I was inspired to write them from watching her experiences and discoveries. You will observe that while some recipes are easy for children to make, others require adult help—yet you will be amazed to see how skilled our little ones can be.

savory
le salé

Spring rolls • *Rouleaux de printemps*   192

Vegetable latkes • *Paillassons de légumes*   194

Quinoa and vegetable *croquettes* • *Croquettes de quinoa aux légumes*   196

Kale and pea pancakes with smoked salmon and *crème fraîche* • *Pancakes au chou frisé et
aux petits pois avec saumon fumé et crème fraîche*   200

Sweet potato, parsley, and roasted hazelnut tartlets • *Tartelettes à la patate douce et
au persil avec noisettes grillées*   203

Gingered butternut squash and fennel soup with olive oil and
parsley *croûtons* • *Soupe à la courge musquée et au fenouil avec gingembre et
croûtons persillés à l'huile d'olive*   205

Lamb and herb meatballs with mint-flavored cucumber salad and
yogurt sauce • *Boulettes d'agneau aux herbes, salade de
concombre à la menthe, et sauce au yaourt*   206

Pasta gratin • *Gratin de pâtes*   210

sweet
le sucré

Raspberry and red currant *financiers* • *Financiers aux framboises et aux groseilles rouges*   214

Strawberry and yogurt mousses with *petits beurres* • *Mousses aux fraises et au yaourt avec petits beurres*   216

Summer fruit crumble with vanilla *crème fraîche* • *Crumble aux fruits de l'été et crème fraîche vanillée*   220

Mini pavlovas with fresh fruit • *Petits pavlovas aux fruits frais*   223

Red berry ice pops • *Bâtonnets glacés aux fruits rouges*   224

Teff and cocoa nib cookies with black sesame seeds and *fleur de sel* • *Cookies à la farine de teff, graines de sésame noir, grué de cacao, et fleur de sel*   226

Lulu's chocolate and olive oil cake with roasted hazelnuts • *Le gâteau au chocolat de Lulu avec huile d'olive et noisettes grillées*   229

Chocolate and raspberry tart • *Tarte au chocolat et aux framboises*   231

Chocolate and coconut milk *petits pots de crème* with meringue • *Petits pots de crème meringuée au chocolat et au lait de coco*   234

savory
le salé

Spring rolls

Rouleaux de printemps

Lulu likes to see the ingredients for making spring rolls lined up on the kitchen counter-top. After the first time we made them, she asked that we prepare them again and again. While you will naturally need to help with a few steps of the process, these rolls are perfect for a child's small hands to prepare and hold. If you don't have or like shrimp, fresh crabmeat or smoked salmon also work well in this recipe.

Makes 24 spring rolls

FOR THE
DIPPING SAUCE:

¼ cup (60 ml)
cold water

2 tablespoons
fish sauce

2 tablespoons
lime juice

2 tablespoons blond
cane sugar

1 tablespoon
chopped cilantro

1 tablespoon
chopped mint

FOR THE
SPRING ROLLS:

8 cups water

2 oz (60 g) rice
vermicelli

24 spring roll
rice sheets

2 carrots, peeled and
julienned

½ cucumber, peeled,
seeded, and cut in
thin sticks

1 avocado, pitted, cut
in thin sticks, and
drizzled with lemon
juice

1 small apple, cored,
cut in thin sticks,
and drizzled with
lemon juice

2 tablespoons
chopped mint

12 long chives, cut in
half (24 pieces)

24 cilantro leaves

12 small cooked
cocktail shrimp, cut in
half lengthwise

To prepare the dipping sauce: In a small bowl, whisk all the ingredients together; set aside.

To prepare the spring rolls: In a pot, boil the water. Remove from the heat and add the vermicelli. Let soak for 3 minutes. Drain and rinse under cold water; set aside.

Use a large plate as a working surface, and have all the ingredients handy. Fill a bowl with water at room temperature. Dip a rice sheet in the water for a few seconds, until it softens. Place the sheet on the plate. At the end closest to you, add a few carrot and cucumber sticks. Add a small amount of vermicelli (about ¼ oz; 7 g), then a few avocado and apple sticks, and finally a few mint leaves. Fold the sides of the rice sheet toward the middle. Starting from the area where you have placed the food, roll the sheet, making sure to tuck everything together tightly, like a small package. When you have completed two-thirds of the roll, add a piece of chive, a cilantro leaf, and a piece of shrimp. Finish rolling. Repeat with the other sheets. Serve the spring rolls with the dipping sauce.

Vegetable latkes

Paillassons de légumes

I've made vegetable latkes like these since Lulu was a toddler, trying different types of vegetables for variety and to introduce her to new flavors. Lulu tells me this one is now her favorite recipe. The latkes are simple to make: I cut the vegetables with my mandoline, and Lulu helps mix them and flatten them in the pan. Try them for a light lunch with a salad or to accompany a more substantial meal.

Makes sixteen 3-inch (7.5 cm) latkes

7 oz (200 g) peeled sweet potato (or butternut squash)

3½ oz (100 g) peeled celeriac

3½ oz (100 g) zucchini

2 large eggs

¼ cup (1 oz; 30 g) quinoa flour

2 tablespoons hazelnut meal

1 tablespoon chopped tarragon

1 tablespoon chopped parsley

Sea salt and pepper

Freshly grated nutmeg (optional)

Olive oil

Crème fraîche or Labneh (page 36), to serve

Preheat the oven to 250°F (120°C). Line a rimmed baking sheet with paper towels; set aside.

Finely grate the vegetables—use a mandoline if you have one. In a large bowl, combine them with the eggs, flour, hazelnut meal, tarragon, and parsley. Season with sea salt and pepper and a light dusting of freshly grated nutmeg, if using.

In a large frying pan, heat 1½ tablespoons olive oil over medium-high heat. Reduce the heat to medium. Drop in three dollops of batter, about ¼ cup each to make one latke. Flatten each with a spatula and cook for 2 to 2½ minutes, or until lightly browned. Flip and cook on the other side for another 2 minutes, until lightly browned. Transfer to the baking sheet and keep warm in the oven while you cook the rest of the latkes, adding extra paper towels between the layers of pancakes. Add more oil to the pan and repeat the process until you run out of ingredients.

Serve with a dollop of *crème fraîche* on the latkes and a salad on the side. Lulu loves hers with soft goat cheese spread on top.

Quinoa and vegetable *croquettes*

Croquettes de quinoa aux légumes

I was quite happy to see some of the pickiest eaters among Lulu's friends gobble these nutritious *croquettes* down. Sometimes, when bits of broccoli show through the coating, the *croquettes* look like they have little trees painted on them. Once our *mise en place* is ready, Lulu is fantastically helpful with mixing the ingredients and then shaping the *croquettes* in the pan.

Makes ten 3-inch (7.5 cm) croquettes

FOR THE LEMON-FLAVORED MASCARPONE CREAM:

8 oz (1 cup; 227 g) mascarpone cheese or *crème fraîche*

1 tablespoon lemon juice

Sea salt and pepper

Olive oil, to drizzle

FOR THE *CROQUETTES*:

⅓ cup (1½ oz; 40 g) quinoa flakes

¼ cup plus 2 tablespoons (90 ml) whole or 2% milk

½ cup (2¾ oz; 80 g) dry quinoa

1 cup (235 ml) salted water

Sea salt

3½ oz (100 g) broccoli or cauliflower florets

Olive oil, grapeseed oil, or coconut oil

1 shallot or ¼ red onion, finely chopped

½ cup (50 g) finely grated carrot

½ cup (50 g) finely grated zucchini

⅓ cup (1½ oz; 40 g) finely grated Parmesan cheese or Comté cheese

1 tablespoon finely chopped parsley

1 garlic clove, minced

2 tablespoons tapioca starch

1 large egg

Ground pepper, to taste

To prepare the mascarpone cream: In a bowl, mix the mascarpone with the lemon juice. Season with sea salt and pepper to taste. Drizzle with olive oil and refrigerate until ready to use.

To prepare the *croquettes*: In a bowl, stir the quinoa flakes into the milk; let rest for 10 minutes.

In a small pot, combine the dry quinoa, salted water, and a pinch of sea salt. Bring to a boil, then turn down the heat, cover, and simmer for 12 to 14 minutes, or until the water is absorbed. Remove from the heat and keep covered for 5 minutes.

Transfer the quinoa to a bowl and fluff it with a fork; let cool.

Meanwhile, blanch the broccoli for 3 minutes in salted boiling water (page 386). Drain and let cool. Chop lengthwise and set aside.

In a frying pan, heat 1 tablespoon olive oil over medium heat. Add the shallot, carrot, and zucchini or cauliflower. Cook for 2 minutes, stirring occasionally with a wooden spoon, until the vegetables soften. Remove from the heat and add to the bowl of cooked quinoa. Stir in the broccoli or cauliflower, soaked quinoa flakes, cheese,

continued

parsley, garlic, tapioca starch, and egg. Season with sea salt and pepper.

At this point, you can cover the preparation with a plate and refrigerate for a few hours until ready to use.

In a large frying pan, heat 2 tablespoons olive oil over medium heat. Place three 3-inch (7.5 cm) rounds (¾-inch [2 cm] thick) of the quinoa mixture in the pan—I use a ring mold to obtain a uniform shape. Cook about 2 to 3 minutes, until lightly browned;

flip gently and cook on the other side for another 3 minutes; transfer the croquettes to a plate lined with paper towel. Repeat with the rest of the quinoa mixture, adding olive oil to the pan between each batch. Serve with the lemon-flavored mascarpone cream (or Labneh, if you prefer; page 36), and a side salad. If you have leftovers, reheat in a nonstick frying pan for 1 to 2 minutes on each side.

Kale and pea pancakes
WITH SMOKED SALMON AND *CRÈME FRAÎCHE*
Pancakes au chou frisé et aux petits pois avec saumon fumé et crème fraîche

Lulu calls these "the green pancakes" and enjoys them best with fresh goat cheese spread on top (she loves fresh goat cheese spread on almost anything). Philip and I like ours with *crème fraîche* and a slice of smoked salmon (preferably wild Alaskan salmon) folded on top. When I bake a batch, I also freeze leftovers for a handy meal when I'm short on time.

Makes ten to twelve 4-inch (10 cm) pancakes

FOR THE PANCAKES:

1 cup (4½ oz; 125 g) peas (fresh or frozen)

2 cups (3½ oz; 100 g) chopped kale leaves

2 tablespoons cilantro leaves

8 mint leaves

1 garlic clove

Sea salt and pepper

1 batch Flax Gel (page 30)

¼ cup (60 ml) *crème fraîche* or ¼ cup buttermilk

2 large eggs, separated

¼ cup (1 oz; 30 g) quinoa flour

¼ cup (¾ oz; 25 g) hazelnut meal

½ teaspoon baking powder

½ teaspoon baking soda

Sunflower oil, to cook

FOR THE GARNISH:

Crème fraîche or soft goat cheese

Smoked salmon

Dill, finely chopped

Fleur de sel

Blanch the peas for 1 minute in salted boiling water (page 386). Transfer to an ice water bath to cool; then drain.

In the bowl of a food processor, combine the peas, kale, cilantro, mint, and garlic. Season with sea salt and pepper, and pulse several times. Add the flax gel and purée the mixture, scraping the sides of the bowl as you go, until the texture is very fine. Transfer to a bowl and stir in the *crème fraîche*, egg yolks, quinoa flour, hazelnut meal, baking powder, and baking soda.

Whip the egg whites with a pinch of sea salt until soft peaks form. Fold gently into the vegetable purée.

In a large frying pan, heat 1 tablespoon sunflower oil over medium heat. Pour ¼ cup batter in the pan and repeat for as many pancakes as the pan can hold. Cook for about 1½ to 2 minutes, until bubbles form on the surface. Flip gently with a spatula; fry for 1 to 2 minutes on the other side until cooked through. Transfer to a plate lined with a paper towel, and repeat until you run out of batter, adding oil to the pan as needed.

When ready to serve, spread *crème fraîche* or fresh soft goat cheese on each pancake, and top with a small slice of folded smoked salmon. Garnish with dill and a dash of *fleur de sel*.

Sweet potato, parsley, and roasted hazelnut tartlets

Tartelettes à la patate douce et au persil avec noisettes grillées

Lulu has quickly learned to roll a crust, arrange it in a tart mold, and spread a filling on top with great care. She tells me this one is her favorite vegetable tart, and she always claps her hands delightedly when she knows this is what we are cooking for dinner.

You will need: eight 4½-inch (11.5 cm) tartlet molds or one 11-inch tart mold.

Makes 8 tartlets or one 11-inch (28 cm) tart

Rustic Crust with Teff Flour (page 60) or Savory Crust with Oat (page 106)

1 sweet potato (about 1 lb; 450 g)

2 tablespoons olive oil, plus more to drizzle

½ red onion, finely chopped (makes 1 cup packed)

1 leek, white part only, finely chopped

1 garlic clove, minced

Sea salt and pepper

3 tablespoons hazelnut meal

1 tablespoon whole hazelnuts

3 large eggs

¼ cup (2 oz; 60 g) *crème fraîche*

¼ cup (60 ml) whole or 2% milk

¼ cup (1 oz; 30 g) finely grated Parmesan cheese

⅓ cup (¾ oz; 20 g) packed parsley leaves, finely chopped

Dash of nutmeg (optional), ground or freshly grated

Preheat the oven to 375°F (190°C). Roll and cut the dough ⅕-inch (0.5 cm) thick to fit inside the molds. Arrange the dough inside the molds and, using a fork, make small holes in the bottom. Place in the fridge while you prepare the filling.

Peel and finely grate the sweet potato; set aside. In a frying pan, heat the olive oil over medium heat. Add the onion and leek; cook, stirring frequently, for 5 minutes, without browning. Add the garlic and continue to cook for 1 minute. Add the sweet potato, and season with sea salt and pepper. Cook for 5 more minutes, stirring frequently, until the vegetables are soft. Transfer to a clean bowl.

Clean and dry the frying pan. Cook the hazelnut meal for 2 minutes over medium heat, stirring frequently; remove from the heat, transfer to a bowl, and set aside to cool. Return the pan to the stove and toast the hazelnuts for 2 minutes over medium heat. Remove from the heat and let cool. Chop the nuts coarsely; set aside.

In a bowl, beat the eggs with the *crème fraîche* and milk. Beat in the Parmesan, chopped parsley, and roasted hazelnut meal; season with pepper. Stir the sweet potato mixture into the egg batter. Divide between the tartlet crusts. Add a dash of nutmeg on top, if using, and drizzle with olive oil.

Bake the tartlets for 30 to 35 minutes (40 minutes for a large tart), or until light brown. Serve warm with the chopped hazelnuts on top, fresh parsley leaves to decorate, and a side salad.

Gingered butternut squash and fennel soup
WITH OLIVE OIL AND PARSLEY *CROÛTONS*

Soupe à la courge musquée et au fenouil avec gingembre et croûtons persillés à l'huile d'olive

I will never forget the day Lulu asked me how we make soup. She was barely four but already so curious to understand the magic that was happening in the pot as I stirred the vegetables. I explained that it depended, because there are many kinds of soups, all different in texture and color. *"Orange!"* she exclaimed. Our conversation inspired this soup, which we prepare often when butternut squash is in season. Generally in soups and stews I prefer to use mace over nutmeg. It has a slightly sweeter and more subtle flavor. Make sure to prepare the *croûtons*, as children especially find them indispensable with soup.

Serves 6; makes 11 cups (2.6 liters)

FOR THE OLIVE OIL AND PARSLEY *CROÛTONS*:

8 slices country bread of your choice, diced

2 tablespoons olive oil

2 garlic cloves

2 teaspoons finely chopped parsley

Sea salt and pepper

FOR THE SOUP:

2 tablespoons unsalted butter

1 tablespoon olive oil

2 celery stalks, diced

1 red onion or shallot, diced

1-inch (2.5 cm) piece of fresh ginger, chopped

2 garlic cloves, minced

1 rosemary sprig

1 oregano sprig

1 tomato, peeled, seeded, and diced

1 butternut squash or red kuri squash (about 3 lb; 1.35 kg), peeled, seeded, and diced (makes 1¾ lb; 800 g)

1 fennel bulb, diced (about 7 oz; 200 g)

1 piece of mace or a dash of nutmeg

4 to 4½ cups (about 1 liter) Homemade Vegetable Stock (page 96), or chicken stock

Sea salt and pepper

TO SERVE:

Crème fraîche

Grated pecorino cheese

Fresh parsley, chopped

To prepare the *croûtons*: Preheat the oven to 375°F (190°C). Line a baking sheet with parchment paper. Put all ingredients in a plastic bag, and shake to coat the bread. Arrange in a single layer on the baking sheet and bake for 10 minutes, or until the *croûtons* are crispy. Remove from the oven and let cool.

To prepare the soup: In a large pot, melt the butter over medium heat; add the olive oil. Add the celery, onion, and ginger. Cook for 2 to 3 minutes, stirring occasionally; without browning. Add the garlic, rosemary, and oregano, and continue to cook for 1 minute. Add the tomato and cook for another minute. Add the butternut squash and fennel, and cook for 5 minutes. Add the mace and stock. Season with sea salt and pepper. Cover and simmer for 20 minutes. Remove from the heat, discard the herbs and mace, and transfer to the bowl of a food processor; purée until smooth, working in batches if necessary.

Serve the soup in large bowls with a dollop of *crème fraîche, croûtons*, grated pecorino cheese, and fresh parsley.

Lamb and herb meatballs

WITH MINT-FLAVORED CUCUMBER SALAD AND YOGURT SAUCE

Boulettes d'agneau aux herbes, salade de concombre à la menthe, et sauce au yaourt

I use different kinds of meat when I make meatballs, but I find lamb particularly flavorful. These are wonderfully soft and a lot of fun to prepare with Lulu, who gobbles them up. When I have a busy day, I prepare the meatballs ahead of time, as they reheat well. The cucumber salad with yogurt sauce has a refreshing, mellow taste that makes it the perfect complement to the more complex flavor of lamb.

Makes thirty 1¾-inch meatballs

FOR THE CUCUMBER SALAD:

1 cucumber, thinly sliced with a mandoline

Pinch of sea salt

1½ tablespoons rice vinegar

½ tablespoon blond cane sugar

Pepper

3 tablespoons almond oil or olive oil

1 tablespoon finely chopped mint

FOR THE YOGURT SAUCE:

1 cup (8 oz; 225 g) whole plain yogurt

1 tablespoon finely chopped red onion

1 tablespoon chopped mint

1 tablespoon chopped chives

Sea salt and pepper

Olive oil, to drizzle

FOR THE LAMB MEATBALLS:

1 carrot, peeled

1 celery stalk

½ of a red onion

½ cup (2 oz; 60 g) pine nuts

1 lb, 3½ oz (550 g) ground lamb

⅓ cup mixed finely chopped mint, basil, and parsley

1 large egg

¼ cup (1 oz; 30 g) almond meal

Sea salt and pepper

⅓ cup (2 oz; 55 g) white rice flour, to coat the meatballs

⅓ cup (80 ml) olive oil

2 garlic cloves, minced

1 tablespoon tomato paste

1 tablespoon balsamic vinegar

4 tomatoes, finely chopped

¾ to 1 cup (236 ml) chicken stock

1 bay leaf

1 teaspoon brown sugar

6 mint leaves

6 basil leaves

To prepare the cucumber salad: Place the cucumber in a strainer over a bowl. Season with sea salt and let rest for 30 minutes to release water. Transfer to a bowl; set aside.

Meanwhile, in a small bowl, combine the rice vinegar and sugar. Season with pepper and whisk in the almond oil. Add the mint, and toss the dressing with the cucumber. Refrigerate until ready to use.

To prepare the yogurt sauce: In a bowl, combine the yogurt with the onion, mint, and chives. Season with sea salt and pepper, and drizzle with olive oil. Refrigerate until ready to use.

continued

To prepare the meatballs: In the bowl of a food processor, pulse the carrot to finely chop; remove from the bowl and set aside. Repeat with the celery stalk. Finely chop half of the red onion; slice the other half, and set aside. Chop ¼ cup (1 oz; 30 g) pine nuts; set aside.

In a large bowl, combine the ground lamb with the chopped herbs, onion, carrot, and chopped pine nuts. Stir in the egg and almond meal. Season with sea salt and pepper. Roll the mixture into 30 balls. Add rice flour to a large plate; roll each meatball in the flour and tap the excess out.

In a large frying pan, heat half of the olive oil over medium heat. Add the meatballs, making sure not to overcrowd the pan. Brown them for a few minutes on each side, about 8 minutes total. Remove from the pan and set aside on a plate. Work in batches and add more oil, if necessary, until all the meatballs are browned.

In the same frying pan, cook the sliced onion for 2 minutes. Add the garlic and cook for 1 minute. Add the tomato paste and cook for another minute. Add the balsamic vinegar, tomatoes, and chopped celery; cook for 3 minutes. Add the stock, bay leaf, sugar, and the rest of the pine nuts. Season with sea salt and pepper, and add the mint and basil leaves. Return the meatballs to the pan and cover. Simmer for 30 to 45 minutes, or until the meat is well cooked and the sauce is reduced. Serve the meatballs with the yogurt sauce, cucumber salad, and steamed basmati rice.

Pasta gratin

Gratin de pâtes

This comfy pasta gratin makes for a happy family. I am particularly fond of rounding out the taste of the sauce with ricotta; Lulu thinks it gives the sauce a lovely pink color. You can use the sauce for pasta served on its own too, so freeze any leftovers. If your family likes food on the spicy side, add a dash of cayenne pepper to the sauce when you cook it.

You will need: one 12-by-8-inch (30.5 by 20 cm) baking dish.

Serves 6

2 slices (1½ oz; 40 g) toasted bread

1 tablespoon parsley

¾ cup (3 oz; 90 g) grated Parmesan cheese

12 oz (340 g) rigatoni

Olive oil

¼ red onion, chopped

3 oregano sprigs

2 thyme sprigs

3 garlic cloves

1 carrot, peeled and grated (3½ oz; 100 g)

1 tablespoon tomato paste

¼ cup (60 ml) dry white wine or white vermouth

1 lb, 5¼ oz (600 g) tomatoes, cored and diced, plus 1 tomato, sliced

1 bay leaf

1½ teaspoons brown sugar

Sea salt and pepper

1 cup (8 oz; 225 g) whole ricotta cheese

3 tablespoons finely chopped basil leaves

¼ cup (1 oz; 30 g) pine nuts

4½ oz (125 g) mozzarella cheese, diced

Ground nutmeg, to finish

Place the slices of toasted bread and parsley in the bowl of a food processor; pulse into fine crumbs. Transfer to a bowl and combine with ¼ cup (1 oz; 30 g) Parmesan cheese; set aside.

Cook the pasta in a large pot of salted boiling water, following the instructions on the package. Remove from the heat, drain, and set aside.

Preheat the oven to 400°F (200°C). Brush the baking dish with olive oil; set aside.

In a large sauté pan, heat 2 tablespoons olive oil over medium heat. Add the onion and oregano and thyme; cook for 5 minutes on low to medium heat, stirring occasionally, without browning. Add the garlic and cook for 1 minute. Add the carrot and cook for 2 minutes. Stir in the tomato paste and cook for another minute. Add the wine and cook for 1 minute. Add the tomatoes, bay leaf, and sugar; season with sea salt and pepper; cover and simmer on low heat for 15 minutes. Uncover and cook for another 5 minutes, or until the sauce is slightly reduced. Discard the oregano, thyme, and bay leaf. Transfer to the bowl of a food processor with the ricotta, and purée until smooth.

In a large bowl, toss the pasta with the sauce, basil, pine nuts, and the rest of the Parmesan cheese. Transfer the pasta to the prepared baking dish. Scatter the mozzarella cheese and sliced tomato over the pasta. Top with the breadcrumbs; add a drizzle of olive oil and sprinkle with nutmeg. Bake the gratin for 30 minutes, or until lightly golden and crispy. Serve with a green salad on the side.

sweet
le sucré

Raspberry and red currant *financiers*

Financiers aux framboises et aux groseilles rouges

A *financier* is usually made with brown butter, giving it a rich, hazelnut-like aroma. Lulu loves to watch the color of butter in the pot transform. We use tangy raspberries and red currants here because they contrast beautifully with the richness of the brown butter, but other berries such as small blackberries are also delectable in this recipe.

You will need: 8 *financier* molds (mine measure 1 by 3½ inches [⅖ by 9 cm]).

Makes 8 **financiers**

8 tablespoons (4 oz; 113 g) unsalted butter, plus more for the molds

1 to 2 tablespoons white rice flour, for the molds

1 vanilla bean, split lengthwise and seeds scraped out

¾ cup plus 1 tablespoon (3½ oz; 100 g) almond meal

¼ cup (30 g) quinoa flour

3½ oz (100 g) confectioner's sugar, sifted, or blond cane sugar, plus more to serve

Pinch of sea salt

4 large egg whites, lightly beaten with a whisk or fork

2 oz (60 g) raspberries

2 oz (60 g) red currants

Preheat the oven to 375°F (190°C). Butter the molds. Coat them with rice flour and tap out the excess; set aside.

In a small pot, melt the butter over low to medium heat. Cook until it starts to turn golden in color and develops a hazelnut-like aroma. Remove from the heat, and add the vanilla bean and seeds. Cover and leave to infuse for 10 minutes.

In the meantime, combine the almond meal, quinoa flour, sugar, and a pinch of sea salt in a large bowl. Beat in the egg whites. Strain the butter and discard the vanilla bean. Stir the butter into the batter quickly. Divide the batter between the molds and stud each with raspberries and red currants. Bake for 20 to 25 minutes, or until the edges of the cakes start to brown slightly. Remove from the oven and let cool for 5 minutes before unmolding. Let cool completely on a rack. Serve dusted with confectioner's sugar.

Strawberry and yogurt mousses

WITH *PETITS BEURRES*

Mousses aux fraises et au yaourt avec petits beurres

These light, yogurt-based strawberry mousses are the perfect treat to enjoy in spring when strawberries have just been picked. I prefer to make them with *fromage blanc,* but it's hard to find outside France, so I use thick plain yogurt—like Greek yogurt—when I'm in the States. I serve the mousses with *petits beurres,* which we eventually use as edible spoons to scoop the mousse out of the jar.

Serves 6

1 lb, 10½ oz (700 g) strawberries, hulled

1¾ oz (50 g) raspberries

Juice of 2 limes (3 to 4 tablespoons)

¾ cup (5¼ oz; 150 g) blond cane sugar

2 gelatin sheets (0.14 oz; 4 g)

1 vanilla bean, split lengthwise and seeds scraped out

7 oz (200 g) whole milk Greek yogurt or *fromage blanc*

2 large egg whites

Pinch of sea salt

2 tablespoons toasted slivered almonds, chopped

Shredded mint leaves, to serve

Petits beurres, to serve (see page 218)

Dice 9 oz strawberries and toss them gently in a bowl with the raspberries, the juice of 1 lime, and 3 tablespoons sugar. Place in the fridge so the strawberries macerate while you prepare the mousse.

In a bowl, cover the gelatin sheets with plenty of water; set aside for 15 minutes.

In the bowl of a food processor, combine the rest of the strawberries, ½ cup (3½ oz; 100 g) sugar, the juice of the other lime, and the seeds of the vanilla bean. Purée until smooth. Take ¼ cup of the purée and heat in a small pot over low heat. Squeeze the gelatin sheets to remove the excess water and add to the warm strawberry purée; stir until gelatin dissolves. Add to the rest of the strawberry purée and stir in the yogurt; set aside.

Whip the egg whites with a pinch of sea salt. When they start to form peaks, add 1 tablespoon sugar. Beat for 1 more minute until stiff. Fold into the strawberry and yogurt purée. Divide the mousse between six 1-cup (236 ml) glasses and refrigerate for a few hours to set.

To serve, divide the macerated fruit, toasted almonds, and mint between the glasses. Serve with *petits beurres* on the side.

Petits beurres

These butter cookies have a scalloped edge and rectangular shape. They are classic in the French food repertoire, and I enjoyed them very much as a child growing up in France.

You will need: a 1¾-by-2½-inch (4.5 by 6.5 cm) cookie cutter for *petits beurres,* or another cookie cutter of your choice.

Makes 18 cookies

1 tablespoon golden flax meal

2½ tablespoons hot water

4 tablespoons (2 oz; 60 g) unsalted butter

2 tablespoons water

¼ teaspoon sea salt

2 teaspoons pure vanilla extract

½ cup (2¾ oz; 80 g) brown rice flour or white rice flour

⅓ cup (1½ oz; 40 g) oat flour

⅓ cup (1½ oz; 40 g) cornstarch or tapioca starch

1 teaspoon baking powder

¼ cup (1¾ oz; 50 g) blond cane sugar

In a bowl, combine the flax meal and water. Stir and let rest for 10 minutes; the mixture will become gelatinous. In a pot, combine the butter, water, and sea salt. Heat until the butter is melted. Add the vanilla and set aside for 15 minutes, stirring occasionally.

In a bowl, combine the flours, cornstarch, baking powder, and sugar. Make a small well in the middle. Add the liquid flax meal and butter preparation to the dry ingredients, and work together with a wooden spoon to form a ball. Separate the dough into two balls, transfer to a plate, and cover. Refrigerate for at least 3 hours or overnight.

Preheat the oven to 350°F (180°C). Line a rimmed baking sheet with parchment paper.

Take the balls of dough out of the fridge and leave to rest at room temperature for 5 minutes. Roll the dough to a ¼-inch (0.5 cm) thickness and cut out the cookies. Transfer them to the lined baking sheet, leaving 2 inches (5 cm) between them. Bake for 15 to 18 minutes, or until the edges start to become golden in color. Remove from the oven and transfer cookies to a rack to cool completely. Store in an airtight container for up to 1 week.

Summer fruit crumble
WITH VANILLA *CRÈME FRAÎCHE*

Crumble aux fruits de l'été et crème fraîche vanillée

With the Irish heritage from Philip's side of the family, crumbles are essential. We find this one—a blend of summer stone fruit with aromas of ginger and lemon—incredible. Choose fruit when it is at its peak. Lulu often prefers to prepare individual crumbles, so she likes to use ramekins or small bowls instead of a larger baking dish. Don't forget to serve the flavored *crème fraîche* on the side, as it complements the dish remarkably well.

Note: If you make individual crumbles, reduce the cooking time to 25 to 30 minutes depending on the size of the dishes.

You will need: one 10-by-7-inch (25.5 by 18 cm) baking dish.

Serves 6

FOR THE VANILLA-FLAVORED *CRÈME FRAÎCHE:*

8 oz (227 g; 1 cup) *crème fraîche*

1 teaspoon confectioner's sugar, sifted

1 vanilla bean, split lengthwise and seeds scraped out

FOR THE CRUMBLE TOPPING:

¾ cup (3¼ oz; 95 g) millet flour

¾ cup (2½ oz; 75 g) rolled oats

½ cup (2½ oz; 70 g) sliced almonds

¼ cup (1¾ oz; 50 g) blond cane sugar

½ cup packed (2¾ oz; 80 g) dark Muscovado sugar

Zest of 1 organic lemon, finely grated

A few drops of lemon oil

1-inch (2.5 cm) piece of fresh ginger, finely grated

7 tablespoons (3½ oz; 100 g) unsalted butter, cold and diced

FOR THE FRUIT:

Unsalted butter, for the mold

3 nectarines, pitted, peeled, and diced

2 peaches, peeled, pitted and diced

2 apricots, pitted and diced

10½ oz (300 g) strawberries, hulled and diced

1 tablespoon lemon juice

2 tablespoons cornstarch

3 tablespoons blond cane sugar

Confectioner's sugar, to dust

To prepare the *crème fraîche:* Place the *crème fraîche* in a small bowl. Stir in the sugar and vanilla seeds. Cover and refrigerate until ready to use. This can be prepared the day before.

To prepare the crumble topping: In a bowl, combine the millet flour, rolled oats, sliced almonds, and sugars. Add the lemon zest, lemon oil, and ginger. Add the butter and, using your fingertips, work until coarse crumbles form; cover and refrigerate until ready to use.

To prepare the fruit: Preheat the oven to 350°F (180°C). Butter the baking dish; set aside.

In a large bowl, combine the fruit. Toss gently with the lemon juice, cornstarch, and sugar. Arrange the fruit in the dish and cover with the crumble topping.

Bake for 40 minutes, or until the fruit bubbles and the top is golden. Dust with confectioner's sugar and serve luke warm with vanilla-flavored *crème fraîche* on top.

Mini pavlovas with fresh fruit

Petits pavlovas aux fruits frais

A pavlova is a very popular summer dessert among my Irish relatives. It didn't take me long to understand why: these fruit-topped meringues are an extraordinary way to finish a meal on a light note. Lulu, in particular, gets excited when she knows meringue is going to be part of our dessert.

The meringues will be a tad crispy on the outside while staying moist on the inside. It's best not to try this recipe if the weather is hot and humid because the meringues will absorb the moisture from the air and stay soft. Although they look elegant and labor-intensive, pavlovas are easy to make, even with children.

Serves 6

4 large egg whites (5 oz; 140 g), at room temperature

1 cup (7¾ oz; 220 g) fine white sugar, plus 1 teaspoon

1 teaspoon pure vanilla extract

1 tablespoon cornstarch, sifted

1 teaspoon white vinegar

1 cup (236 ml) heavy cream

9 oz (250 g) strawberries, hulled and cut in half

Raspberries and currants, to taste

Preheat the oven to 300°F (150°C). Cut six 4-inch (10 cm) circles of parchment paper and place them on a baking sheet; set aside.

In the bowl of stand mixer fitted with the whisk, whisk the egg whites until stiff peaks form. Gradually add 1 cup sugar, whisking well. The meringue is ready when it is stiff and glossy, and the mixture has tripled in volume and stands up when the whisk is lifted. In a small bowl, combine the vanilla, cornstarch, and vinegar; stir until combined. Fold this mixture into the meringue.

Spoon the mixture into the rounds, using a spatula to even it out. Reduce the oven to 250°F (120°C) and bake for 1 hour. Turn the oven off and use a wooden spoon to keep the door cracked open. Allow the meringues to cool completely in the oven for at least 1 hour.

Whisk the cream with the remaining teaspoon of sugar until soft peaks form. Spread the whipped cream over the meringues, and top with the berries. Serve or refrigerate until ready to serve.

Red berry ice pops

Bâtonnets glacés aux fruits rouges

Have you seen the face of a child light up at the sight of an ice pop? It's like magic. Lulu is incredibly enthusiastic about the red color of these ice pops. Ideally, we make them when we're able to pick our own berries—we have a few strawberry plants and red currant and raspberry bushes in our garden—and eat them on a hot summer day.

Note: If you can't find red currants, replace them with an additional 6 oz (170 g) strawberries.

You will need: ten 2½-oz (0.75 ml) ice pop molds and wooden sticks.

Makes 10 ice pops

8¾ oz (250 g) raspberries

8¾ oz (250 g) strawberries

6 oz (170 g) red currants

1¼ cups (295 ml) Lemon Thyme–Infused Syrup (see below)

8 mint leaves

2 tablespoons lime juice

In a blender, purée the fruit with the syrup and mint. Add the lime juice. Pass through a *chinois* or fine sieve, and then pour the fruit purée into the ice pops molds. Freeze for 30 minutes. Insert wooden sticks and return to the freezer until the ice pops are completely set.

Lemon thyme–infused syrup

Sirop parfumé au thym citron

Use this syrup in the preceding ice pops recipe, or serve it with lightly stewed fruit or a fresh fruit salad. It also comes in handy to moisten the base of a sponge cake.

Makes 2 cups (475 ml)

2 cups (472 ml) water

1 cup (7 oz; 200 g) blond cane sugar

3 lemon thyme sprigs

2 tablespoons lemon or lime juice

In a pot, combine the water and sugar. Bring to a simmer and cook until the sugar is dissolved. Remove from the heat and add the lemon thyme. Cover and set aside to infuse for 1 hour. Strain and discard the thyme. Add the lemon or lime juice and let cool completely. This syrup keeps in the fridge for up to 1 week.

Teff and cocoa nib cookies

WITH BLACK SESAME SEEDS AND *FLEUR DE SEL*

Cookies à la farine de teff, graines de sésame noir, grué de cacao, et fleur de sel

I baked these crisp cookies for the first time the day before we left on a two-day road trip to Prince Edward Island. Lulu especially could not keep her hands off them, and by the time we reached our destination, they had all been eaten. The bits of cocoa nibs eaten with *fleur de sel* leave a beautiful finish in the mouth. I can't tell you exactly how long they keep because they never last in our house for more than two or three days (if we're lucky). I imagine one week is a good guess.

Makes 36 cookies

½ cup (2½ oz; 75 g) teff flour

¼ cup (1½ oz; 40 g) white rice flour

¼ cup (1 oz; 30 g) millet flour

2 tablespoons (¾ oz; 20 g) tapioca starch or cornstarch

¼ teaspoon *fleur de sel*

8 tablespoons (4 oz; 113 g) unsalted butter, diced and softened

¼ cup (1¾ oz; 50 g) blond cane sugar

2 tablespoons (¾ oz; 20 g) dark Muscovado sugar

1 tablespoon pure vanilla extract

¼ cup (1 oz; 30 g) cocoa nibs

2 tablespoons (¾ oz; 20 g) black sesame seeds

In a bowl, combine the flours, tapioca starch, and *fleur de sel*; set aside.

In the bowl of a stand mixer fitted with the paddle blade, combine the butter and sugars. Beat until creamy in texture and light in color, scraping the sides of the bowl as needed. Stir in the vanilla, then beat in the dry ingredients. Add the cocoa nibs and black sesame seeds, and beat until just incorporated.

Form the dough into two balls of equal size. Place a ball in the middle of a large piece of plastic film on your working surface. Using the palm of your hand, flatten it into a 5-inch (12.5 cm) disk. Cover with another piece of plastic film. Repeat with the other ball. Transfer the disks onto plates and refrigerate for at least 2 hours, or overnight.

Preheat the oven to 350°F (180°C). Line two rimmed baking sheets with parchment paper; set aside.

Take the cookie disks out of the fridge and let them sit at room temperature for 5 to 10 minutes, or until they are easier to roll. Leave the plastic film on top of the disk, and roll out. The dough may break in a few places, but just patch it as you roll. When the dough is ⅕-inch (0.5 cm) thick, remove the plastic film. Using a cookie cutter of your choice—mine is a 1¾-inch (4.5 cm) flower-shaped mold—cut the cookies. Transfer them to the baking sheets. Bake for 14 minutes. Remove from the oven and let cool for 5 minutes before transferring to a rack to cool completely. The cookies harden as they cool. Store in an airtight container.

Lulu's chocolate and olive oil cake

WITH ROASTED HAZELNUTS

Le gâteau au chocolat de Lulu avec huile d'olive et noisettes grillées

This cake has rich accents of dark chocolate and hazelnut that won't go unnoticed—close your eyes, imagine Nutella, and you get the idea. We like to bake it in a large baking pan or in pretty paper muffin cups that can be transported more easily. For fun or as a special treat, try the dark chocolate icing with sprinkles—it's utterly irresistible!

Note: Lulu and I once made this with a combination of 2½ oz (75 g) dark chocolate and 1¾ oz (50 g) hazelnut-flavored chocolate, and we swooned even more.

You will need: a muffin pan or a 10-by-7-inch (25.5 by 18 cm) cake pan.

Makes 12 muffins or one 10-by-7-inch (25.5 by 18 cm) cake

⅓ cup (80 ml) olive oil, plus more for the pan

½ cup (3½ oz; 100 g) blond cane sugar, plus more for the pan

1 cup (3½ oz; 100 g) hazelnut meal

⅓ cup (1¾ oz; 50 g) teff flour

4½ oz (125 g) dark chocolate (70% cocoa)

1 teaspoon pure vanilla extract

4 large eggs

Pinch of sea salt

Preheat the oven to 350°F (180°C). If using a baking dish, oil the dish, coat with sugar, and tap out the excess; if making muffins, line the pan with paper liners; set aside.

Scatter the hazelnut meal on a baking sheet. Roast for 8 to 10 minutes, or until fragrant (make sure it does not burn). Remove from the oven and let cool. In a bowl, combine the roasted hazelnut meal and teff flour; set aside.

Melt the chocolate in a double boiler (*bain-marie;* page 386). Stir in the olive oil and vanilla.

In the meantime, add the eggs, sugar, and sea salt to the bowl of a stand mixer fitted with the whisk. Beat on high speed for 8 minutes, or until the batter is white and the volume has doubled. Remove the bowl from the mixer, and gently fold in the chocolate and olive oil preparation, making sure to keep the preparation airy. Fold in the flour mixture in the same manner.

Using an ice cream scoop, divide the batter between the muffin cups, or pour into the cake pan. Bake small cakes for 20 minutes and a large cake for 25 to 30 minutes, or until the blade of a sharp knife inserted in the middle comes out clean. Remove from the oven and let cool.

Dust with unsweetened cocoa and confectioner's sugar, or finish with Chocolate Ganache Icing (see page 230).

Chocolate ganache icing
Glaçage au chocolat noir

When I want to dress up a chocolate cake, I like to coat it simply, with a thin layer of melted chocolate that reveals the sublime flavors of dark chocolate. This recipe is wonderful in that way; it's also very easy to prepare.

3½ oz (100 g)
dark chocolate
(64% cocoa)

3 tablespoons
heavy cream

3 tablespoons
sprinkles or chopped
dry-roasted hazelnuts

Melt the chocolate in a double boiler (*bain-marie*; page 386). Remove from the heat and beat in the heavy cream. Using a small cake spatula, spread a thick layer of ganache over each cake. Top with sprinkles or chopped hazelnuts.

Chocolate and raspberry tart

Tarte au chocolat et aux framboises

As far as I am concerned, chocolate and raspberries are perfect together. When Lulu and I bake this tart, she sometimes asks that we leave the raspberries out (she tells me she is a chocolate purist), but I personally prefer the tart with the berries. Choose what tastes best to you, depending on whether you are a chocolate purist too.

You will need: one 9-inch (23 cm) tart mold.

Makes one 9-inch (23 cm) tart

Sweet Crust (see page 232)

3½ oz (100 g) dark chocolate (64% cocoa)

3½ oz (100 g) hazelnut-flavored chocolate (Valrhona)

¾ cup plus 2 tablespoons (200 ml) heavy cream

2 tablespoons blond cane sugar

2 large eggs

3 oz (85 g) raspberries

Unsweetened cocoa powder, to serve

Preheat the oven to 350°F (180°C).

Roll the crust to ⅕-inch (0.5 cm) thickness and cut to fit inside the mold—keep the leftovers for another use. Arrange the dough inside the mold and, using a fork, make small holes in the bottom. Refrigerate for 1 hour. Preheat the oven to 350°F (180°C). Blind bake the crust for 12 minutes (page 386). Remove the parchment and beans, and bake for 3 to 5 more minutes, or until light golden. Remove from the oven and set aside. Reduce oven temperature to 250°F (120°C).

Melt the two chocolates in a double boiler (*bain-marie;* page 386). In a small pot, combine the heavy cream with the sugar and bring to a simmer. Pour over the melted chocolate and stir until smooth. Beat in the eggs, one at a time, until well incorporated. Pour the ganache into the crust, spreading to smooth, and stud with the raspberries. Bake for 40 minutes, or until the chocolate is set. Remove from the oven and let cool completely on a rack. To serve, dust with sifted cocoa powder.

Sweet crust
Pâte sucrée

My sweet crusts are never prepared too sweet, so that the topping can have the spotlight. I like to add accents or nuts, such as the almond meal in this recipe. I often prepare this dough the night before.

Note: You can also make this crust by hand—using your hands or a wooden spoon—following the same instructions. I like to mix with my hands to get a good feel for the texture.

Makes one 11-inch (28 cm) tart or six 4½-inch (11.5 cm) tartlets

⅔ cup (3 oz; 80 g) quinoa flour or millet flour

⅓ cup (2 oz; 55 g) sweet rice flour

⅔ cup (3 oz; 80 g) almond meal

⅓ cup (1½ oz; 40 g) cornstarch

¼ cup (1 oz; 30 g) confectioner's sugar, sifted

¼ teaspoon fine sea salt

8 tablespoons (4 oz; 113 g) unsalted butter, diced

1 batch Flax Gel (page 30)

1 to 2 tablespoons water, if needed

In the bowl of a stand mixer fitted with the dough hook, combine the flours, almond meal, cornstarch, confectioner's sugar, and sea salt. Add the butter and beat on medium speed until crumbles form. Add the flax gel and beat until incorporated. If you need to, add 1 to 2 tablespoons water, one at a time, and beat until the dough detaches from the side and forms a ball—it will be sticky. Dust the dough with rice flour. If you are making tartlets, divide the dough into 6 small balls of equal size; otherwise, flatten the dough into a 6-inch (15 cm) circle. Wrap in plastic film and refrigerate for at least 1 hour. Take out of the fridge at least 10 minutes before rolling.

Chocolate and coconut milk *petits pots de crème*
WITH MERINGUE
Petits pots de crème meringuée au chocolat et au lait de coco

My mother used to make *petits pots de crème* when I was a child, and I also have a recipe for them in my first book, but they are so popular in our home that Lulu and I felt inspired to create a new recipe for this book. These custards have a deep chocolate flavor while the texture stays light. When serving them as a simple, everyday dessert, we omit the meringue, but it's fun to add it for a special occasion.

The secret to creating the best *pots de crème* is choosing great ingredients, of course, but a gentle water bath is essential to cook the custards properly.

Note: When you use whole milk, the texture of the creams is a tad denser, they cook more quickly, and the dessert is silkier.

You will need: eight ½-cup (120 ml) heat-resistant jars and a pastry bag fitted with a tip of your choice.

Serves 8

FOR THE CHOCOLATE CREAMS:

1 cup (236 ml) unsweetened coconut milk

1⅓ cups (315 ml) whole or 2% milk (see Note)

Pinch of fine sea salt

5 cardamom pods, crushed

1-inch (2.5 cm) piece of fresh ginger, peeled and sliced

1 teaspoon pure vanilla extract

2 oz (60 g) bittersweet dark chocolate (Valrhona, 70% cocoa)

2 large eggs

¼ cup (1¾ oz; 50 g) blond cane sugar or coconut sugar

FOR THE MERINGUES:

2 large egg whites

2 oz (⅔ cup; 60 g) confectioner's sugar, sifted

To prepare the chocolate creams: Preheat the oven to 320°F (160°F).

In a pot, combine the coconut milk, milk, sea salt, cardamom pods, and ginger. Bring to a simmer without boiling. Remove from the heat, cover, and let infuse for 30 minutes. Strain, discarding the cardamom pods and seeds and ginger, and return the milk to the pot with the vanilla. Reheat over low heat, and set aside.

In the meantime, melt the chocolate in a double boiler (*bain-marie;* page 386).

In a bowl, beat the eggs with the sugar. Pour the infused milk into the melted chocolate, and whisk until it is a uniform consistency. Add the chocolate to the egg mixture, stirring constantly. Pour into the jars and place them in a baking dish; if foam forms on the surface, remove it with a slotted spoon. Add water to the baking dish halfway up the jars to make a water bath (*bain-marie;* page 386). Bake creams for 30 to 35 minutes, or until the cream looks nearly set when you jiggle the jars

continued

lightly. Remove from the oven and let cool completely. If you are in a hurry, refrigerate until the creams set completely. Enjoy them plain, or dress them up with the meringues on top.

To prepare the meringues: Preheat the oven to 400°F (200°C).

In the bowl of a stand mixer fitted with the whisk, beat the egg whites until soft peaks start to form. Gradually add the sugar while beating; continue until the meringue looks glossy. Spoon into the pastry bag and pipe on top of the cooled chocolate creams. Bake for 8 minutes, or until the meringues turn light brown in color. Remove from the oven and enjoy.

main courses
les plats de résistance

MOST EVENINGS, we eat dinner together between six and seven—not too soon after our afternoon *goûter* so that we have an appetite, but not so late that we're starving. Our simple weekday dinners often include a soup or a side salad (see the "Soups, Savory Tarts, and Salads" chapter for recipes) and the main course.

I've noticed over time, and through writing my books, that I think of a main course as food more likely to be served for dinner—maybe because dinner, more than other meals, is the one that pulls us all together around the table. I tend to have more time to spend preparing dinner too. Perhaps you do as well?

During summer, everyone's appetite can become somewhat capricious, and we prefer things like ratatouille with a piece of whole fish that's been lightly seasoned and cooked on the grill. With colorful winter squash and late potato crops arriving in the fall, a potato cake or oven-roasted root vegetables are favorite choices. In the colder months—which mean many snow days and sledding afternoons in New England where we live—I stick to the fall leftovers with warming dishes like a steaming *hachis parmentier* and exotic-flavored red lentil *crêpes,* foods that fill you up. When spring finally returns, I naturally lean toward cleaner flavors again, with an abundance of delicate spring vegetables and crispier textures. That's when I look for asparagus, artichokes, radishes, and fava beans again.

Of course, there are also the spontaneous cravings for a specific food at unexpected times. Sometimes when it's freezing cold outside, I want only a lean cut of meat with a humble bowl of salad on the side. At other times in summer, all I think about is an appealing dish of lasagna, when it's meant instead to make us feel cozy sitting by a crackling fire with our bellies full. Some meals appear to have no obvious season, and that's perfectly fine too.

I strive to keep our meals balanced, with something cooked and something raw to satisfy our hunger. Some meals are assembled extemporaneously, with whatever ingredients I am able to find in the fridge and at the back of the pantry, but others require solidly written recipes. That's what I have in this chapter. I hope you will enjoy them as much as we do, whenever you feel like it, with family and friends. Or just on your own.

vegetables and side dishes
les plats de légumes et les accompagnements

meat and fish
les viandes et les poissons

Blue potato and red snapper *papillotes* with sugar snap peas • *Papillotes de vitelottes et de perche rouge aux pois mangetout*   278

Fish and vegetable cakes • *Galettes de poisson et de légumes*   280

Oven-baked yellowtail snapper • *Vivaneau à queue jaune rôti au four*   284

Sole rolls with leek sauce, edamame, and romanesco • *Roulades de soles avec sauce au poireau, édamames, et chou romanesco*   287

Oven-roasted monkfish with clams and herb ricotta stuffing • *Rôti de lotte farci à la ricotta aux herbes, avec praires*   288

grains
les céréales

Asparagus and pistachio pesto pasta with spring green vegetables, feta, and olives • *Pâtes au pesto d'asperges et de pistaches, avec légumes verts printaniers, feta, et olives*   294

Pea risotto with lemon, basil oil, and steamed lobster • *Risotto aux petits pois et au citron avec huile au basilic et homard vapeur*   296

Black rice with sautéed green vegetable medley, parsley oil, and grilled salmon • *Riz noir et sa poêlée de légumes verts avec huile au persil et saumon grillé*   299

Red beet gnocchi with Parmesan and parsley sauce • *Gnocchi aux betteraves rouges avec sauce au Parmesan et au persil*   303

Saffron-flavored carrot risotto with bay scallops and pistachios • *Risotto à la carotte et au safran avec coquilles St. Jacques et pistaches*   304

Linguini with arugula pesto, roasted cherry tomatoes, and fennel • *Linguini au pesto de roquette avec tomates cerises et fenouils grillés*   308

Spaghetti with roasted butternut squash, peas, ricotta, mint, and bresaola • *Spaghetti avec courge musquée rôtie, petits pois, ricotta, menthe, et bresaola*   311

Vegetarian lasagna • *Lasagnes végétariennes*   313

My favorite lasagna • *Mes lasagnes préférées*   316

vegetables and side dishes

les plats de légumes et
les accompagnements

Summer ratatouille

Ratatouille d'été

My mother always spent a lot of time preserving ratatouille in summer, when zucchini, eggplants, and tomatoes were plentiful in her garden. I am very fond of warm ratatouille, but serving it cold to accompany a summer buffet has also become a favorite. When I make it, I like that the vegetables are finely diced and finished with a splash of olive oil and balsamic vinegar at the end. This version keeps in the fridge for 3 to 4 days. Prepare it a day ahead, if you like, as this is the type of dish in which flavors develop over time.

Serves 6

1 lb (450 g) eggplants (about 2 medium), cut in ½-inch (1.25 cm) pieces

Sea salt

6 tablespoons olive oil, plus ¼ to ⅓ cup (60 to 80 ml)

1 lb (450 g) zucchini, cut in ½-inch (1.25 cm) pieces

2 shallots, finely chopped

3 garlic cloves, minced

1 yellow bell pepper, cut in ½-inch (1.25 cm) pieces

1 orange bell pepper, cut in ½-inch (1.25 cm) pieces

1 lb, 12¼ oz (800 g) tomatoes, peeled, seeded, and cut in ½-inch (1.25 cm) pieces

2 thyme sprigs

1 tablespoon finely chopped tarragon

1 bay leaf

Pepper

Chopped parsley

Chopped basil, to taste

2 tablespoons balsamic vinegar

Place the eggplant in a colander and sprinkle with ¾ teaspoon sea salt. Let rest for 30 minutes to allow juice to release. Rinse and pat dry.

In a large pot, heat 2 tablespoons olive oil over medium heat. Add the eggplant and cook for 5 minutes, without browning, stirring occasionally. Remove from the heat, transfer to a bowl, and set aside.

In the same pot, heat 2 more tablespoons olive oil. Add the zucchini and cook for 5 minutes, without browning, stirring occasionally. Remove from the heat and set aside with the eggplants.

In the same pot, heat 2 more tablespoons olive oil. Cook the shallots for 2 minutes. Add the garlic and cook for another minute. Add the peppers and cook for 5 minutes, without browning, stirring occasionally. Add the tomatoes and cook for 5 minutes. Return the eggplant and zucchini to the pot. Add the thyme, tarragon, and bay leaf, and season with sea salt and pepper. Simmer, uncovered, for about 75 minutes, stirring occasionally, until the vegetables are soft. Discard the thyme and bay leaf, and stir in the parsley and basil.

Stir in the remaining olive oil and 2 tablespoons balsamic vinegar. You can serve the ratatouille warm as a main course or cold as an accompaniment.

Romanesco gratin

Gratin au chou romanesco

Romanesco looks like a cross between cauliflower and broccoli, but I find that its sweet taste and soft green color make it largely superior. I purposely use a light hand when seasoning this gratin so the earthy flavor of the Romanesco comes through even more. If you cannot find it—it has a short growing season—use broccoli, cauliflower, or even multicolored cauliflower to add a rainbow to your plate.

Serves 4

Olive oil for the dish, plus 2 tablespoons

2 lb (1.9 kg) Romanesco (2 heads), cut in florets

2 garlic cloves, minced

2 tablespoons chopped parsley

3 tablespoons (1½ oz; 45 g) chopped walnuts

3 tablespoons *crème fraîche*

3 tablespoons whole or 2% milk

1¾ oz (50 g) finely grated manchego cheese or cheddar cheese

Sea salt and pepper

Dash of nutmeg, ground or freshly grated

Preheat the oven to 400°F (200°C). Oil an 8½-by-12-inch (21.5 by 30.5 cm) baking dish; set aside.

Steam the Romanesco for 8 to 10 minutes, keeping it al dente. In a large bowl, combine the garlic, parsley, walnuts, *crème fraîche,* milk, and cheese; season with sea salt and pepper. Coat the Romanesco with this mixture and transfer to the oiled dish. Add a dash of nutmeg and drizzle with 2 tablespoons olive oil. Bake for 20 to 25 minutes, or until the gratin starts to color slightly. Remove from the oven and serve as a side.

Oven-roasted root vegetables

Légumes racines rôtis au four

When I roast root vegetables, I like to use a large baking sheet. This gives them plenty of space so they roast and brown instead of steam, which they'll do if they're crowded into a small area. I also like to select them for their color; the wilder they look—like yellow carrots, purple potatoes, and striped beets—the better. Serve these colorful jewels with grilled fish and grains like quinoa.

Serves 4

1 bunch (about 6) slender carrots, cut into 4-inch (10 cm) lengths

1 bunch (about 3) beets, peeled and cut in wedges

1 bunch pink radishes, stemmed and cut in half

10 small potatoes, peeled and cut in wedges

1 cup cauliflower florets (yellow, purple, green, or white) or Romanesco

Fine sea salt and pepper

1 teaspoon ground cumin

3 garlic cloves, finely chopped

1 tablespoon clover honey

¼ cup (60 ml) olive oil

1 tablespoon chopped fresh oregano or marjoram, thyme, or tarragon

1 tablespoon fresh parsley

Fleur de sel, to serve

Preheat the oven to 400°F (200°C). Line a large rimmed baking sheet with parchment paper.

In a large mixing bowl, toss together the carrots, beets, radishes, potatoes, and cauliflower. In a small bowl, combine sea salt and pepper, cumin, garlic, honey, olive oil, oregano, and parsley. Coat the vegetables with this mixture, transfer to the baking sheet, and spread out evenly. Roast the vegetables for 40 to 50 minutes, or until tender when pierced with a skewer. Stir them occasionally. Remove from the oven, sprinkle with *fleur de sel,* and serve warm.

Potato celeriac cake

Gâteau de pommes de terre et de céleri rave

I always have room for plenty of potato recipes in my cooking repertoire; they are comforting and delicious. These potatoes, layered in a cake with thin slices of celeriac and the aromas of butter and thyme, are sophisticated and homey all at once. Enjoy this dish as a main course with a salad or as a side with grilled meat such as a roasted rack of lamb.

Serves 6

3½ oz (100 g; 7 tablespoons) unsalted butter, melted, plus more for the pan

4 medium Yukon Gold potatoes, peeled and thinly sliced with a mandoline

Sea salt and pepper

Freshly grated nutmeg

½ tablespoon finely chopped thyme

1 lb, 8¾ oz (600 g) celeriac, peeled and thinly sliced with a mandoline

Preheat the oven to 400°F (200°C). Butter a 7-by-4-inch (18 by 10 cm) dish, and cover the bottom and sides with a large piece of parchment paper; set aside.

Arrange a layer of the sliced potatoes in the bottom of the prepared dish. Brush with melted butter and season with sea salt, pepper, nutmeg and thyme. Add a layer of celeriac, brush with more melted butter, and season as before. Repeat layers of potatoes and celeriac, with butter and seasoning, until you run out of ingredients.

Press each layer down before starting another. Cover the top with another piece of parchment paper, and place a dish on top to weigh it all down.

Bake for 30 minutes, then remove the top dish and top piece of parchment paper. Continue to bake for 45 minutes, or until all the vegetables are soft when pierced with a knife. Remove from the oven, place a plate on top, and flip the dish. Unmold and remove the second piece of parchment paper. Cut the cake into wedges, and serve.

Round zucchini stuffed with millet and vegetables

Courgettes rondes farcies au millet et aux légumes

I always look for the globe variety at my local farmers' market when I want to prepare stuffed zucchini. You can also make this recipe with four regular zucchini, halved lengthwise, but the round ones are adorable and can be stuffed so nicely. Serve with a green salad.

Serves 4

2 tablespoons olive oil, plus more for the dish and to drizzle

2 tablespoons raisins, soaked in water

8 medium (about 6½ oz; 180 g each) globe zucchini

Sea salt and pepper

¼ red onion, peeled and finely chopped

1 teaspoon ground coriander

2 thyme sprigs

2 garlic cloves, peeled and minced

½ orange bell pepper, diced

2 tomatoes, blanched (page 386), peeled, cored, seeded, and diced

1½ cups (6 oz; 170 g) cooked millet

¼ cup pine nuts

2 oz (60 g) crumbled feta cheese

½ cup (2 oz; 60 g) grated manchego or Parmesan cheese

1 tablespoon finely chopped basil

1 tablespoon finely chopped parsley

Preheat the oven to 375°F (190°C). Oil a 10-by-7-inch (25.5 by 18 cm) baking dish.

Cut a small top off each zucchini. Scoop out the flesh (do not puncture the outer skin). Season with salt and pepper; set aside. Keep 1 cup packed (6 oz; 170 g) finely chopped zucchini flesh. Place the zucchini shells in the baking dish; set aside.

In a sauté pan, heat 2 tablespoons olive oil over medium heat. Add the onion, coriander, and thyme. Cook, stirring occasionally, for 2 minutes. Add the garlic and continue to cook for 1 minute. Add the bell pepper and cook for 1 to 2 more minutes. Add the tomatoes and reserved zucchini. Stir, and season with salt and pepper. Cook over low heat, uncovered, for 7 minutes, stirring occasionally. Remove from the heat and discard the thyme. Stir in the millet, pine nuts, cheeses, fresh herbs, and raisins. Stuff the zucchini with this preparation and put the tops back on. Drizzle generously with olive oil and add just enough water to cover the bottom of the baking dish. Bake the zucchini for 45 minutes to 1 hour, or until the outer skin is tender.

To cook millet al dente, toast 1 cup millet in olive oil in a pot for 1 minute before adding 2 cups water. Bring to a boil, then simmer covered for 12 to 15 minutes, or until the water is absorbed. One cup of dry millet yields about 2½ cups cooked millet.

Zucchini, tomato, and potato *tian*

Tian aux courgettes, aux tomates, et aux pommes de terre

When summer arrives at our door, nothing beats the joy of melt-in-the-mouth, fresh-scented vegetables baked slowly as in a *tian*. My variant of this traditional French dish combines a selection of red onions, tomatoes, and potatoes, as well as yellow and green zucchini for extra color (using just green zucchini is fine too). Enjoy this dish with grilled meat or fish on a hot summer day as we often do.

Serves 6

Olive oil, for dish and to drizzle

1 medium green zucchini

1 medium yellow zucchini

1 medium red onion, peeled

5 medium Yukon Gold potatoes, peeled

4 medium tomatoes

4 garlic cloves, peeled, crushed, and minced

1 tablespoon chopped thyme

1 tablespoon chopped parsley

Sea salt and pepper

Set the oven temperature to 320°F (160°C). Oil a 12-by-9-inch (30.5 by 23 cm) baking dish with olive oil; set aside.

Using a sharp knife, a mandoline, or another slicing device, slice the green and yellow zucchini into paper-thin rounds. Do the same with the red onion and the potatoes. With a serrated knife, cut the tomatoes into thin slices. In a small bowl, combine the garlic, thyme, and parsley; set aside.

In the baking dish, arrange the vegetables in tight, overlapping layers in the following order: green zucchini, yellow zucchini, red onion, potato, and tomato. Season with sea salt and pepper, and add some of the herb/garlic mixture between the layers. Repeat until you run out of ingredients. Drizzle generously with olive oil. Bake for 60 to 75 minutes, or until the vegetables are tender when pierced with a fork. Serve the *tian* warm with grilled meat or fish.

Red lentil *crêpes* filled with sautéed mushrooms and butternut squash

Crêpes aux lentilles corail avec leur poêlée de champignons et de courge musquée

I see these as a cross between an Indian *dosa* and a French *crêpe*. Red lentils also make my version more interesting nutritionally, with protein, folate, and vitamins C and E. Once I grind the lentils into a fine powder, I prepare the *crêpe* batter the way I typically would with one of my French *crêpe* recipes. Then I spice it up with an Indian touch before finishing with a filling that is, once again, assuredly French in looks. These *crêpes* make a perfect meal to warm up with after a day spent out in the winter cold.

Serves 4
(makes eight 8½-inch [21.5 cm] crêpes)

FOR THE *CRÊPES*:

¾ cup (5¼ oz; 150 g) red lentils, sorted

¼ cup (1½ oz; 45 g) potato starch

½ teaspoon ground cumin

½ teaspoon ground coriander

¼ teaspoon turmeric

¼ teaspoon sea salt

Pepper

2 large eggs

1 cup (236 ml) whole or 2% milk

1 cup (236 ml) water

1 tablespoon chopped cilantro

1 tablespoon melted sunflower oil, grapeseed oil, or coconut oil, plus more to cook

FOR THE MUSHROOM AND BUTTERNUT SQUASH FILLING:

4 tablespoons olive oil

1 large shallot, finely chopped

1 teaspoon ground cumin

3 garlic cloves, minced and divided

1 lb, 7 oz (650 g) peeled butternut squash, cut in 1-inch (2.5 cm) pieces

½ cup (120 ml) Homemade Vegetable Stock (page 96), or chicken stock

1 large leek, white part only, finely chopped

9 oz (250 g) peeled crimini mushrooms, thinly sliced

Sea salt and pepper

1 tablespoon chopped cilantro

½ cup (3.5 oz; 100 g) *crème fraîche*

Grated cheddar cheese

To prepare the *crêpes*: Place the lentils in a spice grinder, coffee grinder, or food processor, and grind to a very fine powder. Transfer to a clean bowl and add the potato starch, cumin, coriander, turmeric, sea salt, and pepper. Make a well in the middle of the mixture, and break the eggs into it. Combine the milk and water in a large cup; start to pour them over the eggs while whisking all the ingredients together. Whisk until the mixture is a uniform consistency, then add the cilantro and sunflower oil. Cover and refrigerate for at least 1 hour or overnight.

In a *crêpe* pan, warm 1½ teaspoons sunflower oil over medium to high heat; wipe off the excess oil with a paper towel. When the pan is hot, pour in enough batter to

continued

cover the bottom (about ⅓ cup; 80 ml). Swirl quickly to coat the bottom of the pan, and cook for 1 to 2 minutes, until small bubbles form on the surface. Using a spatula, flip the *crêpe* and cook on the other side for 1 to 2 more minutes. Transfer the *crêpe* to a plate. Brush the pan with oil and stir the batter well with a whisk between each *crêpe*, and repeat until you run out of batter.

To prepare the filling: In a frying pan, heat 2½ tablespoons olive oil over medium heat. Add the shallot and cumin. Cook over low to medium heat, without browning, until the shallot is soft. Add 2 garlic cloves and continue to cook for 1 minute. Add the butternut squash and cook for 4 minutes, stirring occasionally, until the vegetables are well coated. Add the stock and cover. Simmer for 8 to 10 minutes, or until the vegetables are tender. Transfer to a clean bowl; set aside.

In the same pan, heat 1½ tablespoons olive oil over medium heat. Add the leek and mushrooms. Cook for 2 minutes, stirring occasionally. Add the remaining garlic clove, and season with sea salt and pepper. Cover and cook for 5 minutes, or until the vegetables are soft and the juices have evaporated. Return the butternut squash to the pan and stir in the fresh cilantro. Keep warm on the stove.

To assemble, place a *crêpe* flat on the working surface in front of you. Spread 1 tablespoon *crème fraîche* over the surface with a little brush. In the bottom third of the *crêpe*, add a layer of vegetables, and sprinkle with cheddar cheese. Roll the *crêpe* closed and keep it in the frying pan for 30 seconds. Fill the other *crêpes* in the same manner. Serve them with an endive or arugula salad (see Vegetable Tart with Pear and Roquefort, page 112).

Sunchoke, potato, and duck *hachis parmentier*

Hachis parmentier de canard aux pommes de terre et aux topinambours

Lulu always licks her lips when she knows this is what we are having for dinner. To me, this dish is the quintessential comfy French family dinner. We always enjoy ours with a large green salad on the side, also undeniably French.

For a twist on this classic, I like to combine sunchokes with potatoes, which adds a subtle artichoke flavor. If you are able to find duck confit legs, this is a beautiful dish for you. Otherwise, ground beef is also a wonderful choice.

Serves 4 to 6

FOR THE VEGETABLE MASH:

1 lb, 12½ oz (800 g) potatoes

1 lb, 3½ oz (550 g) sunchokes

Sea salt and pepper

1 cup (236 ml) warm whole milk (add more if necessary)

1 tablespoon olive oil

FOR THE DUCK PREPARATION:

4 duck confit legs (1 lb, 9½ oz; 720 g)

1 tablespoon olive oil, plus more for the dish

1 large shallot, diced

1 carrot, peeled and finely chopped

¼ cup (60 ml) dry white wine or white vermouth

½ cup (120 ml) chicken stock

Sea salt and pepper

1 tablespoon finely chopped parsley

1 tablespoon finely chopped tarragon

½ cup (2 oz; 60 g) finely grated manchego cheese or Parmesan cheese

Dash of ground nutmeg

To prepare the vegetable mash: Peel the potatoes and sunchokes, and dice them coarsely. Bring a large pot of salted water to a boil. Add the vegetables and cook for 10 to 15 minutes, or until tender. Strain and purée with a ricer. Season with sea salt and pepper. Stir in enough warm milk to reach the desired texture, then stir in the olive oil; set aside.

To prepare the duck: Preheat the oven to 400°F (200°C). Oil a 10-by-7-inch (25.5 by 18 cm) baking dish; set aside.

Slice the meat off the duck legs. Chop coarsely; set aside.

In a sauté pan, heat 1 tablespoon olive oil over medium heat. Add the shallot and cook over low to medium heat for 3 minutes. Add the carrot and cook for 4 more minutes. Add the duck meat and cook for 3 minutes, stirring occasionally. Add the wine and cook for 2 to 3 minutes. Add the chicken stock, and season with sea salt and pepper. Cover and simmer for 15 minutes, or until the juice reduces slightly. Transfer to the bowl of a food processor, add the parsley and tarragon, and pulse into smaller pieces (a few seconds).

Layer the meat on the bottom of the oiled dish, and top with the mashed vegetables. Sprinkle with the grated cheese. Add a dash of nutmeg, drizzle with olive oil, and season with pepper (the cheese gives salt to the dish). Bake for 30 to 35 minutes, or until the top is golden and crispy. Serve with a green side salad.

continued

Hachis parmentier with ground beef

2 tablespoons olive oil, plus more for the dish and to drizzle

1 large shallot or ¼ red onion, finely chopped

1 celery stalk, diced

1 teaspoon ground coriander

1 tablespoon sun-dried tomato paste

1 tomato, peeled and diced

1 lb (450 g) ground beef (You can also use leftovers of a beef roast.)

¼ cup (60 ml) chicken stock

2 bay leaves

Sea salt and pepper

1 tablespoon chopped parsley

1 oz (30 g) finely grated manchego cheese

Pinch of ground nutmeg

Preheat the oven to 400°F (200°C). Oil a 10-by-7-inch (25.5 by 18 cm) baking dish; set aside.

In a sauté pan, heat 2 tablespoons olive oil over medium heat. Add the shallot, celery, and coriander. Cook over low to medium heat for 4 minutes. Add the tomato paste and tomato, and cook for 4 more minutes. Add the ground beef and cook for 3 minutes, stirring until the pieces separate. Add the chicken stock and bay leaves, and season with sea salt and pepper. Cover and simmer for 15 minutes, or until the juice reduces slightly. Remove from the heat, and discard the bay leaves. Transfer to the bowl of a food processor, add the parsley, and pulse into smaller pieces (a few seconds).

Layer the meat on the bottom of the oiled dish, and top with the mashed vegetables. Sprinkle with the grated cheese. Add a pinch of nutmeg, drizzle with olive oil, and season with pepper. Bake for 30 to 35 minutes, or until the top is golden and crispy. Serve with a green side salad.

My grandmother's stuffed potatoes

Pommes de terre farcies de ma grand-mère

My grandmother often baked this humble, country-style dish with leftovers from a *pot-au-feu* (a traditional French recipe that consists of a one-pot beef stew)—it was one of my favorite dishes of hers. I use ground veal with some extras—carrot, tarragon, and *crème fraîche*—that make it my own. It is now one of Lulu's favorite family meals too.

To keep them moist, cook the potatoes in a Dutch-oven casserole or sauté pan large enough to hold them all side by side. Be sure to buy good-quality potatoes that will stay firm once they're cooked. The best ones are homegrown or those I find at my farmer's market during the peak of the season.

Serves 4

2½ lbs (1 kg, 200 g) potatoes (about 12 organic Yukon Gold or red potatoes, depending on size)

Sea salt and pepper

1 large carrot, peeled

¼ large red onion, peeled

2 tarragon sprigs, finely chopped

¼ cup parsley

1 lb (450 g) ground veal or lamb

3 tablespoons *crème fraîche*

1 large egg

2 tablespoons olive oil

⅓ cup (80 ml) chicken stock

1 bay leaf

Peel the potatoes. Slice the top of each lengthwise. Using a small spoon or a melon baller, scoop out a small well in each potato—enough to hold some of the filling. Season with sea salt and pepper; set aside.

In the bowl of a food processor, combine the carrot, red onion, tarragon, and parsley. Pulse until finely chopped. Transfer to a large bowl and combine with the ground veal. Stir in the *crème fraîche* and egg. Season with sea salt and pepper, and mix well. Stuff the potato shells with the filling. Add the tops.

Warm the olive oil in a *cocotte* (Dutch-oven casserole) or sauté pan large enough to hold the potatoes in one layer. Place the stuffed potatoes in the bottom, side by side. Cook over low to medium heat for 4 minutes. Add the stock and bay leaf. Reduce the heat, cover, and simmer for 35 to 40 minutes, or until the shells of the potatoes are tender when pierced with a fork. Serve with sautéed greens, such as kale or broccoli rabe, and a salad.

meat and fish

les viandes et les poissons

Veal scallopini

WITH POTATOES, PEARS, PROSCIUTTO, AND SAGE

Roulades de veau à la sauge aux pommes de terre avec poires et prosciutto

These cute veal rolls look like precious bundles of yumminess, dressed up like small presents with the cooking thread tied around them. Lulu always claps her hands when she sees that's what I am bringing to the table. Make sure to serve with slices of crusty country bread to soak up the scrumptious sauce.

Serves 4

1 lb (450 g) fingerling potatoes (roughly equal in size)

8 veal scallopini (about 2½ oz [70 g] each; 1 lb, 3¾ oz [560 g] total)

Sea salt and pepper

16 sage leaves

4 slices prosciutto, cut in quarters lengthwise

8 slices (about 2 oz; 60 g) of Cantalet cheese or fontina cheese

2 red pears, peeled, cored, and sliced

3 tablespoons olive oil

1 large shallot, finely chopped

1 bay leaf

¼ cup (60 ml) dry white wine or white vermouth

Wash the potatoes. Steam for 15 minutes, or until they can be pierced with a toothpick. Let cool and peel. Slice 4 potatoes in half and keep the rest whole; set aside.

Arrange the veal scallopini flat on a working surface in front of you. Season with sea salt and pepper. Place a sage leaf in the middle of each piece, and cover with a slice of prosciutto. Place half of a fingerling potato, a slice of cheese, and a slice of pear on top of the prosciutto. Roll up to make a bundle. Wrap the bundle with the a slice of prosciutto, and top with a sage leaf. Tie a piece of cooking string around the meat bundle to hold it

together. Repeat with the others to make eight bundles.

Heat the oil in a deep pan over medium heat. Add the shallot and sauté for 2 minutes. Add the bay leaf and place the meat bundles in the pan; cook for 3 minutes on each side. Pour in the white wine and cook for 1 more minute. Add the rest of the pears and potatoes; stir. Cover and turn down the heat to low. Simmer for 20 minutes. Serve two bundles per person, with the pears, potatoes, and sauce spooned over the top. A grain like quinoa or millet is also a nice accompaniment, if you want a more substantial meal.

Lamb stew

WITH SPRING VEGETABLES

Navarin d'agneau et ses légumes printaniers

When I prepare a *navarin d'agneau* (a French springtime lamb dish accompanied by a medley of baby spring vegetables cooked with white wine and a *bouquet garni*) at home, I prefer to use brightly colored vegetables, so I steam them separately for a short time and only add them to the pot with the meat near the end so that they keep their vibrant colors.

This is a bit of a special occasion dish as, from start to finish, it takes around two hours. You can, however, make it a day ahead, preparing the vegetables and the meat separately. It is worth the effort—a beautiful and scrumptious way to celebrate the arrival of spring with all the pretty young vegetables.

Serves 8

2 tablespoons olive oil

4 lb (1.8 kg) lamb leg (deboned) or lamb shoulder, cut in 2-inch (5 cm) chunks

1 shallot, finely chopped

2 celery stalks, diced

3 garlic cloves, minced

3 tablespoons cornstarch

½ cup (118 ml) dry white wine or white vermouth

2½ cups (590 ml) meat stock (such as chicken stock)

Sea salt and pepper

Bouquet garni (2 thyme sprigs, 1 rosemary sprig, 2 parsley stems, and 2 bay leaves tied together with a cooking string)

1 bunch small carrots, peeled and cut in sticks (keep a few of the green tops)

2 bunches radishes (keep a few of the green tops)

3 bunches of mini turnips (keep a few of the green tops)

2 fennel bulbs, cut in quarters

2 small zucchini, cut in half and then into 8 sticks each

1 cup (4½ oz; 125 g) peas (fresh or frozen)

½ cup lima beans (fresh or frozen) or cooked fava beans (page 102)

½ tablespoon finely chopped mint

½ tablespoon finely chopped parsley or cilantro

In a large, heavy-bottomed pot, heat the olive oil over medium heat. Working in batches, brown the meat for 8 to 10 minutes on each side, or until nicely brown. Add the shallot and celery, and cook for 2 to 3 minutes, stirring occasionally. Add the garlic and cook for 1 minute. Stir in the cornstarch to coat the meat, then add the white wine. Once the wine is absorbed, add the stock. Stir and season with sea salt and pepper. Bring to a simmer. Add the *bouquet garni,* cover, and simmer for about 90 minutes, stirring occasionally.

In the meantime, steam the carrots, radishes, turnips, and fennel separately for 15 minutes; set aside. Steam the zucchini for 5 minutes.

Add the steamed vegetables, peas, and lima beans to the pot of lamb and cook for 10 more minutes. Ladle the stew onto plates, and sprinkle each serving with fresh mint and parsley. Serve with oven-roasted potatoes on the side.

Chicken stuffed with herbs, walnuts, and grainy mustard

Poulet farci aux herbes et aux noix et à la moutarde à l'ancienne

I love the Sunday tradition of roasting a chicken. I like to stuff my chicken with a mixture of nuts, shallots, garlic, fresh herbs, and mustard, which creates a sauce full of incredible flavors—delicious with mashed celeriac and potato on the side.

Note: Use a larger chicken than the recipe calls for if you want leftovers for another dish, such as the Vanilla-Flavored Chicken *Clafoutis* (page 274).

Serves 4

FOR THE OVEN-
ROASTED CHICKEN:

1 organic chicken
(4½ lb; 2 kg)

4 garlic cloves, peeled

1 large shallot, peeled

2 tablespoons (¾ oz; 20 g) hazelnuts

2 tablespoons
(¾ oz; 20 g) pecans

2 tablespoons finely chopped parsley

2 tablespoons finely chopped cilantro

¼ cup (2 oz; 60 g) mascarpone cheese

1 tablespoon
moutarde à l'ancienne
(grainy mustard)

¼ cup (60 ml) olive oil

Sea salt and pepper

2 bay leaves

FOR THE MASHED
CELERIAC AND
POTATO:

14 oz (400 g) peeled celeriac, diced

1 lb, 5¼ oz (600 g) peeled russet potatoes, diced

1⅔ cups (375 ml) whole or 2% milk

1 tablespoon
(½ oz; 14 g) unsalted butter, diced

Sea salt and pepper

To prepare the chicken: Preheat the oven to 400°F (200°C).

Rinse the chicken and pat dry; set aside.

In the bowl of a food processor, combine 2 garlic cloves, the shallot, hazelnuts, pecans, parsley, and cilantro. Purée until smooth. Transfer to a clean bowl and stir in the mascarpone, mustard, and 1 tablespoon olive oil; season with sea salt and pepper. Spoon the mixture into a pastry bag without a tip; set aside.

Carefully stretch out the chicken skin on top and, using the pastry bag, pipe the stuffing uniformly under the skin, being careful not to tear the skin. Massage the chicken with the rest of the olive oil. Place 2 garlic cloves and 2 bay leaves inside the chicken. Tie the legs of the chicken close to the body with cooking string. Place the chicken in a large oven dish and roast for 30 minutes. Reduce the heat to 350°F (180°C) and continue to roast for 75 to 90 minutes, or until the internal temperature reaches 165°F (74°C), checked by inserting a meat thermometer in a few places.

To prepare the mashed celeriac and potato: Fill a large pot with salted water and bring to a boil. Cook the celeriac and potatoes for about 15 to 20 minutes, or until cooked through. Strain and purée with a ricer. Heat the milk; pour it slowly over the vegetable purée, mixing as you go, until you reach your desired consistency. Stir the butter into the warm mash, and season with sea salt and pepper to taste.

Vanilla-flavored chicken *clafoutis*

WITH CHERRY TOMATOES

Clafoutis au poulet vanillé et aux tomates cerises

This savory *clafoutis* is a dish I keep in my repertoire for the times I have leftovers of our Sunday roasted chicken.

You will need: a 10-inch (25.5 cm) quiche mold.

Serves 4

2 tablespoons olive oil, plus more for the mold

2 lemon thyme sprigs

¼ cup finely chopped red onion or 1 large shallot

1 tablespoon honey

7 oz (200 g) cooked chicken (from leftovers of a roasted chicken) or chicken breast, chopped

1 vanilla bean, split lengthwise and seeds scraped out

12 oz (340 g) cherry tomatoes (different sizes and colors)

1 tablespoon sherry vinegar

4 large eggs

2 tablespoons quinoa flour

2 tablespoons hazelnut meal

1 cup (236 ml) milk or goat milk

2 tablespoons finely chopped parsley

Sea salt and pepper, to taste

1¾ oz (50 g) crumbled fresh soft goat cheese

2 oz (60 g) chopped pecans (or hazelnuts)

Preheat the oven to 375°F (190°C). Oil the quiche mold; set aside.

In a frying pan, heat 1 tablespoon olive oil over medium heat. When warm, add the thyme and onion. Cook for 2 minutes, stirring without browning, until soft. Add the honey and cook for 1 minute. Add the chicken, vanilla bean and seeds, and cherry tomatoes and cook on low heat for 10 minutes, stirring, until the tomatoes start to soften. Add the sherry vinegar and cook for 1 minute. Remove and discard the thyme and vanilla bean. Transfer chicken and vegetables to the quiche mold; set aside.

In a bowl, beat the eggs with the quinoa flour and hazelnut meal. Stir in the milk, 1 tablespoon olive oil, and the parsley. Season with salt and pepper.

Pour the egg batter over the chicken and vegetables. Add the crumbled cheese and chopped nuts. Bake the *clafoutis* for 35 to 40 minutes or until the flan is set.

Serve warm with a side salad.

Chicken drumsticks

WITH SPICES AND COCONUT MILK

Pilons de poulet aux épices et au lait de coco

When I'm thinking about comfort food that involves chicken, I like to imagine the sauce that will come with it, something wonderful to flavor a bowl of steaming grains such as brown rice, millet, or quinoa on the side. The sauce in this chicken dish is packed with many of my favorite aromas, from an array of fresh-scented herbs and spices—what's not to love about saffron?—to the flavors of lime juice and coconut milk. I always hope there will be leftovers for the next day so I can have a quiet lunch at home when Lulu is at school and Philip is at the office.

Serves 4

12 chicken drumsticks, between 4 and 5 oz (115 to 140 g) each

1 teaspoon ground coriander

1 teaspoon ground cumin

½ teaspoon turmeric

1-inch (2.5 cm) piece of fresh ginger, peeled and finely grated

1 strand saffron (0.03 oz; 1 g)

½ teaspoon sea salt

Pepper, to taste

3 garlic cloves, minced

Zest of 1 lime, finely grated

4 tablespoons lime juice

⅓ cup (80 ml) olive oil

1 tablespoon fresh basil or cilantro, chopped

1 tablespoon fresh mint, chopped

1 tablespoon fresh parsley, chopped

12 cherry tomatoes, cut in half, or 2 tomatoes, cut into 8 pieces each

1 dry lime leaf or 1 bay leaf

½ red onion, thinly sliced with a mandoline

¼ cup (60 ml) water

½ cup (120 ml) unsweetened coconut milk

Skin the drumsticks by pulling the skin toward the end of the bone and using a pair of scissors to cut it off. Set aside in a large baking dish.

In a small bowl, combine the coriander, cumin, turmeric, ginger, saffron, and sea salt. Season with pepper to taste. Add the garlic and the lime zest and juice. Stir in the olive oil and fresh herbs. Coat the chicken with the sauce and place in the fridge for a few hours so that the flavors develop—although you can cook the chicken right away if you wish.

Preheat the oven to 400°F (200°C). Add the tomatoes, lime leaf, onion, and water to the baking dish. Bake the chicken for 20 minutes. Reduce the temperature to 375°F (190°C) and continue to cook for 40 minutes, stirring a few times, until the chicken is cooked through. Stir the coconut milk into the sauce in the pan and continue to cook for 10 more minutes.

Serve over a grain like millet, quinoa, or short brown rice, with Radish, Fennel, and Apple Salad (page 136) on the side.

Blue potato and red snapper *papillotes*

WITH SUGAR SNAP PEAS

Papillotes de vitelottes et de perche rouge aux pois mangetout

This is one of my favorite *plats complets* (all-in-one meal). Cooking *en papillote,* which consists of steaming small portions of food in a folded pouch of parchment paper or foil, is a classic French technique that I use a lot in my cooking. So many delicious things happen inside a *papillote* when the flavor of one food gradually mingles with the one next to it. Because the ingredients essentially steam in their own juices, I always make sure to include a lot of fresh herbs and slice my vegetables thin so they will cook easily.

Note: I use red snapper fillets in this recipe, but you can use flounder, haddock, or another type of white fish fillet instead (which I often do when I can't find red snapper). A wonderful variant is made with Jerusalem artichokes (one per *papillote,* peeled and finely sliced) layered on top of the potatoes. I never fail to use them when they are in season.

Serves 4

4 red snapper fillets, with skin (150 to 200 g each)

Sea salt and pepper

Olive oil

1 lb, 5¼ oz (600 g) blue potatoes, peeled and thinly sliced with a mandoline

3 garlic cloves, minced

20 cherry tomatoes (mixed colors), cut in half

16 pitted Castelvetrano olives (a variety of green olive)

2 Meyer lemons, 1 thinly sliced and the other cut in wedges

4 thyme sprigs

2 cups (5 oz; 150 g) sugar snap peas, cut in half

Preheat the oven to 400°F (200°C).

Cut four 15-inch (38 cm) sheets of parchment paper. Pat the fish dry with paper towels, then season with sea salt and pepper. Place the sheets of parchment paper on the working surface. Drizzle the centers with olive oil. Make a bed of potatoes on each sheet. Season with sea salt and pepper, and drizzle with more olive oil. Add garlic to each, and top with the fish, skin side up. Add the cherry tomatoes and olives. Top each with 2 slices of lemon, and add parsley and 1 thyme sprig. Drizzle with more olive oil. Lift the wider edges of the paper and fold them over the top. Crimp the side edges by pleating them over and over, or secure with string. Leave enough space between the ingredients and the edge of the paper for the pouches to puff.

Set the pouches in a rimmed baking sheet. Cook for 25 to 30 minutes, or until the potatoes are cooked through. In the meantime heat 1 tablespoon olive oil in a frying pan. Add the sugar snap peas and sauté for 2 minutes. Season with salt and pepper. Serve the *papillotes* on plates directly from the oven and open them at the table. Add additional wedges of lemon if desired and serve with the sugar snap peas.

Fish and vegetable cakes

Galettes de poisson et de légumes

Fish cakes are not the kind of food I ate when I was a child simply because they are not traditionally French, but I've learned to enjoy them after living so long in English-speaking countries. Now that I have my own family, fish cakes have become even more appealing. Lulu simply loves these, and her father and I do too.

I especially like to load my fish cakes with a wide selection of vegetables and fresh herbs—celeriac, potatoes, and zucchini here—which is a twist on the more common fish cakes that use only potatoes. The result lends a bolder flavor to the cakes, which are particularly scrumptious accompanied by labneh and peppery arugula.

Serves 4 (makes ten 3½-inch [9 cm] cakes)

12¼ oz (350 g) russet potatoes

7 oz (200 g) celeriac or sweet potato

1 cup (236 ml) water, plus 2 tablespoons

Sea salt and pepper

⅓ cup (1½ oz; 40 g) quinoa flakes

⅓ cup (60 ml) whole or 2% milk

5 tablespoons olive oil, plus more for frying

1 lb (450 g) cod, haddock, or flounder fillet

2 tablespoons dry white wine or white vermouth

5¼ oz (150 g) zucchini, finely grated

1 garlic clove, minced

2 tablespoons finely chopped parsley

2 tablespoons finely chopped chives, plus more to serve

6 basil leaves, finely chopped

Zest of 1 organic lemon or lime, finely grated

2 large eggs

⅓ cup (1¾ oz; 53 g) white rice flour, to coat the fish cakes (or more if needed)

Lemon wedges, to serve

Labneh (page 36), *crème fraîche,* or sour cream, to serve

Peel the potatoes and celeriac (you should have 1 lb [450 g] of vegetables total) and slice them. Add to a pot and cover with 1 cup (236 ml) water; season with sea salt and cover. Bring to a simmer and cook for 10 to 12 minutes, or until the vegetables are cooked through. Transfer to a large bowl and mash with a fork. Season with pepper and set aside.

In a small bowl, combine the quinoa flakes and milk. Stir and set aside for 10 minutes. In the meantime, heat 2 tablespoons olive oil in a frying pan over medium heat. Add the cod fillet, and season with sea salt and pepper. Cook for 1 to 2 minutes. Add 2 tablespoons water and 2 tablespoons white wine. Cover and cook on low heat for 7 to 8 minutes, or until the fish is just cooked through and starts to flake. Transfer to a bowl. Use a fork to flake the fish. Add to the bowl of mashed vegetables; set aside.

In the same pan, heat 1 tablespoon olive oil over medium heat. Add the zucchini and garlic, and season with sea salt and pepper. Cook for 2 to 3 minutes, or until the zucchini softens. Transfer to the bowl with

continued

the fish and vegetables. Stir in the parsley, chives, basil, quinoa flakes and milk, and lemon zest. Break the eggs into the bowl and stir until well combined. Cover and place in the fridge for 1 to 2 hours.

Prepare a plate with ¼ cup white rice flour. Using your hands, make patties about 3½ inches (9 cm) in diameter and ½ inch (1.25 cm) thick. Coat them lightly in the flour on both sides, and repeat until you run out of fish mixture.

Preheat the oven to 250°F (120°C). In a large frying pan, heat 2 tablespoons olive oil over medium heat. Cook 3 or 4 fish cakes (or as many your pan can hold) for 4 to 5 minutes on one side, then flip and cook on the other side until golden brown, adding more oil if needed. Transfer to a plate covered with a paper towel and place in the oven to keep warm while you cook the other fish cakes.

Serve with labneh drizzled with olive oil, chopped chives, wedges of lime, lightly sautéed (or steamed) green vegetables such as broccoli rabe (an utter favorite), and a large bowl of baby arugula dressed with Everyday Salad Dressing with Shallot (page 115).

Oven-baked yellowtail snapper

Vivaneau à queue jaune rôti au four

I prefer to buy my fish whole when I can, cleaned but with the head still on. This is most likely a cultural thing, as we often buy whole fish at a *poissonnerie* (fishmonger) in France. Then I try not to fuss too much with it, keeping the flavors intact.

This is a recipe where the fish is lightly infused with aromas of ginger, lime, and fresh herbs before being cooked on a bed of thinly sliced onion and fennel. It's delicate and makes a beautiful presentation. For a full meal, serve it with something simple, like a bowl of steaming rice (or any other grain you like) or even roasted potatoes, on the side.

Serves 4

2 tablespoons minced ginger

3 tablespoons finely chopped cilantro

1 tablespoon finely chopped basil

2 limes, peeled and finely chopped, plus 1 lime, thinly sliced

Sea salt and pepper

1 yellowtail snapper (1½ lb; 680 g), cleaned and scaled

1 red onion, thinly sliced

2 fennel bulbs, thinly sliced

6 stems of small cherry tomatoes (with about 8 tomatoes on each)

Olive oil

Preheat the oven to 400°F (200°C). Line a baking sheet with parchment paper; set aside.

In a small bowl, combine the ginger, cilantro, basil, and chopped lime. Season with sea salt and pepper; set aside. Score the skin of the fish with 3 diagonal cuts. Stuff the cuts with the ginger, herb, and lime preparation; put the rest inside the fish.

Make a bed with the onion and fennel on the lined baking sheet. Place the fish on top. Add the cherry tomatoes and drizzle with olive oil. Top with the lime slices. Cook the fish for 30 minutes, or until the flesh flakes easily when tested with a fork. Serve with a grain such as rice or quinoa, or potatoes, and extra lime if desired.

Sole rolls

WITH LEEK SAUCE, EDAMAME, AND ROMANESCO

Roulades de soles avec sauce au poireau, édamames, et chou romanesco

We used to eat *roulades de sole* with a *beurre blanc* sauce as part of a multicourse meal when my mother had guests over for a family gathering—and when everyone was there, we sometimes had nearly forty people at the table. My version of this dish is greener, with the addition of edamame, and comes together quickly. Serve it with a grain on the side.

Serves 4; makes 1½ cups (350 ml) leek sauce

FOR THE LEEK SAUCE:

1 tablespoon olive oil

1 shallot, finely chopped

1 leek, white part only, finely chopped

¼ cup (60 ml) dry white wine or white vermouth

½ cup (120 ml) heavy cream or unsweetened coconut milk

½ cup (120 ml) chicken stock

2 tablespoons coarsely chopped parsley

Sea salt and pepper

FOR THE VEGETABLES:

Sea salt

2 cups (5 oz; 140 g) shelled green edamame (fresh or frozen)

2 cups (7 oz; 200 g) Romanesco florets

1 tablespoon olive oil

1 garlic clove, minced

Pepper

FOR THE ROULADES:

8 Dover sole or flounder fillets

Sea salt and pepper

8 thin lemon slices

8 parsley leaves

8 toothpicks or cooking string

Olive oil, to drizzle

To prepare the leek sauce: In a frying pan, heat the olive oil over medium heat. Add the shallot and leek; cook, without browning, for 10 minutes, stirring occasionally, until the vegetables are soft. Add the wine and let evaporate for 1 to 2 minutes. Add the cream, stock, and parsley, and simmer for 3 minutes. Season with sea salt and pepper to taste. Transfer to the bowl of a food processor and purée until smooth. Keep warm on the side.

To prepare the vegetables: Blanch the edamame and Romanesco in salted boiling water for 3 to 4 minutes (page 386). Transfer to an ice water bath; drain and set aside. In a frying pan, heat the olive oil over medium heat. Cook the vegetables with the garlic clove for 2 minutes. Season with pepper; keep warm on the side.

To prepare the roulades: Preheat the oven to 400°F (200°C).

Rinse the fish under cold water and pat dry. Lay the fillets on a clean working surface, and season with sea salt and pepper. Roll up each fillet to make a bundle. Place a slice of lemon and a piece of parsley on top of each bundle and secure with a toothpick or cooking string tied around it. Transfer the fish to a baking dish and drizzle with olive oil. Bake for 15 to 20 minutes. Place 2 bundles on each plate. Drizzle with the leek sauce. Serve with the sautéed vegetables; more leek sauce; and black rice ramen, quinoa, steamed white rice, or brown rice.

Oven-roasted monkfish

WITH CLAMS AND HERB RICOTTA STUFFING

Rôti de lotte farci à la ricotta aux herbes, avec praires

When I catch sight of beautiful monkfish fillets at my local store, I can never pass them by. The sweet flavor and dense texture of the fish somehow remind me of the meat in a lobster tail—ideal in a dish like this one. Here, I like to stuff a mixture of ricotta, finely grated zucchini, and fresh herbs between the fillets and then wrap the roast between thin slices of prosciutto for a balance of flavors. Then I cook it *en papillote* so the ingredients steam in their own juices and the aromas mingle nicely. The clams on the side are a must, as is a piece of your favorite bread to soak up the sauce.

Serves 4

½ cup (5¼ oz; 150 g) whole milk ricotta cheese

¼ cup finely chopped zucchini

1 tablespoon finely chopped parsley

2 shallots, finely chopped

1 tablespoon finely chopped basil

Sea salt and pepper

2 tablespoons olive oil, plus more to drizzle

24 littleneck clams

1 celery stalk, diced

2 lemon thyme or thyme sprigs

½ cup (120 ml) dry white wine or white vermouth

1½ tablespoons heavy cream

4 slices prosciutto

2 equal-size pieces monkfish (10 oz [280 g] each)

2 small tomatoes, thinly sliced (makes 8 to 10 slices)

1 long parsley sprig

In a small bowl, combine the ricotta with the zucchini, parsley, half of the shallots, and basil. Add a dash of sea salt and pepper and 1 tablespoon olive oil; set aside.

Brush the clams under cold water to remove any remaining sand; set aside.

In a frying pan, heat 1 tablespoon olive oil over medium heat. Add the celery, the rest of the shallots, and the lemon thyme; cook for 2 to 3 minutes, without browning, until soft. Add the clams and white wine, and cover. Increase the heat. Bring to a simmer and cook for 5 to 10 minutes, or until all the clams are open. Remove from the heat and add the heavy cream—you will reheat the clams close to the time you serve them.

Preheat the oven to 420°F (215°C). Cut a 15-by-20-inch (38 by 51 cm) piece of parchment paper and three or four 14-inch (35.5 cm) pieces of string (long enough to tie around the roast). Drizzle the parchment paper with olive oil. Arrange the strings across the parchment parallel to you and equally spaced to the length of the fish. Place a slice of prosciutto along each string. Top with the first piece of monkfish, perpendicular to you and across all four strings. Season with sea salt and pepper; spread half the ricotta mixture on top. Top with half the tomato slices and the rest of the ricotta. Top with the other piece of fish. Wrap the prosciutto

continued

around the fish and top with the rest of the tomato slices. Lay the parsley across the top, and tie each string so the roast is tightly closed. Drizzle with 1 tablespoon of the clam sauce and olive oil. Lift the wider edges of the paper and fold them over the top of the roast. Crimp the side edges by pleating them over and over, or secure with string. Leave enough space between the ingredients and the edge of the paper for the pouch to puff.

Set the parcel in a rimmed baking sheet or a baking dish. Bake for 35 minutes. Remove from the oven, open the *papillote,* and slice the roast into thick pieces. Serve with the reserved clams and sauce; oven-roasted sweet potatoes; and a grain such as black rice, Lulu's favorite.

grains
les céréales

Asparagus and pistachio pesto pasta

WITH SPRING GREEN VEGETABLES, FETA, AND OLIVES

Pâtes au pesto d'asperges et de pistaches avec légumes verts printaniers, feta, et olives

Adding green pesto is among my favorite ways to dress a plate of pasta, soup, or potatoes when I have little time to cook. Here, the pasta is combined with pretty green spring vegetables and accented with salty feta and olives. It's the perfect spring dish.

Note: The pesto will keep in the fridge for up to a week, or you can freeze it in 8-oz (236 ml) Mason jars. If you freeze it, take it out to thaw for a few hours before you plan to use it; I often put it in the fridge the night before to use the next day.

Serves 4; makes 2 cups (472 ml) pesto

FOR THE PESTO:

1 bunch (1 lb; 450 g) asparagus

1 cup (¾ oz; 20 g) packed basil leaves

1 teaspoon finely grated lime zest

1 garlic clove

3 tablespoons (1½ oz; 45 g) shelled unsalted pistachios, pine nuts, or walnuts

½ cup (2 oz; 60 g) packed finely grated Parmesan cheese

Sea salt and pepper

¾ cup (175 ml) olive oil

Squeeze of lime juice, to taste

FOR THE PASTA:

12¼ oz (350 g) pasta of your choice

2 tablespoons olive oil

1 cup (3½ oz; 100 g) green peas, fresh or frozen

1 cup cooked fava beans (page 102)

Asparagus tips (reserved from making the pesto), diced

1 garlic clove, minced

Sea salt and pepper

¾ to 1 cup (236 ml) asparagus and pistachio pesto, to taste

2 oz (60 g) feta cheese, crumbled

⅓ to ½ cup pitted kalamata olives, to taste

To prepare the pesto: Cut 1 inch (2.5 cm) off the bottom of each asparagus stem, then cut the tips off and set them aside for the pasta. You'll be left with 4-inch (10 cm) stems, making about 6¼ oz (180 g). Blanch the asparagus stems in salted boiling water for 2 minutes (page 386). Transfer to an ice water bath to cool; drain and set aside.

In the bowl of a food processor, combine the asparagus, basil, lime zest, garlic, pistachios, Parmesan, and a pinch of sea salt and pepper; pulse to finely chop. Add the olive oil and continue to work to obtain a paste. Stir in the lime juice. Taste for seasoning and set aside.

To prepare the pasta: Cook the pasta per the instructions on the package.

Meanwhile, heat the olive oil in a frying pan over medium heat. Add the peas, fava beans, reserved asparagus tips, and garlic; sauté for 3 to 4 minutes, or until lightly cooked but still crunchy and green. Season with sea salt and pepper.

Toss the pasta with the pesto, and divide it between four plates. Top with the green vegetables, feta, and olives. Serve immediately.

Pea risotto

WITH LEMON, BASIL OIL, AND STEAMED LOBSTER

Risotto aux petits pois et au citron avec huile au basilic et homard vapeur

Once I cooked this spring pea risotto for a large group of friends and family at a garden lunch in the middle of May to celebrate Philip's birthday. I remember how everyone enjoyed this light meal and how courageous I felt serving it, knowing that two good Italian friends (who are always hungry) were sitting there with us. When they called for seconds, I knew that I had done something right.

While the lobster is a perfect complement to this spring dish, I've also served it with oven-roasted racks of lamb with scrumptious results, as on Philip's birthday. When fava beans are also available, I make sure to add them to favorite spring recipes like this one.

Serves 4; makes ⅓ cup (80 ml) basil oil

FOR THE BASIL OIL:

Sea salt

1 cup packed fresh basil leaves

⅔ cup (160 ml) olive oil

FOR THE RISOTTO:

5½ cups (1.3 liters) fish or chicken stock

4 small lobster tails (3 oz [90 g] each)

2 tablespoons olive oil

1 tablespoon (1 oz; 14 g) unsalted butter

2 lemon thyme sprigs, or thyme sprigs

Zest of 1 lemon, finely grated

1 leek, white part only, finely chopped

1 large shallot, finely chopped

1½ cups (10½ oz; 300 g) carnaroli rice, or Arborio rice

½ cup (60 ml) dry white wine or white vermouth

1 cup (4½ oz; 125 g) shelled fresh peas

½ cup cooked fava beans (page 102) (optional)

½ cup (2 oz; 60 g) finely grated Parmesan cheese, plus more to serve

2 to 3 tablespoons mascarpone cheese or *crème fraîche*

1 tablespoon finely chopped parsley

1 tablespoon finely chopped mint

Lemon juice, to serve

To prepare the basil oil: Cook the basil leaves in a large pot of salted boiling water for 15 seconds. Drain and transfer to an ice water bath to cool; squeeze out the excess water and chop coarsely. Transfer to a blender or the bowl of a food processor, add the olive oil, and purée until smooth. Strain through a fine sieve or *chinois;* use immediately or pour into an airtight container. The oil will keep in the refrigerator for up to 3 days.

To prepare the risotto: In a pot, heat the stock and keep warm; set aside.

Steam the lobster for 10 to 15 minutes, or until the meat is cooked through. Let cool and remove the meat from the tails; set aside.

In a large, heavy-bottomed pot, heat the olive oil and butter over medium heat. Add the lemon thyme and lemon zest; cook for 1 minute. Add the leek and

continued

shallot. Sauté for 4 minutes, without browning, until soft. Add the rice and stir for 1 minute to coat. Add the white wine and cook until all the liquid is absorbed. Add the stock, 1 cup (240 ml) at a time, stirring constantly, and waiting until it is absorbed before adding more. When you have only ½ cup (120 ml) stock left, add the peas, fava beans, and the remaining stock; continue to cook until the rice is al dente. Stir in the Parmesan cheese, mascarpone, parsley, and mint. Remove from the heat and cover. Let rest for 2 minutes. Discard the lemon thyme.

Serve the risotto in shallow bowls and squeeze a little lemon juice on top. Drizzle with the basil oil, top with the lobster, and add more Parmesan if desired.

Black rice with sautéed green vegetable medley, parsley oil, and grilled salmon

Riz noir et sa poêlée de légumes verts avec huile au persil et saumon grillé

"This is my favorite type of rice!" Lulu exclaimed the first time she ate black rice. I am like her. Given the choice, I would always choose black rice over other kinds for its bolder texture and dramatic color.

This dish, in particular, is one of the food combinations I craved during my second pregnancy. I like how it offers so many things in one go: body and purity of flavor in the rice and crunchy green vegetables and an undeniable mood booster in the fish, which I prefer slightly undercooked. I highly recommend serving it with the herb-flavored oil and labneh, but if you prefer to keep it simple, it is still delicious without them.

Serves 4

3 small zucchini

3 tablespoons olive oil

1 shallot, finely chopped

2 cups (12¾ oz; 360 g) black rice

4 cups (945 ml) water or Homemade Vegetable Stock (page 96)

Sea salt

1 oregano stem

1 cup (4½ oz; 125 g) shelled peas (fresh or frozen)

1 cup (5 oz; 140 g) shelled edamame (fresh or frozen)

2 cups (5¼ oz; 150 g) sugar snap peas, cut in half

2 garlic cloves

Squeeze of lemon or lime juice

FOR THE GRILLED SALMON:

4 skinned wild salmon steaks, 4½ oz (125 g) each

Sea salt and pepper

1 tablespoon olive oil

FOR THE GARNISH:

2 cups sprouted micro greens, purple watercress, or a blend of both

Labneh (page 36), to serve

Parsley or basil oil, to serve (pages 88 and 296) (optional)

Fleur de sel, to serve

Using a vegetable peeler, slice the zucchini lengthwise into thin strips; stop when you get to the soft center, and use the leftovers for something else, like a soup or the Cocoa, Walnut, and Zucchini Muffins (page 146). Set aside.

In a pan, heat 1 tablespoon olive oil over medium heat. Add the shallot and cook without browning, stirring occasionally, for 2 minutes. Add the rice and stir for 1 minute to coat. Add the water and season with sea salt. Add the oregano. Cover and simmer for 30 minutes, or until the water is absorbed and the rice is al dente. Remove the oregano, and keep the rice warm covered on the side.

While the rice is cooking, blanch the shelled peas and edamame in salted boiling water for 2 minutes (page 386). Drain and transfer to an ice water bath; set aside.

In a frying pan, heat 2 tablespoons olive oil over medium heat. Add the sugar snap peas and zucchini. Cook, without browning, for 2 to 3 minutes, or until the

continued

zucchini softens but the sugar snap peas are still crunchy and bright green. Add the blanched peas and edamame and the garlic; cook for 2 more minutes, stirring occasionally. Remove from the heat and drizzle a squeeze of lemon juice on top.

To prepare the salmon, rinse and pat dry. Season the flesh with sea salt and pepper. In a frying pan, heat the olive oil over medium heat. Add the salmon, skin side down. Cook for 3 to 4 minutes. Flip on the other side and continue to cook for 3 minutes, or to your preferred doneness. I do not cook mine completely through so that it stays tender.

To serve, plate the salmon steaks individually, add the sautéed green vegetables with the black rice, micro greens, and a dollop of labneh. Finish with a dash of *fleur de sel* and a drizzle of parsley or basil oil. If you are too short of time to prepare the herbed oil, simply add freshly chopped parsley or basil and drizzle with olive oil.

Red beet gnocchi

WITH PARMESAN AND PARSLEY SAUCE

Gnocchi aux betteraves rouges avec sauce au Parmesan et au persil

Like many of her six-year-old girlfriends, Lulu loves the color pink. And since she adores gnocchi, I created this recipe for her. The bright fuchsia dumplings against the delicate white in the sauce are simply stunning and oh so appetizing!

Note: If you are serving this dish in the summer, add freshly cooked corn sliced off the cob. Toss in some lightly sautéed langoustines for a more substantial meal.

Serves 4; makes about sixty 1½-inch (4 cm) gnocchi

1 small beet
(3½ oz; 100 g), peeled
and diced

1 tablespoon olive oil

3 medium potatoes
(1 lb; 450 g)

½ cup (2 oz;
60 g) finely grated
Parmesan cheese

1 large egg

⅓ cup (1¾ oz; 53 g)
white rice flour

⅓ cup (2 oz; 55 g)
sweet rice flour

Sea salt and pepper

FOR THE PARMESAN
AND PARSLEY SAUCE:

¼ cup (1 oz; 30 g)
pine nuts

1½ cups (356 ml)
whole or 2% milk

¾ cup (3 oz; 90 g)
finely grated
Parmesan cheese

2 tablespoons finely
chopped parsley
or basil

Olive oil, to drizzle

Steam the beet until tender. Transfer to the bowl of a food processor and purée with the olive oil until smooth; set aside.

Boil the potatoes in a large pot of water until tender. Cool slightly, then peel; you want 14 oz (400 g) potatoes once they are peeled. Pass them through a ricer with the beet purée; stir to combine completely. Stir in the Parmesan, egg, and flours until smooth. Season with sea salt and pepper. Divide the dough into 4 pieces and roll into 1-inch (2.5 cm) thick logs. Cut the logs into ½-inch (1.25 cm) pieces, and make a small imprint on each gnocchi with a fork or gnocchi board; set aside.

To prepare the sauce: In a pan, toast the pine nuts for a few minutes over low to medium heat, until lightly golden; set aside.

Combine the milk and Parmesan cheese in a pot. Whisk together and heat. Cook for 2 minutes, stirring constantly, until the cheese melts and the sauce thickens. Keep warm on the side over a low flame.

Bring a large pot of salted water to a boil. Drop in a first batch of gnocchi—about 12, but do not overcrowd the pot—and cook for 1 to 2 minutes, or until the gnocchi rise to the surface. Remove with a slotted spoon and transfer to a serving dish. Cover with plastic film while you continue to cook. Repeat with the other gnocchi, in as many batches as you need.

When ready to serve, spoon some sauce into the bottom of four shallow plates. Add the gnocchi and spoon a little more sauce over them. Sprinkle with parsley or basil. Garnish with the pine nuts, sprinkle with extra cheese if desired, and drizzle with olive oil. Serve immediately.

Saffron-flavored carrot risotto

WITH BAY SCALLOPS AND PISTACHIOS

Risotto à la carotte et au safran avec coquilles St. Jacques et pistaches

I am a cook with many risotto recipes up my sleeve. In fact, when I tell Lulu we are having risotto for dinner, she invariably asks, *"Lequel?"* ("Which one?"). The beauty of this carrot-based recipe is that while it's simple comfort food for an everyday meal, it can also be turned into a more sophisticated dish when friends come over by adding the scallops and all the garnishes—many of my recipes are designed this way. What's not to love about that?

Serves 4

1 lb, 8¾ oz (600 g) carrots

5 tablespoons olive oil

2 tablespoons unsalted butter

2 thyme sprigs

¾ cup (175 ml) unsweetened coconut milk

5½ cups (1.3 liters) chicken stock

¾ teaspoon saffron threads

1 shallot, finely chopped

1 leek, white part only, finely chopped

1½ cups (10½ oz; 300 g) Arborio rice or carnaroli rice

½ cup (120 ml) dry white wine or white vermouth

½ cup (2 oz; 60 g) finely grated Parmesan or pecorino cheese, plus more for garnish

Sea salt and pepper

¾ lb (340 g) bay scallops

1½ tablespoons (⅔ oz; 20 g) shelled unsalted green pistachios, finely chopped

1 tablespoon finely chopped parsley

Pistachio oil, to serve

Micro greens, to serve

Peel the carrots and pulse them in the bowl of a food processor until they are finely chopped; set aside.

In a large, heavy-bottomed pot, heat 2 tablespoons olive oil with 1 tablespoon butter over medium heat. Add the carrots and thyme, and cook for 3 minutes. Add ¼ cup (60 ml) coconut milk, ¼ cup (60 ml) chicken stock, and ¼ teaspoon saffron; cook for 5 minutes, stirring occasionally, until the carrots are soft. Remove from the heat, discard the thyme, and reserve ⅓ cup (80 ml) of the carrot preparation. Transfer the rest to the bowl of a food processor with ¼ cup (60 ml) chicken stock, and purée until smooth; set aside.

Heat the rest of the stock in a pot with ½ teaspoon saffron; keep warm.

In a large pot, heat 2 tablespoons olive oil with 1 tablespoon butter. Add the shallot and leek. Sauté for 4 minutes, without browning, until soft. Add the rice and stir for 1 minute to coat. Add the white wine and cook, stirring constantly, until all the liquid is absorbed. Add the warm stock, 1 cup (236 ml) at a time, stirring constantly and waiting until each cup is absorbed before adding more. When you add the last cup of broth, also add the puréed carrots. Once most of the liquid is absorbed, check the rice to see whether you need more broth—the rice should stay

continued

slightly al dente. Stir in the Parmesan cheese and the rest of the coconut milk. Season with sea salt and pepper, to taste. Cover and remove from the heat.

In a sauté pan, heat 1 tablespoon olive oil over medium heat. Add the scallops and cook for 1 minute on each side. Season with sea salt and pepper.

Serve the carrot risotto in bowls. Top with the sautéed scallops and reserved carrots. Garnish with the pistachios, chopped parsley, and a little more shaved Parmesan; drizzle with pistachio oil. Top with micro greens, if using, and serve immediately.

Linguini with arugula pesto, roasted cherry tomatoes, and fennel

Linguini au pesto de roquette avec tomates cerises et fenouils grillés

A platter of vegetarian pasta is often a dish we have on Saturdays, when I am looking for a simple way to nourish us with scrumptious, healthy foods before our afternoon activities resume. Once the vegetables are prepared, they can be left nearly unattended while they bake, which is another reason why this dish is attractive on busy days. Arugula has a sharp, peppery taste that makes it a great addition to the hazelnut pesto, which can also be prepared ahead of time.

Serves 4; makes 1¼ cups (295 ml) pesto

FOR THE ARUGULA AND ROASTED HAZELNUT PESTO:

4 tablespoons (1½ oz; 40 g) hazelnuts

1 cup (¾ oz; 20 g) basil leaves

2 garlic cloves, peeled and sliced

2 cups (2½ oz; 70 g) packed arugula

½ cup (2 oz; 60 g) finely grated Parmesan cheese

Sea salt and pepper

¾ cup (175 ml) olive oil

FOR THE ROASTED CHERRY TOMATOES, FENNEL, AND RED ONION:

1 lb, 5¼ oz (600 g) cherry tomatoes, mixed colors and sizes if you can find them

1 fennel bulb, thinly sliced into sticks

½ red onion, thinly sliced with a mandoline

4 garlic cloves, peeled and minced

2 tablespoons finely chopped marjoram leaves

4 thyme sprigs

⅓ cup (80 ml) olive oil

1 tablespoon honey

Sea salt and pepper

FOR THE LINGUINI:

12¼ oz (350 g) linguini

Crumbled feta cheese, to taste

Arugula leaves, to garnish

In a frying pan, toast the hazelnuts for 1 to 2 minutes over medium heat, until slightly golden. Remove from the heat and rub the nuts with a kitchen towel to remove the skins. Let cool.

In the bowl of a food processor, combine the hazelnuts, basil, garlic, arugula, Parmesan, and a pinch of sea salt and pepper and pulse to finely chop. Add the oil and continue to work to obtain a paste. Use about two-thirds for the linguini in this recipe; the rest can be refrigerated for up to a week or frozen for later use.

To prepare the vegetables: Preheat the oven to 375°F (190°C).

In a large baking dish, combine the cherry tomatoes, fennel, and onion. Add the garlic and fresh herbs. Drizzle with olive oil and honey, then season with sea salt and pepper. Bake for 40 minutes, stirring occasionally. Reduce temperature to 250°F (120°C) to keep the vegetables warm. Remove the thyme sprigs to serve.

To prepare the linguini: Cook the linguini according to the instructions on the package. Toss with the pesto and top with the roasted vegetables. Garnish with the feta and a few leaves of fresh arugula. Serve immediately.

Spaghetti with roasted butternut squash, peas, ricotta, mint, and bresaola

Spaghetti avec courge musquée rôtie, petits pois, ricotta, menthe, et bresaola

So many wonderful things happen in this autumnal spaghetti dish: slices of butternut squash roasted in olive oil, garlic, and coriander mingle with creamy ricotta, bright peas, earthy nuts, and savory cured meat.

Over time, I have cooked different versions of this dish, inviting friends to come and enjoy it with us. I settled on this one after Lulu licked her lips, asking for more and saying, *"C'est super bon, maman"* ("It's really nice, Mummy").

Note: Bresaola is air-dried, salted beef, aged for two or three months before it becomes hard and dark red in color. If you cannot find bresaola, use slices of prosciutto or serrano ham instead.

Serves 4

4 tablespoons (2 oz; 60 g) walnuts or hazelnuts

1 organic butternut squash (about 3 lb; 1.36 kg)

2 garlic cloves, minced and divided

4 tablespoons olive oil

2 teaspoons ground coriander

Sea salt and pepper

12 oz (340 g) spaghetti

1 large shallot, finely chopped

½ cup (125 g) whole milk ricotta cheese

1 tablespoon chopped cilantro

1 tablespoon chopped mint

1 cup (4½ oz; 125 g) green peas (fresh or frozen)

Finely grated Parmesan cheese, to taste

16 slices bresaola

Pumpkin seed oil or olive oil, to drizzle

In a frying pan, toast the walnuts for 2 to 3 minutes, or until fragrant. Remove from the heat and chop coarsely; set aside.

Preheat the oven to 375°F (190°C).

Cut the top off the butternut squash; set aside. Cut the bottom part in half and remove the seeds. Cut half of it into ½-inch (1.25 cm) slices. Pat the slices dry and transfer to a large bowl. Coat with 1 clove minced garlic, 2 tablespoons olive oil, and 1 teaspoon ground coriander. Season with sea salt and pepper, and toss gently. Transfer to a baking sheet and bake for 25 to 30 minutes, or until the squash slices are cooked through and lightly roasted; set aside.

In the meantime, peel the rest of the squash. Dice and steam for 15 minutes, until tender. Using a ricer, purée the squash; set aside.

Cook the pasta according to the instructions on the package. Reserve ¾ cup (180 ml) of the cooking water.

In a frying pan, heat 2 tablespoons olive oil over medium heat. Add the rest of the ground coriander with the shallot, and sauté for 4 to 5 minutes, without browning,

continued

until soft. Add the rest of the garlic and cook for 1 minute. Add the ricotta, puréed squash, and ½ cup cooking water from the pasta. Stir and simmer for 1 to 2 minutes to heat. Toss the pasta in the sauce (add more pasta water if needed). Add the cilantro, mint, and peas, and cook for 1 minute—the peas should stay green and crunchy.

Divide the pasta between 4 plates and top with grated Parmesan to taste. Garnish with slices of bresaola, roasted butternut squash, and walnuts, and drizzle with pumpkin seed oil. Serve immediately with a side salad.

Vegetarian lasagna

Lasagnes végétariennes

At times, you may prefer a light type of lasagna, and a vegetarian one like this is the perfect answer for that craving. Mine has an obvious tone of fall aromas with its lightly caramelized onions, sautéed spinach, and mushrooms mixed with a creamy, ricotta-based, winter squash purée. Red kuri squash is my first choice when it's seasonal, but butternut squash is a great option too. I also like to use gluten-free brown rice pasta for this dish.

Note: There is no need to peel the red kuri squash. Just wash it thoroughly before cutting.

Serves 4

4 tablespoons olive oil, plus more for the dish

1 package dry lasagna (10 oz; 280 g)

1 medium red onion, thinly sliced

1 thyme sprig

1 bay leaf

1 teaspoon brown sugar

1 teaspoon sherry vinegar

1 lb, 2 oz (500 g) red kuri squash, seeded and diced (see Note)

2 carrots, peeled and diced

4 cups (6 oz; 125 g) packed spinach leaves

Sea salt and pepper

8¾ oz (250 g) crimini mushrooms, peeled and sliced

6 sage leaves, chopped

2 tablespoons chopped parsley

2 cups (1 lb; 450 g) whole milk ricotta cheese

2½ oz (70 g) fontina cheese, grated

Dash of freshly grated nutmeg

½ cup (120 ml) heavy cream

½ cup (2 oz; 60 g) finely grated Parmesan cheese

Preheat the oven at 400°F (200°C). Oil a 12-by-8-inch (30.5 by 20 cm) baking dish; set aside.

Precook your lasagna sheets for a few minutes (I don't cook mine all the way through, because they will finish cooking once layered with the vegetables); set aside.

In a nonstick frying pan, heat 2 tablespoons olive oil over medium heat. Add the onion, thyme, and bay leaf. Turn the heat down to low, cover, and cook for 10 minutes. Stir in the brown sugar and vinegar, and continue to cook, uncovered, for 5 to 10 more minutes; set aside.

In the meantime, steam the squash and carrots until tender when pierced with a

fork. Using a food mill or ricer, purée the vegetables into a bowl.

In the same sauté pan you used for the onions, heat 1 tablespoon olive oil over medium heat. Add the spinach and a pinch of sea salt. Cook for 1 minute, or until just wilted; put in a separate bowl and set aside.

Return the pan to the stove, add 1 tablespoon olive oil, and heat again over medium heat. Add the mushrooms and season with sea salt and pepper. Cook for 5 minutes, stirring occasionally, until the mushrooms have released their water and are browned; set aside.

Mix the chopped herbs, ricotta, onions, and one-third of the grated fontina cheese

continued

into the butternut squash preparation. Season with sea salt and pepper and a dash of nutmeg. In a small pot, combine the cream with the rest of the fontina cheese and season with pepper. Heat and whisk until melted; set aside.

Cover the bottom of the lasagna pan with lasagna sheets. Spread with half of the sqaush purée and half of the spinach and mushrooms. Cover with more lasagna sheets and spread with the rest of the squash purée. Add the rest of the spinach and mushrooms. Cover with the rest of the lasagna sheets. Pour the cream over the pasta and finish with the grated Parmesan. Bake the lasagna for about 30 minutes, or until the top looks crispy. Serve with a side salad.

My favorite lasagna

Mes lasagnes préférées

On a freezing cold day, a dish of lasagna will make many faces beam. Maybe it's the creaminess of the sauce that does it. Over the years, I've made many different kinds of lasagna, but I always come back to this more traditional meat-based dish, which never fails to appeal to young and old alike. In case you didn't know, a reheated dish of lasagna tastes wonderful the next day when the pasta has absorbed some of the sauce. And the meat and tomato sauce is also excellent served as a Bolognese with spaghetti, linguini, or the pasta of your choice.

FOR THE MEAT AND
TOMATO SAUCE:

2 tablespoons olive oil

2 thyme sprigs

1 teaspoon ground
coriander

1 large shallot or
1 small red onion,
finely chopped

2 celery stalks, finely
chopped

3 garlic cloves,
minced

1 tablespoon
tomato paste

2 carrots, peeled and
finely grated

1 small zucchini,
finely grated

1 small turnip, finely
grated (optional)

1 lb (450 g) ground
veal (or use ⅓ lb
[150 g] ground pork,
⅓ lb [150 g] ground
veal, and ⅓ lb [150 g]
ground beef)

1 large can (28.2 oz;
800 g) diced tomatoes

1 bay leaf

Sea salt and pepper

FOR THE
WHITE SAUCE:

4¼ tablespoons
(2 oz; 60 g)
unsalted butter

¼ cup plus
2 tablespoons
(1¾ oz; 50 g)
cornstarch

3 cups (700 ml)
whole or 2% milk

Sea salt and pepper

Nutmeg, ground or
freshly grated,
to taste

FOR THE LASAGNA:

1 package (10 oz;
280 g) dry lasagna

1 cup (4¼ oz; 120 g)
finely grated
Parmesan cheese

Olive oil, to drizzle

Dash of nutmeg,
ground or freshly
grated

To prepare the meat and tomato sauce: In a sauté pan, heat 2 tablespoons olive oil over medium heat. Add the thyme, coriander, shallot, and celery. Cook for 3 minutes, stirring occasionally, until soft. Add the garlic and cook for 1 minute. Add the tomato paste and cook for 1 minute. Add the grated carrots, zucchini, and turnip (if using), and cook for 5 minutes, stirring occasionally. Add the meat and cook for 5 minutes, stirring frequently, until the meat is cooked. Add the tomatoes and bay leaf, and season with sea salt and pepper. Turn down the heat and simmer, uncovered, stirring occasionally, for 30 minutes, or until the sauce is slightly reduced. Remove from the heat, and discard the bay leaf and thyme. Transfer the sauce to the bowl of a food processor and purée until smooth; set aside.

To prepare the white sauce: In a pot, melt the butter over medium heat. Add the cornstarch all at once and stir rapidly until a uniform consistency. Add the milk and whisk vigorously. Season with sea salt

continued

and pepper; continue to whisk until the sauce simmers and thickens. (When small bubbles appear, it should have thickened sufficiently.) Cook for 1 more minute, then remove from the heat and add a pinch of nutmeg; set aside.

To prepare the lasagna: Prepare the lasagna sheets according to the instructions on the package. (Some need to be precooked and some don't. I like to precook my brown rice pasta for 1 to 2 minutes in boiling salted water, because it will finish cooking once layered with the meat and white sauce.)

In the meantime, preheat the oven to 400°F (200°C). Grease a 12-by-8-inch (30.5 by 20 cm) baking dish. Spread one-third of the white sauce in the bottom of the dish. Add a layer of lasagna and cover with half of the meat and tomato sauce. Sprinkle with ¼ cup (½ oz; 14 g) Parmesan. Add another layer of lasagna, another third of the white sauce, the rest of the meat and tomato sauce, and another ¼ cup (½ oz; 14 g) Parmesan. Cover with another layer of lasagna. Add the last third of the white sauce, and sprinkle with the rest of the Parmesan. Drizzle with olive oil, and add a dash of nutmeg.

Bake the lasagna for 45 minutes, or until golden brown in color. Serve with a large salad of mixed greens on the side.

sweet treats for the family

les desserts de famille

WHENEVER I BRING a tasty-looking dessert to the dining table, everyone smiles—especially little ones who have been champing at the bit. Dessert always has this amazing power on people, especially when it is *fait maison* (homemade) because somehow it is always tastier. At home, I am used to hearing, *"C'est quoi le dessert?"* ("What's for dessert?") It's a natural question to ask since there always is one, simple and casual for our everyday meals, a little more elaborate when guests are over for dinner.

Making a dessert is a deeply pleasurable activity for me—in fact, my family and friends tell me I am known for my eye-catching desserts. Of course, my desserts are largely inspired by my French roots, because that's what lives strongly in me.

Quite often, I want to taste fruit after a meal, so my desserts are filled with gorgeously plump apricots, fragrant strawberries, cheerful cherries, or calming apples, with lots of zest, vanilla, and scented herbs picked fresh from the garden. In hot weather, Summer Fruit *Papillotes* and Lavender

Ice Cream (page 330) showcase bright, sun-ripened fruits that reveal an intense burst of color once the casings are torn open, exquisite for the eye. In fall, favorite apples are lightly sautéed in butter and sugar to accompany a smooth, melt-in-the-mouth Goat Milk *Panna Cotta* (page 339). Sometimes, dessert is a humble yet mouthwatering fruit tart that everyone I know welcomes with open arms—and mouths. These tarts look very French and feel personal to me. They are a family tradition I keep alive.

What I crave even more than fruit is CHOCOLATE—in capital letters. Oh, the joy of chocolate! While flipping through the pages of this book, you will undoubtedly notice my deeply anchored love affair with the stuff. At home, we take chocolate seriously. It is perfect in both an everyday cake for *l'heure du goûter*—such as Lulu's Chocolate and Olive Oil Cake (page 229)—or in the graceful Chocolate Celebration Cake (page 378) for memorable occasions. It shares first place with fully ripened fruit in Pear and Chocolate Crumbles (page 368), and it looks decadent in the dreamy Tiramisu Cake (page 381) that never fails to please.

While some desserts are purposely prepared family style, others are made individually so that everyone has his or her own to enjoy—just in case anyone felt somewhat reluctant to share. Desserts have such incredible power over people. Here, you will find a recipe for every taste and occasion.

fruit, creams, and *clafoutis*
les fruits, les crèmes, et les clafoutis

for the love of tarts
pour l'amour des tartes

Apricot galette with pistachios • *Galette aux abricots et aux pistaches*   352

Raspberry and lime mascarpone tartlets • *Tartelettes aux framboises et au citron vert à la mascarpone*   354

Meringue and clementine tartlets • *Tartelettes meringuées aux clémentines*   357

Strawberry and almond tart • *Tarte aux fraises et aux amandes*   360

chocolate passion
passion chocolat

Chocolate mousse with salted caramel and matcha tea cookies • *Mousse au chocolat avec caramel au beurre salé et langues chat au thé matcha*   365

Pear and chocolate crumbles • *Crumbles aux poires et au chocolat*   368

Marbled chocolate brownie with raspberries • *Brownie marbré au chocolat et aux framboises*   370

Chocolate mousse tartlets • *Tartelettes à la mousse au chocolat*   372

Chocolate cake, mascarpone cream, and raspberries • *Gâteau au chocolat, crème à la mascarpone, et framboises*   377

Chocolate celebration cake • *Gâteau de fête au chocolat*   378

Tiramisu cake • *Gâteau au tiramisu*   381

fruit, creams, and *clafoutis*
les fruits, les crèmes, et les clafoutis

Baked apricots
WITH LEMON VERBENA
Abricots rôtis au four parfumés à la verveine citronnée

During our family vacations in the south of France every summer, my mother and I always marveled at the beautiful displays of apricots in the stalls of the local markets; their delicate scent was unforgettable. I've realized since then that a fine apricot is rare and that to choose them carefully is key. I prefer my apricots with a deep yellow-orange color and firm to the touch so they don't bruise too quickly—but not hard, because that means they were picked when they were still green.

In this recipe, warm apricots shine in a bath of aromatic juice that, if you are like me, you will want to scoop up with your spoon. I use herbs that I grow in my garden; they grow like weeds, in fact, so I often just choose the ones that look the best. Try the herbs that you find most easily near you.

Serves 4

12 medium apricots, cut in half and pitted

¼ cup (60 ml) coconut oil

1 vanilla bean, split lengthwise and seeds scraped out

1 tablespoon finely grated organic orange zest

Juice of 1 orange

¼ cup (1¾ oz; 50 g) Turbinado raw sugar

¼ cup (60 ml) coconut milk

10 lemon verbena, lemon balm, or mint leaves

Whole milk Greek yogurt, stirred with a fork, to serve

Preheat the oven to 400°F (200°C).

Arrange the apricot halves, cut side up, in a 12-by-8-inch (30.5 by 20 cm) baking dish; set aside.

In a small pot over medium heat, combine the coconut oil, vanilla bean and seeds, orange zest and juice, and sugar. Heat and stir until the sugar dissolves, then add the coconut milk. Pour over the apricots and add the lemon verbena. Bake for 20 to 30 minutes, or until the apricots are tender when pierced with a fork. Serve warm in small bowls with plain Greek yogurt or *crème fraîche* ice cream (page 334).

Summer fruit *papillotes* and lavender ice cream

Papillotes de fruits de l'été et glace à la lavande

Use the same technique as for a savory *papillote* but add sweet ingredients instead; the result is something irresistible. This *papillote* uses a medley of luscious summer fruit that, once the parchment paper is torn open, displays a palette of bright colors that is completely seductive. I love it served with a scoop of lavender-infused ice cream melting slowly right in the middle.

Serves 4

FOR THE LAVENDER ICE CREAM:

4¼ cups (1 liter) whole milk

10½ oz (300 g) blond cane sugar

2 tablespoons edible lavender flowers

1 cup plus 1 tablespoon (250 ml) heavy whipping cream

FOR THE FRUIT *PAPILLOTES:*

4 apricots, cut in quarters and pitted

3½ oz (100 g) cherries, pitted and cut in half

3½ oz (100 g) strawberries, hulled and cut in quarters

3½ oz (100 g) raspberries

3½ oz (100 g) red currants

Juice and zest of 2 limes (about 4 tablespoons)

¼ cup (1¾ oz; 50 g) blond cane sugar

2 vanilla beans, cut in half, split lengthwise, and seeds scraped out

2 tablespoons (1 oz; 30 g) unsalted butter, diced

To prepare the ice cream: In a pot, bring the milk and sugar to a boil, stirring until the sugar is dissolved. Remove from the heat and add the lavender flowers. Cover and let cool. Leave to infuse for 8 hours, or overnight in the fridge. Strain the milk. Whip the cream until firm peaks form, then fold it gently into the infused milk preparation. Transfer to the bowl of an ice cream maker, and churn according to the instructions for the machine. Transfer to a container and place in the freezer until ready to use.

To prepare the *papillotes:* Preheat the oven to 350°F (180°C). Cut four 14-inch (35.5 cm) pieces of parchment paper. Lay them flat on the working surface.

In a bowl, combine the fruit with the lime juice, sugar, and vanilla seeds. Divide the fruit between the four pieces of parchment. Add ½ vanilla bean and ½ tablespoon butter to each *papillote*. Lift the wider edges of the paper and fold them over the top. Crimp the edges by pleating them over and over, or secure with string. There should be enough space between the ingredients and edge of the paper for the pouches to puff.

Set the pouches on a rimmed baking sheet and bake for about 20 minutes, or until the fruit is soft and has released its juice. To serve, open each *papillote,* remove the vanilla bean, and put one scoop of lavender ice cream in the middle of the fruit. Or serve with whole milk Greek yogurt.

Vanilla and coconut ice cream

WITH RASPBERRY SWIRL

Glace à la vanille et à la noix de coco avec coulis de framboises

I have a collection of small multicolored bowls that I particularly like to use when I prepare this dessert. They are the perfect size for everyone to enjoy his or her own serving of ice cream with a crisp *langue de chat* cookie (page 367) stuck upright in it.

The red pattern created by the raspberry sauce against the delicate white of the coconut ice cream makes it almost too pretty to eat. Except that at home, the ice cream disappears in the blink of an eye.

FOR THE RASPBERRY SWIRL:

6 oz (170 g) raspberries

2 tablespoons blond cane sugar

1½ tablespoons cold water

FOR THE ICE CREAM:

1 cup (236 ml) whole milk

1 vanilla bean, split lengthwise and seeds scraped out

½ cup (1½ oz; 40 g) unsweetened coconut flakes

4 large egg yolks

½ cup (3½ oz; 100 g) blond cane sugar

1 can (1¾ cups; 400 ml) unsweetened coconut milk

To prepare the raspberry swirl: In the bowl of a food processor, combine all the ingredients and purée. Pass through a fine sieve or *chinois* and discard the raspberry seeds. Transfer the sauce to a small jar, and refrigerate until ready to use.

To prepare the ice cream: In a pot, combine the milk with the vanilla bean and seeds and coconut flakes. Bring to a simmer over medium heat. Remove from the heat, cover, and leave to infuse for 1 hour. Strain, discarding the vanilla bean and coconut flakes, and reheat.

In the bowl of a food processor fitted with a whisk, combine the egg yolks with the sugar and beat until light and fluffy. With the machine running, slowly pour in the warm milk. Transfer back to the pot and heat, without boiling and stirring constantly, until the custard thickens and coats the spoon. This takes about 5 minutes,

when the temperature reaches 185°F (85°C). Transfer the custard to a clean bowl. Stir in the coconut milk and let cool slightly. Place in the fridge to cool completely.

Transfer the cream to the bowl of an ice cream maker and churn according to the instructions for the machine. Spread half of the ice cream in the bottom of a rectangular container (like a 4½-by-8-inch [11.5 by 20 cm] bread pan lined with parchment paper), or divide between eight ½-cup (120 ml) dishes. Drizzle with a thin layer of raspberry sauce, top with the rest of the ice cream and drizzle with more raspberry sauce. Draw a wooden skewer through the ice cream to create a swirl. Place the ice cream back in the freezer until completely set.

Serve the ice cream with vanilla-flavored *langues de chat* (page 367) and any extra raspberry sauce.

Cherry soup

WITH LEMON THYME AND
GRAPEFRUIT *CRÈME FRAÎCHE* ICE CREAM

Soupe de cerises au thym citron et glace à la crème fraîche au pamplemousse

The month of June makes me joyful because that's when bright, ruby-colored cherries are in season. I'm lucky because I grew up with cherry trees in my parents' garden; now also I have my own to share.

This soup recipe is the one that reminds me the most of my grandmother Marie's traditional *bocaux de cerises* (cherry preserves), in which the cherries are left mostly intact. Here, they are bathed in light syrup—infused with aromas of ginger, lime, and vanilla—and served with zesty *crème fraîche* ice cream that brings a harmonious balance of flavors to the dessert. I prefer the cherries pitted, but sometimes I leave the pits in if I am short on time. Nobody seems to mind either way.

Serves 4

FOR THE GRAPEFRUIT
AND *CRÈME FRAÎCHE*
ICE CREAM:

2 cups (472 ml)
crème fraîche

2 cups (472 ml)
buttermilk

1 tablespoon finely
grated grapefruit zest

½ cup (118 ml)
grapefruit juice

¾ cup (5¼ oz; 150 g)
blond cane sugar

FOR THE
CHERRY SOUP:

1 lb, 5¼ oz (600 g)
fresh cherries, pitted

Juice of 1 lime
(about 2 tablespoons
lime juice)

2 cups (472 ml)
cold water

⅓ cup (2¼ oz; 65 g)
blond cane sugar

1-inch (2.5 cm) piece
of fresh ginger, sliced

1 vanilla bean, split
lengthwise and seeds
scraped out

Zest of 1 lime,
finely grated

3 lemon thyme sprigs

2 lemon verbena
sprigs

To prepare the ice cream: In a large bowl, beat together the *crème fraîche*, buttermilk, grapefruit zest and juice, and sugar until a uniform consistency. Chill for a few hours in the fridge. Transfer to the bowl of an ice cream maker and churn according to the instructions for the machine. Transfer the ice cream to a covered container and place in the freezer until completely set.

To prepare the cherry soup: Place the cherries in a bowl and toss them with the juice of 1 lime to prevent oxidation; set aside.

In a pot, combine the water, sugar, ginger, vanilla bean and seeds, and lime zest. Bring to a simmer, stirring occasionally to dissolve the sugar. Cook for 1 minute and remove from the heat. Add the lemon thyme and lemon verbena, and cover; leave to infuse for 30 minutes. Strain over the cherries, and let cool.

When ready to serve, ladle the cherries and syrup into four bowls, and add a scoop of grapefruit *crème fraîche* ice cream in the middle.

Tapioca pudding

Pudding de tapioca

A list of comfort foods should always include a bowl of creamy tapioca pudding. I keep mine on the lighter side (sometimes you find recipes that call for adding eggs) and top it with fresh raspberries that release their beautiful scarlet juice when they touch the warm pudding. Eat each teaspoon slowly to savor the sweet taste in your mouth.

Serves 4

6 tablespoons (2½ oz; 70 g) small tapioca pearls

1⅔ cups (400 ml) whole milk

1⅔ cups (400 ml) unsweetened coconut milk

¼ cup (1¾ oz; 50 g) blond cane sugar

1 vanilla bean, split lengthwise and seeds scraped out

Raspberries, to taste

Bring a large pot of water to a boil. Pour the tapioca in gradually; reduce the heat and simmer for 5 minutes, stirring occasionally. Drain and set aside.

In the same pot, heat the milk with the coconut milk, sugar, and vanilla bean and seeds. Add the tapioca and cook over low heat, stirring constantly, for 15 to 20 minutes, or until the tapioca pearls are cooked and the texture is creamy. Remove the vanilla bean before serving.

Divide the pudding between small serving bowls and top with a few raspberries. Since the tapioca is warm when you add the raspberries, they will cook slightly and release their juice. Eat lukewarm or at room temperature.

Goat milk *panna cotta*

WITH SAUTÉED APPLES AND COCOA NIBS

Panna cotta au lait de chèvre avec pommes sautées et grué de cacao

The taste of goat milk is subtle in this delicate, silky *panna cotta*. And what comes with it—sautéed apples with raspberries, and crunchy bits of cocoa nibs—is exquisite. Serve the *panna cotta* alone for something soothing, or serve it as suggested with the fruit, cocoa nibs, and crisp delicate cookies for a magnificent dessert for a dinner party.

Note: This recipe can be made with cow's milk too, if you find the taste of goat milk too strong.

Serves 4

FOR THE *PANNA COTTA:*

1 cup (236 ml) goat milk

1 cup (236 ml) heavy cream

1 vanilla bean, split lengthwise and seeds scraped out

1 lemongrass stalk, finely chopped

15 lemon balm leaves

¼ cup (1¾ oz; 50 g) blond cane sugar

1½ teaspoons gelatin powder or 2½ gelatin sheets (5 g)

FOR THE SAUTÉED APPLE AND RASPBERRY TOPPING:

1 large red apple (such as McIntosh), peeled, cored, and diced

Squeeze of lemon juice

1 tablespoon (½ oz; 14 g) unsalted butter

1 tablespoon blond cane sugar

1 cup (3½ oz; 100 g) raspberries

1½ teaspoons (5 g) roasted cocoa nibs

To prepare the *panna cotta:* In a pot, combine the goat milk—¾ cup (175 ml) if you are using gelatin powder, or 1 cup (236 ml) if you are using gelatin sheets—with the heavy cream. Bring to a simmer. Remove from the heat and add the vanilla bean and seeds, lemongrass, and lemon balm. Cover and let infuse for 30 to 60 minutes. Strain and reheat. Stir in the sugar; set aside.

In the meantime, if you are using gelatin powder, pour ¼ cup (60 ml) goat milk into a small bowl. Sprinkle the gelatin on top and let sit for 10 minutes. If you are using gelatin sheets, soak the sheets in a large bowl of water for 15 minutes. Squeeze the water out.

Add the gelatin powder and milk, or the gelatin sheets, to the infused milk mixture; stir until completely dissolved. Divide the liquid between four 6-oz (175 ml) Mason jars or water glasses, and let cool. Place in the fridge for 3 hours, or preferably overnight, until the *panna cotta* sets.

To prepare the topping: Drizzle the apple with lemon juice to prevent discoloration; set aside. In a frying pan, melt the butter over medium heat. Add the diced apple and sugar, and cook for 4 to 5 minutes over low to medium heat, stirring occasionally, until the apple softens. Add the raspberries and cook for 2 more minutes, or until the raspberries start to soften and color the apples slightly; set aside.

When ready to serve, top the *panna cotta* with the fruit and sprinkle with cocoa nibs to taste. Serve with the Teff and Cocoa Nib Cookies (page 226).

Strawberry and almond flan
WITH ORANGE AND COCONUT MILK

Flan aux fraises et aux amandes parfumé à l'orange et au lait de coco

I am totally enamored with this strawberry dessert. And, in fact, friends who have tried it with me share the same feeling of love. It has a pudding-like texture, the cross between a soft flan and a delicate cake, with hints of vanilla, orange, and almond gently coming through. I like it best when strawberries are small and packed with flavor.

Note: I prefer to use fresh berries for this dessert. However, if you are making it out of season you can use frozen berries, just add about 15 minutes more to the cooking time since there's more water released by the frozen fruit. Also note that if you prefer to make this dessert nut free you can substitute the almond flour with millet flour.

You will need: a 10-by-7-inch (25.5 by 18 cm) dish.

Serves 6 to 8

Unsalted butter, for the dish

⅓ cup (2¼ oz; 65 g) blond cane sugar, plus 2 tablespoons to coat the dish

3 large eggs, at room temperature

1 teaspoon finely grated orange zest

2 teaspoons pure vanilla extract

¼ cup (1 oz; 30 g) almond meal

2 tablespoons cornstarch or tapioca starch

1 cup (236 ml) unsweetened coconut milk

12½ oz (350 g) small strawberries or raspberries, hulled and cut in half

Confectioner's sugar, to dust

Preheat the oven to 350°F (180°C). Butter the dish, coat the bottom and sides with 2 tablespoons sugar, and tap out the excess; set aside.

In a bowl, whisk the eggs with the rest of the sugar until well combined. Stir in the orange zest and vanilla. Beat in the almond meal and cornstarch. Stir in the coconut milk. Pour the batter into the prepared dish and stud with the strawberries. Bake for 30 to 35 minutes, or until the batter is set. Let cool completely.

This dessert is best eaten at room temperature. When ready to serve, dust with confectioner's sugar.

Blackberry sabayon gratins

Sabayons gratinés aux mûres

Bushes of blackberries grow wild everywhere near my parents' home in France. They conjure up the loveliest childhood memories of my mother and me picking buckets of them, with which we made jam and whatever else we fancied, like fruit tarts and small gratins similar to these. Here, I cover the berries with a silky sabayon made with apple juice and perfumed with rum for an adult twist on my childhood favorites.

I suggest preparing the gratins ahead of time and placing them under the broiler a few minutes before you want to eat dessert. You can also make this dish with blueberries or raspberries.

You will need: four 4½-by-1¼-inch (11.5 by 3 cm; ¾ cup) ramekins.

Serves 4

FOR THE FRUIT:

1 tablespoon (½ oz; 14 g) unsalted butter, plus more for ramekins

10½ oz (300 g) blackberries

2 tablespoons pure cane sugar

Zest of ½ organic lime, finely grated

FOR THE SABAYON:

¾ cup (175 ml) fresh apple juice

2 tablespoons rum

1 vanilla bean, split lengthwise and seeds scraped out

4 large egg yolks

⅓ cup (2¼ oz; 65 g) blond cane sugar

Confectioner's sugar, to dust

Butter the ramekins; set aside.

In a frying pan, melt the butter over medium heat. Add the blackberries and sprinkle with the sugar and lime zest. Cook for 2 minutes on each side. Remove from the heat and divide between the ramekins; set aside.

In a pot, combine the apple juice, rum, and vanilla bean and seeds. Bring to a simmer over low-medium heat. Remove from the heat, cover, and let infuse for 30 minutes. Strain and discard the vanilla bean; set aside.

In a bowl that is large enough to sit over a double boiler (*bain-marie;* page 386) without its bottom touching the water, beat the

egg yolks with the sugar. Stir in the apple juice. Place the bowl over a pot of simmering water, and cook the sabayon, stirring constantly with a wooden spoon, until the cream thickens and coats the spoon; this takes about 7 minutes. Remove from the heat and set aside.

Preheat the broiler. Pour the cream over the blackberries. Place the ramekins under the broiler for 1 to 2 minutes, or until the top starts to bubble slightly and turn golden brown in color—watch this last step carefully, as the broiling process can happen quickly and varies from one oven to another. Serve the gratins warm and dusted with confectioner's sugar.

Use the egg whites to make *langues de chats* (page 367) or almond *tuiles* (page 345), both of which pair well with this recipe.

Sabayon is the French name for zabaglione, a light, mousselike Italian dessert prepared by whisking eggs, sugar, and generally white wine or liqueur over gently boiling water until the cream thickens.

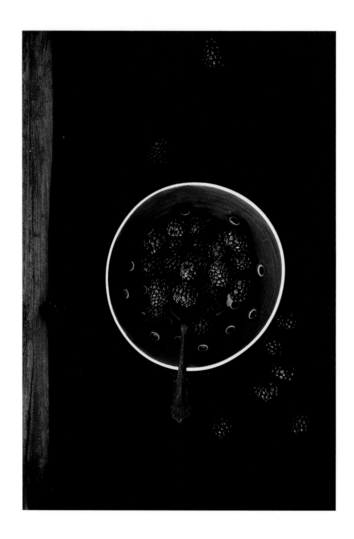

Strawberry floating islands and almond *tuiles*

Iles flottantes aux fraises et tuiles aux amandes

Here, I've taken a favorite classic French dessert—there's a recipe for lavender-flavored *îles flottantes* in my first book—and revamped it with fruit to make an extremely light and refreshing spring dessert to serve when strawberries are beautifully fragrant and sweet. Once plated, the meringue looks light like a cloud floating in the middle of a ruby red bath.

As for Lulu, she loves to dip the *tuiles* in the strawberry sauce and then drink the rest by the glass! This is a smart way too!

You will need: six ½-cup (120 ml) bowls or ramekins, as well as a pastry bag fitted with a wide tip.

Serves 6; makes 18 to 20 tuiles

FOR THE FLOATING ISLANDS:

3 tablespoons sliced almonds

1 lb, 10½ oz (750 g) small sweet strawberries

8 lemon balm or mint leaves

2 tablespoons lime juice

4 tablespoons blond cane sugar

Safflower oil, for ramekins

4 large egg whites

Pinch of sea salt

FOR THE ALMOND *TUILES*:

2 large egg whites

2 tablespoons millet flour

2 tablespoons sweet rice flour

2 tablespoons white rice flour

¼ cup (1¾ oz; 50 g) blond cane sugar

4 tablespoons (2 oz; 56 g) melted unsalted butter

1 teaspoon pure vanilla extract

Sliced almonds, to garnish the *tuiles*

To prepare the floating islands: In a frying pan, toast the sliced almonds for 1 to 2 minutes, or until they start to brown slightly; set aside to cool.

In the bowl of a food processor, purée the strawberries with the lemon balm, lime juice, and 2 tablespoons sugar until smooth. Cover and refrigerate.

Preheat the oven to 300°F (150°C). Oil the bowls, wipe out the excess with a paper towel, and set aside.

Cover a plate with parchment paper; set aside.

In the bowl of a stand mixer with the whisk beat the egg whites with a pinch of sea salt on high speed until soft peaks form. Add 1 tablespoon sugar and beat for 30 seconds. Add another tablespoon of sugar and beat for 30 more seconds. Transfer the egg whites to the pastry bag; make sure there's no air in the bag and the meringue is packed tight. Pipe into the oiled bowls (Lulu loves to help me with this step). Flatten the tops with a spatula, and bake the meringues for 10 to 12 minutes; do not

continued

let them color. Remove from the oven, and let cool for 5 minutes. Run a sharp knife around the edges to release each meringue from its bowl. Flip onto the parchment-covered plate. If you will not be using them right away, cover and keep in the fridge.

When ready to serve, place the meringues in the center of shallow bowls and pour the strawberry sauce around them. Top with sliced almonds and serve with almond *tuiles* on the side.

To prepare the almond *tuiles*: Preheat the oven to 400°F (200°C). Line two baking sheets with parchment paper; set aside.

In a bowl, beat the egg whites with a fork until foamy. Add the flours and beat vigorously. Beat in the sugar, then the melted butter and vanilla, until the batter forms ribbons when drizzled over the bowl. Drop ½ tablespoon batter onto the parchment paper and flatten it slightly (I use a small brush) to create a 2-inch (5 cm) round. Repeat to cover the baking sheets, leaving 2-inch (5 cm) spaces between the cookies. Top with the sliced almonds and bake for 8 to 10 minutes, or until the edges of the cookies start to color—switch the baking sheets, if necessary, so the cookies bake uniformly. Remove baking sheets from the oven and transfer the parchment paper to the kitchen counter. Repeat until you run out of ingredients. Use a spatula to lift and transfer the *tuiles* to a cooling rack and let cool completely.

sweet treats for the family

Cherry and raspberry *clafoutis*

WITH PISTACHIOS

Clafoutis aux cerises et aux framboises avec pistaches

The world of *clafoutis* is a dreamy one in our home. In summer, it welcomes almost any kind of fruit, even if a traditional *clafoutis* is made essentially with cherries. In this version, I add raspberries for extra juiciness and a splash of rum for flavor—which is what my aunts always did with theirs.

Use almond meal for a more subtle dessert or pistachio meal for a more pronounced taste and a touch of green color.

You will need: one 10-inch (25.5 cm) square baking dish (or a 10-by-7-inch [25.5 by 18 cm] baking dish).

Serves 6 to 8

Unsalted butter, for the mold

2 tablespoons blond cane sugar, plus ½ cup (3½ oz; 100 g)

1 lb, 2 oz (500 g) mixed cherries (varieties like Bing and Rainier)

Squeeze of lemon juice

7 oz (200 g) raspberries

1¼ cups (300 ml) whole milk

1 vanilla bean, split lengthwise and seeds scraped out

4 large eggs

½ cup (2 oz; 60 g) almond meal

⅓ cup (1½ oz; 40 g) millet flour

3½ oz (100 g) *crème fraîche*

1 tablespoon rum (optional)

Confectioner's sugar, to dust

Shelled unsalted green pistachios, chopped coarsely

Preheat the oven to 350°F (180°C). Butter the dish, coat with 2 tablespoons sugar, and tap out the excess; set aside.

Pit the cherries and drizzle with lemon juice to prevent discoloration. Arrange them with the raspberries in a single layer in the buttered dish; set aside.

In a pot, heat the milk with ¼ cup (1¾ oz; 50 g) sugar and the vanilla bean and seeds. Bring to a simmer over medium heat. Remove from the heat, cover, and leave to infuse for 30 minutes. Strain and keep warm.

In a large bowl, whisk the eggs with the remaining sugar until well combined. Beat in the almond meal and millet flour. Stir in the *crème fraîche*. Pour in the warm milk while stirring constantly, then add the rum, if using. Pour this batter into the dish with the berries. Bake for 45 minutes, or until the *clafoutis* is set. Remove from the oven and let cool.

When ready to serve, dust with confectioner's sugar and sprinkle with chopped pistachios.

for the love of tarts
pour l'amour des tartes

Apricot galette

WITH PISTACHIOS

Galette aux abricots et aux pistaches

Luscious apricots are remarkable when baked in a modest, rustic-style tart like this one. It is by far one of my favorite summer tarts because the juice the fruit releases is sweet and rich, and its orange-yellow color is intense. But then I'm biased since apricots are my favorite summer fruit—perhaps because you need to exercise patience to find the perfectly ripe ones.

Note: You can use peaches instead of apricots, if that's what you have and like. Score the skin of 3 large peaches in a few places, blanch for 1 minute in boiling water (page 386), cool in ice water, and remove the skins.

Makes one 9-inch (23 cm) galette

Sweet Crust (page 232)

2 tablespoons pistachio meal (see below)

1 tablespoon cornstarch

2 tablespoons blond cane sugar

1 teaspoon pure vanilla extract

1 teaspoon finely grated lime zest

5 to 6 medium apricots, sliced (about 8 slices each), or 3 large peaches (see Note)

1 egg white, lightly beaten

Confectioner's sugar, to serve

1 tablespoon (½ oz; 14 g) shelled unsalted green pistachios, finely chopped, to serve

Line a large baking sheet with parchment paper. Roll the crust to a ⅕-inch (0.5 cm) thickness, cut an 11-inch (28 cm) disk, and transfer to the baking sheet; set aside.

Preheat the oven to 400°F (200°C).

In a bowl, gently toss the pistachio meal, cornstarch, sugar, vanilla, and lime zest to combine. Spread in the center of the crust, leaving a 1-inch (2.5 cm) border. Top with

the slices of apricots. Fold the edges of the crust in to form the *galette*. Brush the border with egg white. Bake for 30 to 35 minutes, or until the crust is lightly golden in color. Remove from the oven and leave to cool for at least 15 minutes before slicing.

When ready to serve, dust the edge with confectioner's sugar, top with chopped green pistachios, and slice in wedges.

To make pistachio meal, place 1 cup shelled unsalted pistachios in a grinder or food processor, and pulse into a fine powder. Keep in the fridge and use as needed.

Raspberry and lime mascarpone tartlets

Tartelettes aux framboises et au citron vert à la mascarpone

I typically make a raspberry tart with fresh, uncooked raspberries to let their beautiful shape and color shine. In this tart, however, I wanted the raspberries to have a melt-in-the-mouth texture, baked with a mixture of eggs, lime, mascarpone, and sugar. The result is absolutely splendid.

You will need: six 4½-inch (11.5 cm) tartlet molds.

Makes six 4½-inch (11.5 cm) tartlets

Sweet Crust (page 232)

3 large eggs, separated

⅓ cup (2¼ oz; 65 g) blond cane sugar

8 oz (227 g; 1 cup) mascarpone cheese

Zest and juice of 1 lime

1 teaspoon pure vanilla extract

Pinch of sea salt

4½ oz (125 g) raspberries

Confectioner's sugar, to serve

Roll and cut the crust to ⅕-inch (0.5 cm) thick to fit inside the molds. Arrange the dough inside the molds and, using a fork, make small holes in the bottom of each. Place in the fridge for 30 to 60 minutes.

Preheat the oven to 350°F (180°C). Blind bake the tartlets for 10 minutes (page 386). Remove and let cool; set aside.

In the meantime, in a bowl, beat the egg yolks with the sugar until light in color. Beat in the mascarpone. Stir in the lime zest and juice, as well as the vanilla extract.

In a separate bowl, whip the egg whites with a pinch of sea salt until stiff peaks form. Gently fold them into the mascarpone mixture.

Divide the cream between the molds and stud with the raspberries. Bake the tartlets for 35 minutes, or until the tops are lightly golden in color. Remove from the oven and let cool for 10 minutes before unmolding onto a cooling rack; let cool completely.

When ready to serve, dust with confectioner's sugar.

Meringue and clementine tartlets

Tartelettes meringuées aux clémentines

I've always had a deep fascination for a lemon tart garnished with a pretty, silky meringue sitting on top. So it seems only natural that I came up with these tartlets, using clementines as the citrus base. I baked them for the first time for a New Year's Eve dinner with friends, who loved the cute-looking meringue sitting on top as much as I do.

You will need: eight 4-inch (10 cm) tartlet molds and a pastry bag fitted with the tip of your choice.

Makes eight 4-inch (10 cm) tartlets

Sweet Crust (page 232)

FOR THE CLEMENTINE TOPPING:

¾ cup (5¼ oz; 150 g) blond cane sugar

Zest of 4 clementines, finely grated (makes about 1 tablespoon)

4 large eggs

½ cup plus 1½ tablespoons (200 ml) fresh clementine juice (about 6 clementines)

1 tablespoon lemon juice

7 tablespoons (3½ oz; 100 g) unsalted butter, cold and diced

FOR THE MERINGUE TOPPING:

1 cup (7 oz; 200 g) blond cane sugar

¼ cup (1¾ oz; 50 ml) water

3 large egg whites

2 to 3 tablespoons confectioner's sugar, to dust

Preheat the oven to 340°F (170°C). Roll and cut the dough to ⅕-inch thick (0.5 cm) to fit inside the molds. Arrange the dough inside the molds and, using a fork, make small holes in the bottom of each. Blind bake the tartlet shells for 20 minutes (page 386). Remove the parchment paper and weights, and bake for another 5 minutes. Remove from the oven and let cool for 5 minutes before umolding. Place the crusts on a cooling rack; set aside.

To prepare the clementine topping: In a bowl that is large enough to sit over a double boiler (*bain-marie;* page 386) without its bottom touching the water, add the sugar, and rub the clementine zest with the sugar until the zest is coated. Beat in the eggs, one at a time, then stir in the clementine

and lemon juices. Place the bowl over a pot of simmering water, and cook, stirring constantly with a wooden spoon, until the mixture thickens and coats the spoon (between 15 and 20 minutes). Remove from the heat and stir in the butter until it melts and is absorbed. Using a hand mixer, whisk for 1 to 2 minutes to emulsify. Divide the cream between the crusts and place in the fridge until it sets completely.

To prepare the meringue topping: In a pot, combine the sugar and water—this will be your syrup. Let the sugar absorb the water; bring to a boil, stirring just until the sugar is dissolved. Cook until the temperature of the syrup reaches 250°F (120°C) on a candy thermometer; remove the pot from the heat.

continued

In the meantime, beat the egg whites in the bowl of a stand mixer fitted with the whisk on medium speed until foamy. Still beating, slowly pour the syrup in, letting it run along the edge of the bowl. Increase the speed of the mixer to high and beat the meringue for 5 minutes until it's stiff and shiny. Transfer to the pastry bag and decorate the tops of the tartlets with the meringue. Refrigerate until ready to use.

Just before you serve the tartlets, dust with confectioner's sugar, and place them under the broiler for barely 30 seconds, or until the top of the meringue starts to brown. Watch this step closely, because it happens quickly and cooking time varies from oven to oven. Remove from the broiler and serve.

Strawberry and almond tart

Tarte aux fraises et aux amandes

I was born in May, when the first blossoms of the season—and strawberries—appear. Maybe this is why I never tire of using these delicate berries in desserts like this delectable tart in which the fruit is baked with a creamy almond filling. This is my go-to tart when I am looking for a quick strawberry dessert.

You will need: one 9-inch (23 cm) tart mold with removable bottom.

Makes one 9-inch (23 cm) tart			
Sweet Crust (page 232)	½ cup (2 oz; 60 g) almond meal	3 tablespoons heavy cream or whole milk	Confectioner's sugar, to serve
1 large egg	¼ cup (1¾ oz; 50 g) blond cane sugar	1 lb, 7 oz (650 g) strawberries, hulled and cut in half	
	1 teaspoon pure vanilla extract		

Preheat the oven to 375°F (190°C). Roll and cut the crust to ⅕-inch (0.5 cm) thick to fit inside the mold (you will have some leftovers). Arrange the dough inside the mold and, using a fork, make small holes in the bottom; set aside.

In a bowl, beat the egg with the almond meal, sugar, vanilla, and cream until all the ingredients are well combined. Arrange the strawberries in the crust and pour the batter over them. Bake the tart for 35 minutes, or until the filling is set. Remove from the oven and leave to cool for 5 minutes before unmolding carefully. Let cool completely on a cooling rack.

When ready to serve, dust with confectioner's sugar.

chocolate passion
passion chocolat

Chocolate mousse

WITH SALTED CARAMEL AND MATCHA TEA COOKIES

Mousse au chocolat avec caramel au beurre salé et langues de chat au thé matcha

A family dinner that includes a bowl of mouthwatering chocolate mousse on the menu is always a happy one. As a child, my brother and I always used a *langue de chat* cookie as a spoon to eat ours; once the first cookie was eaten, we grabbed another one. Lulu has rapidly learned and adopted the same friendly habit. Even if you don't have time to make the cookies, do try the salted caramel on top of the mousse—they are truly amazing together.

Langues de chat (literally, "cat's tongues") are thin, crisp cookies that are supposed to look like, well, cat's tongues. They are perfect for using up leftover egg whites. Lulu simply adores these and often begs for us to bake some together for her school snack. They can accompany many desserts like a *mousse au chocolat,* ice cream, custard, or a fruit salad. Lulu likes them made with green matcha tea, but I also make vanilla-flavored ones.

Note: You can use the remaining egg yolks to make the Blackberry Sabayon Gratins (page 342).

You will need: a pastry bag fitted with a 0.4-inch (1 cm) tip and six 1-cup (236 ml) glasses.

Serves 6

Matcha Tea
Langues de Chat
(see page 367)

FOR THE SALTED CARAMEL:

⅓ cup (2¼ oz; 65 g) blond cane sugar

2 tablespoons (1 oz; 30 g) unsalted butter (If you use salted butter, omit the *fleur de sel.*)

½ cup (120 ml) heavy cream (see Note)

¼ teaspoon *fleur de sel*

FOR THE CHOCOLATE MOUSSE:

⅓ cup plus 2 tablespoons (100 ml) heavy cream

7 oz (200 g) chocolate (70% cocoa), finely chopped

3 egg yolks

5 egg whites

Pinch of sea salt

3 tablespoons blond cane sugar

To prepare the salted caramel: Add the sugar to a pot over medium heat and cook without stirring. The sugar will start melting. Continue to cook on medium to low heat until all the sugar is melted and the caramel is liquid and amber in color. Keeping the heat on low, stir in the butter. Once it's well incorporated, add the cream a little at a time, stirring constantly; be sure you go slowly so the temperature difference between the caramel and cream does not create splatters. When you've added all the cream and it's well incorporated, the caramel is ready. Remove from the heat and stir in the *fleur de sel* (if not using salted butter). Let cool completely. Place in the fridge until

continued

ready to use (I keep mine in a Mason jar). This salted caramel is also delicious drizzled warm on top of vanilla ice cream.

To prepare the chocolate mousse: In a small pot, bring the cream to a boil. Place the chocolate in a bowl and pour the hot cream over it; let rest for 1 minute. Stir the chocolate and cream until all the chocolate is melted and the ganache is smooth. Beat in the egg yolks.

In a separate bowl, beat the egg whites with a pinch of sea salt. While beating, add 1 tablespoon sugar and beat for 30 seconds before adding the second one. Wait another 30 seconds, then add the last tablespoon. Fold the egg whites into the chocolate ganache a little at a time. Divide the chocolate mousse between six serving glasses. Cover and keep refrigerated for a few hours to set.

Serve the mousse topped with the salted caramel, a few *langues de chats,* and fresh berries on the side.

Matcha tea *langues de chat*

These cookies are perhaps Lulu's favorites. Whenever we prepare a batch of them, she never resists the temptation to steal some from the cooling rack while they are still almost too hot to eat. I gladly join in, as I feel just like she does about them. They are wonderful with this chocolate mousse and to accompany ice cream or custard-based desserts.

Makes about 50 cookies

½ cup (2¾ oz; 80 g) brown rice flour

⅓ cup (1½ oz; 40 g) cornstarch or tapioca starch

¼ teaspoon sea salt

1½ teaspoons green matcha tea powder, sifted

8 tablespoons (4 oz; 113 g) unsalted butter, softened

½ cup (3½ oz; 100 g) blond cane sugar

4 large egg whites (4½ oz; 130 g)

1 teaspoon pure vanilla extract

In a bowl, combine the brown rice flour, cornstarch, sea salt, and tea powder; set aside.

In the bowl of a stand mixer fitted with the whisk, beat the butter and sugar until smooth and creamy, scraping the sides of the bowl as you work. Add the egg whites, one at a time, and beat until combined. Stir in the vanilla. Add the flour mixture and beat again until completely smooth.

Preheat the oven to 400°F (200°C). Line two baking sheets with parchment paper. Transfer the batter to the pastry bag. Squeeze onto the prepared baking sheets to form 2⅓-inch (6 cm) sticks; leave at least 2 inches (5 cm) between them, as the cookies spread. Bake for about 8 to 9 minutes, or until the edges start to brown slightly but the center remains green. I put about 14 to 16 cookies on each sheet and then repeat, keeping the batter in the fridge between batches. Transfer the cookies onto a cooling rack while they are still warm, and let cool completely.

The *langues de chat* will keep for 1 week in an airtight container at room temperature. If the weather is humid, they do not stay crisp as long.

To make traditional vanilla-flavored *langues de chat,* simply omit the matcha tea and increase the pure vanilla extract to 1 tablespoon.

Pear and chocolate crumbles

Crumbles aux poires et au chocolat

Pears and chocolate must have been married in a previous life. I never would have imagined it before I tried it, but now I realize how well they invariably pair together. They are scrumptious in this crumble, which is especially cute when baked in individual glasses so you have one to enjoy all by yourself.

Serves 6

FOR THE CHOCOLATE
CRUMBLE TOPPING:

¼ cup (1½ oz; 40 g)
buckwheat flour

¼ cup (1 oz; 30 g)
millet four

½ cup (1¾ oz; 50 g)
hazelnut meal

1 tablespoon
unsweetened
cocoa powder

¼ teaspoon
fleur de sel

¼ cup plus
2 tablespoons
(2½ oz; 75 g)
Turbinado sugar

4 tablespoons (2 oz;
60 g) unsalted butter

1 teaspoon pure
vanilla extract

½ cup (1½ oz; 45 g)
sliced almonds

2 oz (60 g)
dark chocolate
(64% cocoa),
coarsely chopped, or
chocolate chips

FOR THE FRUIT:

Unsalted butter, for
the glasses

6 ripe Bartlett pears,
peeled, cored,
and diced

2 tablespoons
lemon juice

2 tablespoons
Turbinado sugar

Confectioner's sugar,
to serve

Unsweetened cocoa
powder, sifted,
to serve

To prepare the crumble topping: In a bowl, combine the flours, hazelnut meal, cocoa powder, *fleur de sel,* and sugar. Add the butter and vanilla; using your fingertips, work until coarse crumbles form. Mix in the sliced almonds and chocolate chips. Cover and refrigerate the topping for 1 hour.

To prepare the fruit: Preheat the oven to 350°F (180°C). Butter six 1-cup (236 ml) heat-resistant glasses; set aside.

In a bowl, gently toss the pears with the lemon juice and sugar. Divide the fruit between the glasses and top with the cooled chocolate crumble. Bake for 30 to 35 minutes, or until lightly golden in color. Remove from the oven and let cool slightly.

Serve lukewarm, dusted with confectioner's sugar and unsweetened cocoa.

Marbled chocolate brownie
WITH RASPBERRIES
Brownie marbré au chocolat et aux framboises

Those who enjoy the taste of a richer brownie will delight in this family-style marbled chocolate brownie studded with raspberries. It's directly inspired by one made by my lovely friend Elea, whom I met during one of the workshops I taught in Paris in the spring of 2014—we just couldn't stop eating it! In this recipe, I really wanted the flavor of hazelnut to come through, so I roasted the hazelnut meal before making the batter to give the brownie a deep, nutty flavor.

You will need: one rimmed 10-by-7-inch (25.5 by 18 cm) baking dish.

Makes fifteen 1¾-inch (4.5 cm) brownies

11 tablespoons (5¼ oz; 150 g) unsalted butter, melted, plus more for the dish

½ cup (1¾ oz; 50 g) hazelnut meal

¼ cup (1½ oz; 40 g) brown rice flour

1 tablespoon golden flax meal

1 cup (7 oz; 200 g) blond cane sugar

2 teaspoons pure vanilla extract

4 large eggs

5¼ oz (150 g) dark chocolate (70% cocoa), melted

½ cup (4 oz; 113 g) mascarpone cheese

3½ oz (100 g) raspberries, lightly mashed with a fork

Preheat the oven to 350°F (180°C). Butter the baking dish and line with parchment paper; set aside. Spread the hazelnut meal on a rimmed baking sheet and roast for 8 to 10 minutes. Remove from the oven and let cool.

In a bowl, combine the hazelnut meal with the brown rice flour and flax meal; set aside.

In a bowl, beat the melted butter with ¾ cup (5¼ oz; 150 g) of the sugar until well mixed. Add 1 teaspoon vanilla. Beat in three of the eggs, one at a time, until well incorporated. Beat in the melted chocolate, then the flour mixture. Pour three-fourths of the resulting batter into the prepared dish.

In a bowl, beat the remaining egg with the rest of the sugar and the mascarpone cheese until well incorporated. Beat in the remaining teaspoon of vanilla. Pour into the pan over the chocolate batter. Pour in the rest of the chocolate and scatter with the mashed raspberries. Bake for 45 to 50 minutes, or until the blade of a sharp knife inserted in the middle comes out nearly clean. Remove from the oven and let cool completely.

Lift the parchment paper out of the dish and slice the brownies into small (1¾-inch; 4.5 cm) squares. One brownie may be just what you want, as these are definitely richer than others I typically prepare; but I still always go back for seconds.

Chocolate mousse tartlets

Tartelettes à la mousse au chocolat

I often daydream about chocolate desserts. With this one, I envisioned rich chocolate tartlets dedicated to chocolate lovers like us. A chocolate mousse sits on top of a chocolate crust covered with a thin layer of chocolate. Don't let them intimidate you—they look more complicated than they are.

I purposely make these tartlets smaller than usual because they're quite rich in chocolate, so the smaller size is just the right amount.

You will need: eight 3½-inch (9 cm) tartlet molds and a pastry bag fitted with a tip of your choice.

Makes eight 3½-inch (9 cm) tartlets

Sweet Chocolate Crust (see page 374)

1 oz (30 g) dark chocolate (64% cocoa), melted in a double boiler (*bain-marie*)

¼ cup plus 2 tablespoons (90 ml) whole milk

¼ cup plus 2 tablespoons (90 ml) heavy cream, plus 1¼ cups (295 ml), cold

1-inch (2.5 cm) piece of fresh ginger, peeled

6 oz (170 g) dark chocolate (64% cocoa), finely chopped or pulsed into a powder

2 large egg yolks

¼ cup (1¾ oz; 50 g) blond cane sugar

Unsweetened cocoa powder, sifted, to serve

Confectioner's sugar, sifted, to serve

Blind bake the chocolate tartlet crusts as indicated in the Sweet Chocolate Crust recipe. Brush each crust with a thin layer of melted chocolate. Let cool at room temperature or in the fridge until the chocolate hardens.

In a pot, heat the milk over medium heat with ¼ cup plus 2 tablespoons heavy cream and the ginger. When it simmers, remove from the heat and cover. Let infuse for 30 minutes. Strain and reheat to keep warm.

Place the chopped chocolate in a large bowl; set aside.

In another bowl, whisk the egg yolks with the sugar until light in color. Pour the warm milk into the egg mixture while whisking constantly. Return to the pot. Cook over low heat, without boiling,

stirring constantly, until the cream coats the spoon and the temperature reads 185°F (85°C) on a candy thermometer. Pour the warm *crème anglaise* over the chopped chocolate. Let rest for 20 seconds, then stir vigorously to combine.

Whip 1¼ cups (295 ml) cold heavy cream until soft peaks form. Fold into the chocolate mixture in two batches. Cover with plastic film, and refrigerate for about 2 hours.

Transfer the chocolate mousse to the pastry bag and pipe into the tartlet crusts. Dust with cocoa powder and confectioner's sugar, and serve with additional cardamom custard (see Waffles with Stewed Apples and Cardamom Custard, page 40) on the side, if you like. The tartlets are best eaten at room temperature.

Sweet chocolate crust
Pâte sucrée au chocolat

There are times when a tart filling is going to shine just because it's prepared with a chocolate crust—like this one where quality unsweetened cocoa is added.

You will need: eight 3½-inch (9 cm) tartlet molds.

¾ cup (3¼ oz; 95 g) millet flour

⅓ cup (2 oz; 55 g) white rice flour

¼ cup (1½ oz; 40 g) sweet rice flour

⅓ cup (1½ oz; 40 g) almond meal

1 tablespoon (7 g) unsweetened cocoa powder, sifted

Pinch of sea salt

7 tablespoons (3½ oz; 100 g) unsalted butter, diced and softened

¼ cup (¾ oz; 25 g) confectioner's sugar

1 batch Flax Gel (page 30)

1 egg white, lightly beaten, to brush the pastry

In a bowl, combine the flours, almond meal, and cocoa powder with a pinch of sea salt; set aside.

In the bowl of a food processor with a paddle blade, cream the butter with the confectioner's sugar. Beat in the flax gel, then the dry ingredients. Work the dough until it detaches from the sides of the bowl. Remove from the bowl and divide into 8 small balls of equal size. Cover with plastic wrap and refrigerate for 1 to 2 hours.

Preheat the oven to 350°F (180°C). Take the dough out of the fridge, and roll out each ball on a floured working surface to fit inside the tarlet molds (if the dough is too cold, let it rest at room temperature for 5 minutes). Arrange the dough inside the molds. Blind bake the crusts for 10 minutes (page 386). Remove the weights and parchment paper, and brush the bottom of the crusts with egg white. Bake for 10 more minutes. Remove from the oven and let cool for 5 minutes before unmolding. Let cool completely on a rack.

Chocolate cake, mascarpone cream, and raspberries

Gâteau au chocolat, crème à la mascarpone, et framboises

This is the chocolate dessert that I like to prepare when friends gather. I like that from a simple chocolate cake—which we also like to eat on its own—I am able to create a more elegant, prettier dessert that invariably gets oohs and aahs from the crowd.

Note: Replace the butter with vegetable, coconut, or grapeseed oil, if you prefer.

You will need: an 8-inch (20.5 cm) square baking pan and a pastry bag fitted with a tip of your choice.

Makes nine 2½-inch (6.5 cm) cake squares

FOR THE DARK CHOCOLATE CAKE:

6 tablespoons (3 oz; 85 g) unsalted butter, plus more for the pan

⅓ cup (1½ oz; 40 g) almond meal or hazelnut meal

¼ cup (1½ oz; 40 g) buckwheat flour

¼ teaspoon *fleur de sel*

4½ oz (125 g) dark chocolate (70% cocoa)

3 large eggs

½ cup (2½ oz; 70 g) brown sugar, light Muscovado sugar, or coconut palm sugar

FOR THE MASCARPONE CREAM:

½ cup (120 ml) heavy cream, cold

10½ oz (300 g; 1⅓ cups) mascarpone cheese, stirred with a fork

3 tablespoons confectioner's sugar, sifted, plus more to dust

1½ teaspoons pure vanilla extract

FOR THE TOPPING:

7 oz (200 g) raspberries

Confectioner's sugar, to dust

Unsweetened cocoa powder, sifted, to dust

2 tablespoons roasted hazelnuts, coarsely chopped (optional)

To prepare the cake: Preheat the oven to 350°F (180°C). Butter the baking pan and line with parchment paper.

In a bowl, combine the almond meal, buckwheat flour, and *fleur de sel;* set aside. Melt the chocolate and butter in a double boiler (*bain-marie;* page 386); set aside. In the bowl of a stand mixer fitted with the whisk, beat the eggs and sugar until light in color. Fold in the melted chocolate and butter, then the dry ingredients. Mix until just combined. Pour into the pan and bake for 25 minutes, or until the blade of a sharp knife inserted in the middle comes out clean. Remove from the oven and let cool on a rack. Carefully remove the cake from the mold by lifting the edges of the parchment paper. Cut the cake into 9 squares; set aside.

To prepare the mascarpone cream: In the bowl of a stand mixer fitted with the whisk, whip the heavy cream until peaks form; set aside. In another bowl, beat the mascarpone with the confectioner's sugar and vanilla until smooth. Fold in the whipped cream. Transfer to the pastry bag and pipe the cream onto the cake squares.

Add the topping: Arrange the raspberries on top of the cream. When ready to serve, dust with confectioner's sugar and cocoa. Garnish with chopped nuts, if desired; serve on individual plates.

Chocolate celebration cake

Gâteau de fête au chocolat

I keep this multilayered, creamy but light chocolate cake for special occasions, like a birthday or a gathering that requires an impressive conclusion to a meal. I baked it once for Thanksgiving, and when Lulu turned six, this was the cake she asked for—it happened to be Christmas too. Adults and children alike always beg for seconds.

You will need: one 13-by-18-inch (33 by 46 cm) baking sheet, one 8-inch (20 cm) ring mold, and a plastic cake wrap.

Serves 8

FOR THE CHOCOLATE *GÉNOISE:*

½ cup (2 oz; 60 g) cornstarch, sifted

¼ cup (1 oz; 30 g) millet flour

¼ cup (¾ oz; 25 g) oat flour, sifted

¼ cup (1 oz; 30 g) unsweetened cocoa powder, sifted

½ teaspoon baking powder

6 large eggs, separated

Pinch of sea salt

2½ tablespoons (1 oz; 30 g) blond cane sugar

FOR THE CHOCOLATE MOUSSE:

¼ cup (60 ml) whole milk

¼ cup (60 ml) heavy cream, plus ¾ cup (180 ml), cold

4 cardamom pods, crushed

½ vanilla bean, split lengthwise and seeds scraped out

1 gelatin sheet (0.07 oz; 2 g)

2 oz (60 g) dark chocolate (64% cocoa), finely chopped

1 large egg yolk

1 tablespoon blond cane sugar

Unsweetened cocoa powder, to serve

Confectioner's sugar, to serve

Berries (blueberries and blackberries or raspberries), to serve (optional)

To prepare the cake: Preheat the oven to 350°F (180°C). Line the baking sheet with parchment paper; set aside.

In a bowl, combine the cornstarch, flours, cocoa powder, and baking powder; set aside.

In the bowl of a stand mixer fitted with the whisk, beat the egg whites with the sea salt until soft peaks begin to form. Gradually add the sugar while continuing to beat. Beat in the egg yolks until well incorporated. Fold gently into the dry ingredients, making sure to keep the batter light.

Spread the cake batter on the prepared baking sheet and even it out with a spatula. Bake for 8 to 10 minutes, or until the blade of a sharp knife inserted in the middle comes out clean. Remove from the oven and let cool.

Using an 8-inch (20 cm) ring mold, cut two circles out of the cake, making sure to peel the parchment paper off carefully; set aside. Keep the leftover cake for another use, such as a trifle, a tiramisu, or simply a snack.

To prepare the mousse: In a pot, bring the milk, ¼ cup (60 ml) heavy cream,

continued

cardamom pods and seeds, and vanilla bean and seeds to a simmer over medium heat. Remove from the heat, cover, and let infuse for 30 minutes.

In the meantime, soak the gelatin sheet in a large bowl of cold water; set aside.

Put the chocolate in a large bowl, set aside.

In another bowl, beat the egg yolk with the sugar until light in color.

Strain the milk and cream mixture, discarding the vanilla bean and cardamom pods, and reheat. Pour the warm liquid slowly over the egg mixture, stirring constantly. Transfer back to the pot and cook over low heat, without boiling, stirring constantly, until the cream coats the spoon. It starts thickening at about 180°F (80°C). Remove from the heat. Squeeze the water out of the gelatin sheet and stir into the warm cream. Pour the cream over the

chocolate and let rest for 1 minute, then stir vigorously until the chocolate is melted. Let cool for 5 minutes.

Beat ¾ cup (180 ml) cold heavy cream until soft peaks form. Fold it gently into the chocolate cream in two batches.

To assemble the cake: Line an 8-inch ring mold with a plastic cake wrap. Place one circle of chocolate cake on the bottom. Spread half of the chocolate mousse on the cake. Top with the second circle of cake, and finish with the rest of the chocolate mousse. Smooth the surface with a spatula. Cover with plastic wrap and place in the fridge for a few hours, or even overnight. When the mousse is set, carefully remove the ring mold. To serve, dust the cake with cocoa powder and confectioner's sugar, peel off the plastic cake wrap, decorate with the berries (if using), and slice.

sweet treats for the family

Tiramisu cake

Gâteau au tiramisu

This decadent-looking cake is meant to appear a bit messy, with mascarpone cream oozing down the sides. Although a traditional tiramisu is made with ladyfingers, I chose to bake two olive oil sponge cakes here—because I'm really fond of the light sweetness of olive oil–based cakes—and build the layers of my tiramisu with them. It's another wonderful cake to make for special occasions when you have a large group to feed.

You will need: two 9-inch (23 cm) cake pans.

Serves 12

Unsalted butter, for the pans

½ cup (2¾ oz; 80 g) white rice flour, plus more for the pans

1 cup (4½ oz; 125 g) millet flour

⅓ cup (2 oz; 55 g) sweet rice flour

2½ teaspoons baking powder

¼ teaspoon sea salt

4 large eggs

¾ cup (5¼ oz; 150 g) blond cane sugar

¾ cup (180 ml) olive oil

1 tablespoon pure vanilla extract

FOR THE MASCARPONE FILLING:

½ cup (120 ml) strong brewed coffee

2 tablespoons marsala

1 cup (8 oz; 227 g) mascarpone cheese

3 large egg yolks

½ cup plus 2 tablespoons (2¾ oz; 80 g) confectioner's sugar, sifted

1 tablespoon pure vanilla extract

1 cup plus 1 tablespoon (250 ml) heavy whipping cream, cold

Unsweetened cocoa powder, sifted, to taste

Shaved dark chocolate (64% cocoa)

Preheat the oven to 350°F (180°C). Butter the pans, coat them with white rice flour, and tap out the excess; set aside.

In a bowl, combine the flours, baking powder, and sea salt; set aside.

In the bowl of a stand mixer fitted with the whisk, beat the eggs with the sugar until light in color. Beat in the olive oil and vanilla, then add the dry ingredients. Beat until all ingredients are just incorporated. Divide the batter equally between the two cake pans and bake for 20 to 25 minutes, until a sharp knife inserted in the middle comes out clean. Let cool for 5 minutes before unmolding onto a cooling rack. Let cool completely.

To prepare the filling: In a small bowl, combine the coffee and marsala; set aside.

In a large bowl, beat the mascarpone with the egg yolks. Stir in the confectioner's sugar and vanilla.

In another bowl, whip the cream until it forms firm peaks, then fold it gently into the mascarpone mixture; set aside.

Slice a thin layer off the top of each cake. (The tops are not used in the recipe; you can nibble on them.) Place one cake (cut side up) on a cake stand or large plate.

continued

Brush with the coffee mixture. Spread with half of the mascarpone cream, letting a little run over the sides (if you have too much cream, keep some on the side). Dust with cocoa powder and sprinkle with shaved chocolate. Carefully place the second cake on top, cut side up. Brush with the coffee mixture. Cover with the rest of the *mascarpone* cream. Dust with cocoa powder and shaved chocolate. Place the assembled cake in the fridge for a few hours before serving.

acknowledgments
remerciements

I WOULD LIKE TO THANK my mother for instilling in me a passion for homemade and homegrown food, for educating me about food as she took me wandering through farmers' markets and let me cook with her, and for showing how you can express love by preparing a meal for your family and friends. I would not look at food the same way had I not experienced family meals and dinners shared with friends as I did when I was growing up in France.

My heartfelt thanks also go to all the readers of my blog and first book, who have kept following me throughout the years, whether I was able to post regularly or not. And my gratitude goes to all the people who tried and cooked my recipes, sent me heartening notes, and gave me warm and encouraging feedback as I went along. Their words feed my inspiration to cook and my imagination to create new dishes. And thanks to my friends who tell me they love to come to our house for a meal.

Thanks to my agent, Claudia Cross, for helping me through the writing process.

This is the second book that I have pub-

lished with Roost Books. I am extremely grateful to the team I work with and to my editor, Sara Bercholz, in particular.

I would also like to thank my dear, caring mother-in-law, Patricia, who never hesitated to come and stay with us, helping with daily life chores and Lulu when I was pregnant with our son, Rémy, so I could write and finish my book in the last weeks before my manuscript was due.

My gratitude goes to my loving husband, Philip, who—although supporting me completely—gives me critical and constructive advice on the dishes I prepare and the stories I write. And last, I would like to thank my darling daughter, Lulu, who proves to be my most precious muse and companion in the kitchen. When we cook together, she often says something like, *"On met la recette là dans ton livre, hein maman?"* ("Shall we add this recipe to your book, Mummy?") She tells her friends that her mummy is a chef and that she could teach cooking classes in her school. These words sound so sweet to my ears. Ultimately, she is the reason I wrote this book.

index of basic recipes and techniques

index des recettes de base et techniques

BASIC RECIPES • *Recettes de Base*

These simple recipes are called out in the sidebars throughout the book. They are listed here for your convenience, should you want to locate them more easily.

General • *En Général*

Tart Crusts • *Les Pâtes à Tarte*

TECHNIQUES

These simple techniques are used throughout the book. You can refer to them as needed when they are mentioned in a recipe.

Blanching Vegetables •
Blanchir les Légumes

This is a process by which you precook vegetables (or fruit) for a short period of time in a large pot of salted boiling water, then submerge them in ice water to stop the cooking. If you want to keep vegetables—such as peas, basil, edamame, fava beans, and asparagus—green and crunchy, it's important to keep the cooking time short, have sufficient salt in the water, and make sure you transfer the vegetables to an ice water bath right after you drain them.

Blind Baking a Crust •
Précuire une Tarte

This is the process of prebaking a tart crust before adding the filling. Once you have rolled out the crust and placed it in your tart mold, line it with a large piece of parchment paper and top with pie weights, dry rice, or dry beans. Bake the crust for 10 to 15 minutes at the oven temperature indicated in the recipe. The recipe may also instruct you to continue baking the crust for 5 more minutes without the parchment paper and weights before adding the filling.

Using the Double Boiler •
Cuire au Bain-Marie

You can melt or heat ingredients by putting them in a bowl that is then placed over a pot of simmering water. Be sure that the bowl never touches the water and that the water is not boiling too hard. This method is often used to melt chocolate, sugar, and butter in baking.

Using the Water Bath •
Cuire au Bain-Marie

Although the French name for "water bath" is the same as for "double boiler," the technique is different. For a water bath, you place a pan of water in an oven—the hot water provides a constant, steady heat source and ensures slow, even cooking. Place the dish(es) containing the food in a larger pan. Place the pan in the oven, then add enough boiling water to the large pan so that it reaches halfway up the dish(es) containing the food. Take care that the water doesn't spill over into the food when you remove the pan from the oven.

index

index

PRAISE FOR *La Tartine Gourmande*

"Everything about this book is charming: the writing,
the photographs, and the bright, fresh recipes for food you'll
want to make every day. When Béa says this is food 'to inspire,'
she is telling the simple truth. If you're a fan of Béa's blog,
you'll be thrilled to have her stories, pictures, and food bound
together; and if you're new to Béa's work, then you're
in for a treat—delight awaits."

—Dorie Greenspan, author of *Around My French Table*

"As bright as a sunny day in the French countryside,
La Tartine Gourmande will inspire cooks with fresh,
vibrant vegetables and colorful fruits and berries.
From breakfast through dessert, this lushly photographed
book by Béatrice Peltre will have cooks everywhere
licking their lips . . . and their plates!"

**—David Lebovitz, author of *Ready for Dessert*
and *The Sweet Life in Paris***

"A lovely, personal peek into Béatrice's French-kissed
kitchen. A wonderland of tartines, tatins, and tales
of culinary delight. Béa's book takes an inspired look at
gluten-free baked goods and fresh, seasonally inspired
day-to-day creations—Cherry Tomato Tartlets Tatin,
Omelet Wraps with Nori and Crunchy Vegetables, Brown
Butter Pistachio and Poppy Seed *Financiers*. Yes, please."

**—Heidi Swanson, author of *Near & Far*
and *Super Natural Every Day***